RECORDS OF
Washington County,
GEORGIA

RECORDS OF
Washington County,
GEORGIA

Compiled by
Marie De Lamar & Elisabeth Rothstein

CLEARFIELD

Reprinted for
Clearfield Company, Inc. by
Genealogical Publishing Co., Inc.
Baltimore, Maryland
2000, 2006

Originally published by Delwyn Associates,
Albany, Georgia, 1975.
Reprinted with an added index by
Genealogical Publishing Co., Inc.
Baltimore, 1985.
Copyright© 1985 by Genealogical Publishing Co., Inc.
Baltimore, Maryland. All Rights Reserved.
Library of Congress Catalogue Card Number 84-73076
International Standard Book Number 0-8063-1110-X
Made in the United States of America

Publisher's Note

This book is offset from the original mimeographed
edition and thus preserves all the typographical
irregularities of the original.

Contents

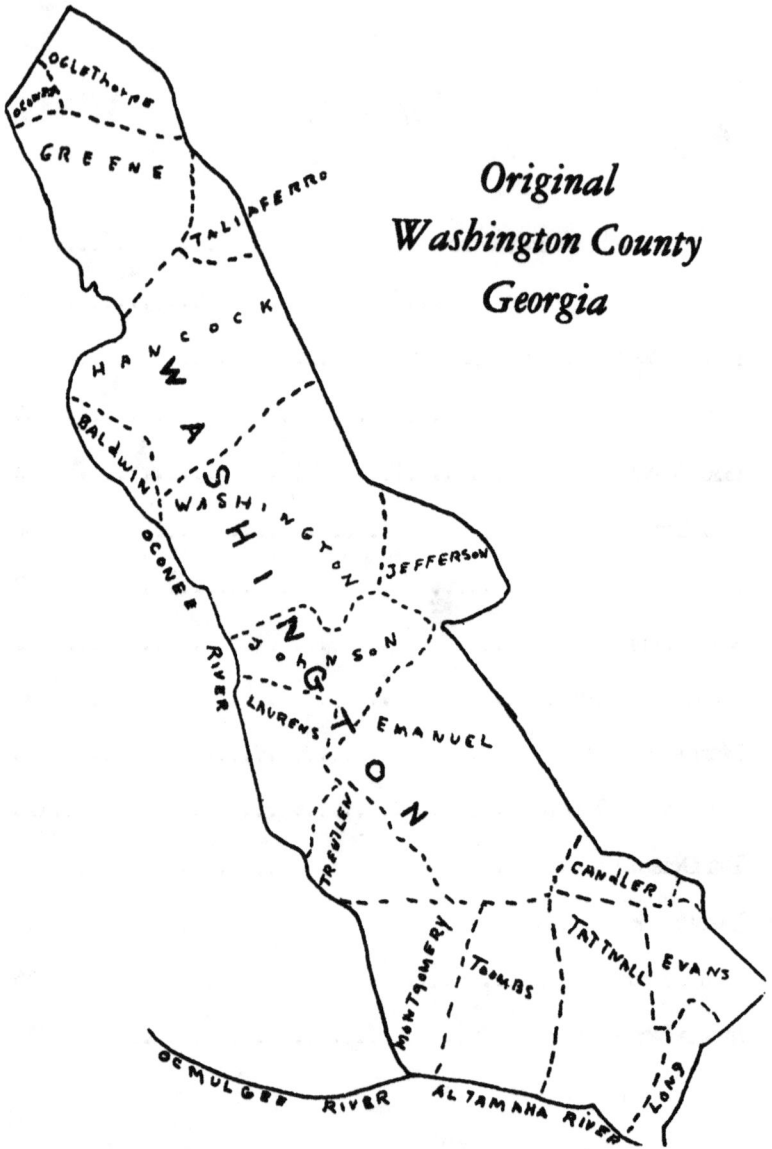

Original
Washington County
Georgia

Note

Washington County was established February 25, 1784 from the Creek Indian Cession of November 1, 1783. The county originally included all the territory "from the Cherokee Corner, north extending from the Ogeechee River to the Oconee River, south to Liberty County."

A part of Washington County was set off to Greene County, 1786; a part to Hancock County, 1793; a part to Montgomery County, 1793; a part to Laurens County, 1811; a part to Baldwin County, 1807, 1812, and 1826; and a part to Johnson County, 1858. The county seat is Sandersville, Georgia.

Washington County and Franklin County, which was erected the same year as Washington County, were the two counties where bounty grants were made to soldiers of the Revolutionary War. These soldiers were eligible for bounty grants upon proof of their service no matter what state they served, and soldiers from every state applied for and received bounty grants—many of them settling on their land.

There was a fire in the Washington County courthouse in 1855 which destroyed many of the early records of the county, and the courthouse was burned by General Sherman on his march to the sea. A few records of the 1840s survive, but generally the extant court records begin after the Civil War. Therefore, the majority of the records given here are from sources other than the courthouse.

HEAD-RIGHT AND BOUNTY GRANTS

While the Revolutionary War was still in progress, The General
Assembly of Georgia passed two Acts relating to the granting of
land but until 1782 the State was overrun and occupied by the
British and the government was so disorganized that the necessary
official machinery for surveying and granting land was never
perfected. As a result both of these Acts became ineffectual,
and are referred to here only as a matter of historical interest.
The first of these was the Act of June 7, 1777 (as amended by
the Act of September 16, 1777) entitled "An Act for opening a
land office and for the better settling and strengthening this
State"; the second was the Act of January 23, 1780, entitled
"An Act for the more speedy and effectual settling and strengthening this State". Actually only a very few surveys were ever
made under those Acts and the first grant of land based on any
of such surveys was not signed and issued until October 22, 1783.
Neither Act provided for a fee-simple grant, but both followed
the Colonial requirement for the annual payment of rent of two
shillings on each hundred acres in the grant, in addition to
settlement and cultivation within nine months. However, both
Acts recognized the fact that many Colonial and State records
had been lost or destroyed during the War and stipulated that
despite their loss those persons who could produce some proof
of an application for survey or an agreement to purchase or
settlement under any Colonial law or grant would be entitled to
confirming grants. One feature of both Acts which was followed
in every subsequent Act was that a man would be entitled to
200 acres as his own head-right plus an additional 50 acres for
his wife, each child and each slave but that in no event could
the total grant exceed 1000 acres.

The first effective land Act was the Act of February 17, 1783
(as amended by the Act of August 1, 1783) entitled "An Act for
opening the land office and for other purposes therein men-
tioned". This Act allowed a man to take up 200 acres upon his
own head-right free of any charge except office fees for survey
and grant, plus an additional 50 acres upon the head of each
member of his family at sales prices ranging from one to four
shillings per acre, and it limited any grant to a maximum of
1000 acres. The rights of persons who had previously received
warrants of survey were ratified and they were declared to be
entitled to grants of land then occupied by them. Those persons who, under legislation passed during the War, had become
entitled to bounty lands, such as citizens who had not molested
their neighbors' families or property, refugees who had served
in militia companies outside of the state, militiamen of the
State and men who had served in the minute battalions were declared entitled to grants without charge except for office fees.
The machinery for granting land, as set up by this Act, was as
follows. The applicant for land would appear before the land
court of the county in which he desired land, composed of

1

five Justices, and after making oath as to the size of his family including slaves, would obtain a warrant of survey. The county surveyor would then lay out his land, keep a copy of the plat of survey in his office and forward a copy to the Surveyor-General. After living on the land a year and cultivating at least three per cent of the acreage, the settler would then apply to the Governor's office for his grant and pay all purchase price due and all office fees. The grant would then be issued and recorded.

The Act of February 25, 1784 which was passed primarily to create and open up Franklin and Washington Counties, made some revisions in the grant laws theretofore enacted. The sales price of land in those two counties was fixed at three shillings per acre and the maximum grant was again limited to 1000 acres. Bounty grants could be located in the new counties and all bounty grants in all counties were no longer to be tax free for ten years but were to be increased by fifteen per cent in acreage. A large section in what later became Greene County was reserved exclusively for bounty grants to men who had served refugees or militiamen. For the first year members of the Executive Council were to act as the land courts for the new counties, prior to their organization.

Under the Act of February 22, 1785 the provisions for payment of a purchase price or consideration for granted land, other than office fees, were removed and therafter all land was granted free. Cultivation was no longer a requisite. However, the restrictions as to the amount of land to which a man was entitled upon his own and his family's head-rights and the restriction as to the 1000 acre maximum grant remained unchanged. No surveys for bounty grants were to be made after February 22, 1786 but as to bounty land surveyed prior to that date a gran could be made upon the warrant at any time thereafter.

No information whatsoever as to the State or County of a man's former residence, or as to names of his wife or members of his family appear upon either the warrant for survey, the recorded plat of survey or the recorded grant. Only the grantee's name is shown on those records in the Surveyor-General's office.

HEADRIGHT AND BOUNTY GRANTS

Some of those listed below received more than one grant; others bought the bounty grants given Revolutionary Soldiers. The date shown is that of the first grant in the instances where more than one grant was recorded.

Abbott, John	1787
Abercrombie, Charles	1791
Acord, John	1786
Adams, John	1786
Mathias	1788
Robert	1785
Adamson, James	1796
Charles	1795
Adcock, James	1785
Adkins, John	1794
Ainsworth, James	1837
Akridge, William	1805
Albert, John	1785
Albritton, Zaca (?)	1818
Alexander, Asa	1785
Arpa	1785
Washington	1785
James	1785
John L.	1785
Robert	1785
Samuel	1785
Vincent	1787
Alford, James	1786
Alison, Henry	1785
Allen, Charles	1794
Edmond	1797
James	1784
Robert	1785
Thomas	1784
Allenthrope, Vincent	1788
Allison, Henry	1784
Amosson, Uriah	1798
Anderson, Alexander	1784
Barclay	1784
Elijah	1785
Henry	1829
John	1794
John	1788
Reuben	1798
William	1784
Andrew, Samuel	1788
Andrews, John	1785
Angelly, Alexander	1787
Anglin, David	1785
Archord, John	1785
Arline, John	1792
Armstrong, Alexander	1789
James	1824
John	1794
Asbury, Jonathan	1795

Ashmore, John	1785
Aubry, Alexander	1784
Jacob	1874
Autry, Absalom	1793
Alexander	1785
John	1786
Autrey, Alexander	1785
Avent, Joseph	1784
Avery, Alexander	1787
Sarah	1821
Samuel	1820
Averett, John	1784
Aycock, Benjamin	1801
Elius	1794
Richard	1785
Ayers, Abraham	1785
Daniel	1784
James	1785
Thomas	1784
William	1784
Bacon, John	1784
Nicholas	1790
Reuben	1787
Bagby, George	1785
Baggs, John	1784
Joseph	1789
Bailey, Azariah	1785
David	1853
William	1717
Baker, Francis	1804
Joseph	1801
Joshua	1789
Thomas H.	1848
Baldwin, David	1785
John	1785
Mordecai	1802
Robert	1785
William	1785
Ballard, Christopher	1793
Joshua	1785
Banks, Elisha Fowler	1794
Gerard	1791
Reuben	1785
Bankston, James	1787
Laurence	1793
Barber, Joseph	1791
Richard	1806
Thomas	1838
Barbre, Isaac	1795

Barbre, Jesse	1788		Benefield, Charles	—
Barcley, John	1786		Bennett, Arthur	1791
Barefield, John	1856		Bennis, heirs of John	1792
Richard	1784		Bentley, Balam	1792
Solomon	1796		John	1784
Barkshare, Richard	1787		William	1791
Barlow, Henry	1804		Benson, John	1789
William	1818		Berry, John	1784
Barnap -	1791		John Sr.	1815
Barnes, John	1830		William	1787
Barnett, Abraham	1787		Berryhill, Andrew	1784
Claiborne	1786		Samuel	1734
Joel	1784		Betsell, John	1788
Joshua	1784		Bevens, William	1794
Samuel	1787		Bibb, Thomas	1791
Barronton, William	1785		Binion, John	1797
Barrow, William	1794		William	1797
Bartemore, Benjamin	1784		Bird, Michael	1792
Bartlett, William	1835		Bishop, James	1734
Barton, Willoughby	1786		Joshua	1785
Barwick, John	1842		Stephen	1784
Basdale, Jeffrey	1798		William	1784
Bass, Esan	1793		Bithea, Philip	1845
Bassett, George	1786		Black, John	1793
Batchelor, Cornelius	1786		William	1787
Bateman, Jason	1831		Blake, John	1799
Theophilus	1816		Blakey, Robert	1805
Bates, John	1785		Blanchard, Benjamin	1795
Beal, Archibald	1784		William	1785
Hezekiah	1784		Bland, Elisha	1807
Beard, Edmund	1785		William	1808
Beasley, Burwell	1785		Blifill, John	1794
John	1818		Bloodworth, Samuel	1784
Richard	1786		Blount, heirs of Jacob	1785
Beaver, Anthony	1798		James	1795
Beavin, William	1793		Richard	1817
Beckcom, Allen	1790		Blunt, James	1791
heirs of Allen			John Gray	1787
Beckcom	1811		Richard	1806
Samuel	1790		William	1787
Sherod	1790		Boatright, Edmund	1837
Simon	1790		George	1829
Solomon	1790		James	1836
Beckham, Allen	1787		Boazman, Jacob	1788
John	1784		Luke	1794
John Y	1818		Bobo, Sampson	1787
Samuel	1786		Bobough, Lewis	1786
Simon	1785		Boggs, Joseph	1802
Solomon	1787		Bonner, George	1787
Bedgood, John R.	1852		Ruth	1784
Richard	1814		Sherwood	1787
Richmond	1840		Bonnet, heirs of John	1788
Samuel	1820		Booker, Gideon	1785
Bedingfield, Joseph	1791		Boon, William	1796
Beezly, Joseph	1791		Borland, Andrew	1791
Bell, John	1785		Boswell, James	1796
Bender, John	1788			

Boon, William	1796	Brinton, John	1790
Borland, Andrew	1791	William	1790
Nathan	1785	Britain, James	1790
Boswell, James	1796	Britt, David	1845
Bowen, Joel	1785	Jesse	1821
Oliver	1786	John	1817
Windal	1838	Brock, Eleazer	1792
Bower, Ephriam	1785	Brooks, Jacob	1785
Bowie, James	1784	9 Jesse	1784
Reason	1784	Rogers	1788
Boyd, Edward	1784	Brown, Allen	1785
Thomas	1791	Andrew	1785
Boykin, Francis	1786	Dempsey	1799
Jesse	1785	Emanuel	1835
William	1798	Frederick	1786
Bozeman, Joseph	1789	Henry	1794
Brack, Benjamin	1794	Hezekiah	1842
Bracken, Isaac	1793	Jean	1794
William	1791	Jesse	1788
Bracker, William	1800	John	1784
Bracks, Eleazer	1785	Joseph	1793
Bradley, Abraham	1785	Mary	1804
Braedy, William	1785	Richard S.	1836
Brandon, Jacob	1784	Thomas	1785
Branham, Spencer	1787	William	1785
Brannan, Samuel	1784	William C.	1847
Brannon, Thomas	1784	Brownen, Isaac	1795
Brantley, Aaron	1820	Browner, Charles	1786
Benjamin H.	1837	John	1787
Edward	1835	Brunson, Ebeneezer	
James	1839	Heirs of	1785
Jeptha	1846	David	1785
John F.	1839	John	1785
Spencer	1845	Brunston, William	1785
Thomas	1784	Bryan, Joseph	1793
Brasill, John	1787	Bryant, David	1790
Braswell, Benjamin	1786	Duncan	1786
Ferdinand	1787	John	1785
George	1788	Buck, William	1814
John	1785	William Sr.	1836
Kindred	1790	Buckhalter, Jacob	1785
Robert	1787	John	1785
Samuel	1786	Joshua	1787
Swanson	1786	Michael	1785
Bray, Thomas	1787	William	1787
Brazwell, Benjamin	1788	Bugg, Jacob	1787
Bready, William	1785	Jeremiah	1784
Breck, William	1816	John	1786
Bremer, John	1793	Nicholas	1784
Brewer, William	1788	Bullard, Wiley	1793
Brewster, Hugh	1786	Burch, Charles	1784
Brewston, John	1785	Edward	1784
Bridges, William	1822	Burford, Daniel	1785
Briggs, John	1787	Leonard	1785
Bright, Levi	1803	Mitchell	1786
Brinkley, John	1804	William	1785

Burgamot, William	1802	Carney, Matthew	1785
Burgamy, William	1797	Onsbey	1784
Burge, John	1793	Carpenter, Peter	1796
Burke, Charles	1785	Carr, Isham	1790
David	1786	Patrick	1784
Nimrod	1788	Thomas	1786
Burkes, Isham	1785	Carrell, William	1784
Burnet, Daniel	1790	Carson, David	1785
Burnett, Daniel	1790	Samuel	1786
John	1784	Thomas	1785
Burney, Brandal	1799	Carswell, Matthew	1805
David	1790	Carter, David	1784
James	1794	Giles	1819
John	1785	Silas	1840
Randal	1786	William	1797
Richard	1788	Cartice, John	1787
Willis	1816	Cartledge, James	1785
Burnhart, George	1788	Samuel	1784
Burns, Andrew	1787	Castavous, Micajah	1784
Burnsides, John	1785	Castellon, Michael	1785
Burris, Hansford	1841	Castleberry, Henry	1784
Burt, Moody	1784	Jacob	1784
Burton, Richard	1784	Jeremiah	1786
Bush, John	1786	John	1786
Levi	1818	Peter	1786
Nathan	1820	Caswell, John	1794
Bussey, Hezekiah	1785	Catching, Joseph	1793
Thomas	1785	Seymour	1784
Butler, Daniel	1789	Catchings, Benjamin	1790
Buttery, Zachariah	1786	Joseph	1784
Byne, Edmund	1786	Cates, Thomas	1793
		Cato, James	1826
Cade, Drury	1788	Caudry, Jonathan	1797
Cader, Francis	—	Cawthon, William	1793
Cahoon, James	1797	Cawthorn, Josiah,	
Cain, John	1786	heirs of	1785
William	1787	Josiah	1785
Calhoun, Abraham	1813	William	1787
Calk, James	1785	Certam, James	1798
Call, Richard	1784	Cessna, John	1786
Cambell, Gilbert	1796	Chambers, John	1784
William	1785	Champlis, Christopher	1784
Camp, Samuel	1787	Chance, Henry	1798
Thomas	1787	Isaac	1791
William	1785	Sampson	1797
Campbell, John	1785	Simpson	1791
William	1785	Vincent	1793
Canady, John	1786	Chandler, Abednego	1792
Candler, Henry	1785	Mordecai	1792
John	1785	Chany, Emanuel	1789
William	1784	Chapman, William	1786
Cannon, Caleb	1801	Chappell, John	1797
Cantey, James	1809	Chavis, Jeremiah	1785
John	1809	Chevalier, Chas.Francis	1788
Carlisle, John	1786	Childers, David	1784
Carnes, Thomas P.	1793	Childress, Richard	1788

6

Childers, Thomas	1784	Connell, Jesse	1791
Childrey, John	1786	Connelly, James	1788
Childs, Moses	1796	John William	1793
Chileney, William	1785	Patrick	1787
Chisolm, John	1785	Conner, Daniel	1798
Childry, Thomas	1784	John	1788
Chivers, Joel	1794	Connor, Daniel	1785
Larkin	1849	Cook, Cornelius	1848
Thomas	1788	David	1788
Christmas, Nathaniel	1786	Giles	1816
Robert	1786	John	1785
Clark, Elijah	1785	McKean	1832
William	1784	Reuben	1787
Clarke, Gibson	1785	Cooke, Heirs of George	1785
John Sr.	1788	Cooksey, William	1799
Clay, David	1786	Coop, Henry	1786
Percibal	1799	Cooper, Isaac	1816
Clayton, John	1789	James	1786
Clemens, Hosea	1799	John	1800
Coalson, William	1787	Joseph	1794
Coats, John	1787	William	1838
Lasley	1790	Coston, John	–
Nathaniel	1785	Thomas	1838
Cobb, Ezekiel	1786	Coup, Henry	1785
James	1790	Michale	1785
Joseph	1786	Coursey, William	1794
Cobbs, James	1808	Cowens, Eleazer	1793
John	1797	Cowen, Edward	1785
Joshua	1804	William	1789
Cochran, William	1787	Cox, Henry	1791
Cocke, Zebulon	1793	John	1791
Cocker, Edward	1787	Josiah	1794
Cockerham, James	1791	Thomas	1801
Cocks, James	1801	William	1793
Cole, Benjamin	1834	Crane, Lewis	1785
Josiah	1785	Crawford, Anderson	1786
William	1786	Charles	1786
Coleman, Curtis	1794	John	1785
Harris	1784	Samuel	1787
James	1786	Strother	1786
Jones	1785	Thomas	1843
John	1784	Cresswell, Da:.vid	1786
Jonathan	1793	Gilbert	1787
Moses	1787	Creswell, James	1787
Thomas	1820	Robert	1787
Collier, William	1784	Samuel	1787
Collins, James	1817	Cribbs, Gilbert	1786
John	1785	Thomas	1784
William	1788	Criddle, Thomas	1790
Colson, Sanders	1793	Crispus, James	1787
Colter, John	1796	Crittenden, John	1801
Comins, David	1790	Crittenton, John	1789
Eleazer	1789	Croker, William	1786
Cone, James	1795	Crookshanks, Patrick	1794
John	1816	Croom, Emra	1852
William	1784	Major	1846

7

Croome, Elijah	1804	Dardien, John	1799
Crosby, George	1791	Darding, John	1785
William	1797	Dardin, John	1794
Cross, Edward	1821	Davenport, LQC	1801
Crumley, Anthony	1785	Thomas	1785
Crutchfield, John	1785	heirs of Thomas	1785
Culbreath, John	1784	David, William	1784
Peter	1784	Davidson, James	1791
Culpepper, John	1786	Joseph	1786
Sampson	1791	Davis, Absalom	1785
Cummins, David	1833	Benjamin	1784
Eli	1831	Blanford	1785
Robert	1794	Chesley	1785
Cunningham, John	1785	Clementus	1786
W.	1785	Diocletion	1821
Cureton, Richard	1784	Enos A.	1849
William	1788	Jacob	1787
Curl, John	1785	James	1784
Currie, John	1789	Joel	1809
Curry, Alexander	1787	heirs of John	1784
David	1793	Joseph	1797
John	1815	Lewis	1786
Robert	1787	Meredith	1799
William	1787	Moses	1785
Cutchings, Meredith	1785	Robert Jr.	1785
Cuthbert, Alex Daniel	1785	Samuel	1785
Cutts, Joseph	1820	Solomon	1786
		Thomas	1794
Dameron, John	1792	William	1785
Dampier, Daniel	1784	Dawson, James	1795
Daniel, Abraham	1786	Richmond	1793
Amos	1804	Day, Ambrose	1788
Benjamin	1786	Henry	1785
Charles	1788	Robert	1784
Edmund	1787	Deampher, Aylesey	1816
Eustis	1788	Dean, John	1784
James	1786	Thomas	1787
Jonas	1811	Dearizeaux, Stephen	1791
John	1788	Deas, DeWitt	1793
Stephen	1810	James	1793
Thomas	1787	Deason, Rachel	1790
William	1785	Debosk, Peter	1797
Daniell, Benjamin	1790	Declendemes, Matthew	1785
Danielly, John	1790	Deek, Joseph	1818
James	1787	Delaplaigne, Peter E.	—
Daniely, Daniel	1784	Delk, Jacob	1808
James	1785	Joseph	1797
Dannard, Jacob	1789	Denkins, Gilbert	1786
Darby, John	1786	Denman, Charles	1785
Richard	1785	Denmark, Shadrack	1806
Darbee, Jacob	1801	Dennard, Rebecca	1808
Darcy, Benjamin	1785	Shadrack	1817
Darcey, James	1785	Dennis, Abraham	1785
Darden, George	1785	Isaac	1788
Jacob	1787	Jacob	1784
Stephen	1787	John	1785

8

Dennison, Daniel	1785	Edwards, Gray	1818
Densby, Jacob	1787	Peter	1785
Dent, John	1830	Eiland, Absalom	1790
Deveaux, Peter	1784	Elands, Absalom	1793
Dickens, Lewis	1840	Elbert, Gen. Sam'l.	1785
Dickenseeds, Edward	1785	Eli, E. B.	1851
Dickson, David	1786	Elliott, Benjamin	1835
James	1788	William	1717
Jeremiah	1794	Ellis, Robert	1786
Michel	1789	Solomon	1787
Reuben	1799	Stephen	1785
Robert	1785	Ely, John	1839
Thomas	1795	Emanuel, Asa	1785
Dillard, George	1798	David	1785
Nicholas	1790	English, Cornelius	1788
Phillip	1800	James S.	1817
Dix, Andrew	1784	John	1794
Dixon, Michael	—	Thomas	1789
Robert	1792	Ennis, Jonathan	1796
Domin, Frederick	1794	Espey, James	1789
Domini, Frederick	1795	Eubank, Daniel	1783
Donnelly, John	1794	Evans, Benjamin	1787
Dooley, George	—	Daniel	1784
Douglas, Alexander	1785	David	1791
Edward	1790	Gibson	1784
John	1785	James	1785
William	1787	John	1784
Dowdey, Richard	1790	Josiah	1787
Dowell, Thomas	1785	Stephen	1785
Downs, William	1784	William	1786
Duckworth, Jacob	1786	Zacheus	1796
Dudley, Elam	1837	Eves, Nathaniel	1785
Duggan, John	1805		
Duhart, Jno. W.	1785	Fagan, Aaron	1798
Duke, Buckner	1785	George	1795
heirs of James	1787	Fail, Thomas	1789
John Taylor	1785	Fair, Jacob	1785
William	1787	Peter	1788
Dukes, Henry heirs of	1809	Fandley, Norris	1786
Duncan, David	1786	Farmer, John	1810
James	1786	Faulconer, Jacob	1791
heirs of Jos.	1787	Feagan, Aaron	1787
Matthew	1785	Featherstone, Howell	1791
Miles	1785	Felps, David	1785
Thomas	1815	Fenn, Eli	1830
Dunn, Luke	1786	Fravier	1784
Durbin, Luke	1786	John	1785
Durden, Frances	1818	William	1786
		Zachariah	1786
Eads, heirs of John	1785	Fenney, Euphama	—
Eady, John	1785	Ferrell, James	1785
Earnest, George	1790	Few, Benjamin	1785
Jacob	1787	Igantius	1785
Eason, Isaac	1840	William	1785
Eaton, Robert	1795	Fields, James	1793
Eckols, Joel	1788	Finchwell, Joseph	1785

9

Finley, James	1784	Fussell, Ezra	1785
Fish, Joseph J.	1827	Fusils, Thomas	1790
Fisher, Metcalf	1840		
Fitzpatrick, Frederick	1840	Gaffold, William	1788
Joseph	1786	Gainer, Jesse	1817
William	1786	Galman, Harmon	1794
Fleming, Robert	1785	Galphin, George & John	1784
William	1785	John	1787
Fling, John	1785	Thomas	1785
Flournoy, Robert	1786	Gamble, John	1784
Thomas	---	Ganer, William	1790
Floyd, James N.	1855	Gardiner, John	1789
Paleman (Pateman?)	1788	Gardner, Lewis	1785
Flucker, George	1788	William	1784
Fluker, Baldwin	1785	Garnel, Eli	1785
William	1785	Garner, Jacob	1805
Folds, George	1784	Redick	1804
Forbes, Benjamin	1838	Garrett, John	1785
Ford, Joshua	1785	Gaston, Alexander	1785
Forehand, Jordan	1821	David	1784
Forrest, Hillory	1839	Gates, Philip	1802
Forsyth, Robert	1786	George, William	1784
Fort, Arthur	1785	Germany, John	1784
Owen	1784	Samuel	1785
Thomas	1785	William	1785
Fortune, Jacob	1785	Gibbs, William	1785
Foson, William	1801	Gibson, Adam	1790
Foster, John	1786	Gidden, Richard	1789
William	1785	Gilbert, Drery	1841
Fouche, Jonas	1788	Thomas	1787
Foulds, George	1786	Giles, John	1797
Fountain, William	1788	Gillett, Elijah	1784
Fowler, Nathan	1786	Gilliland, Thomas	1785
Francis, Cordall	1820	William	1785
Franklin, George	1797	Gilmore, Charles H.	1797
Philimon	1789	James	1805
Samuel O.	1851	John H.	1816
William	1785	Gladen, James	1807
Fraser, Andrew (Frazer)	1785	Glamkin, John	1785
Malikah	1785	Glascock, Thomas	1785
Frederick, Francis	1789	William	1784
Thomas	1786	Glaspy, John	1784
Freeman, Holeman	1784	Glass, Joel	1785
John	1784	John	1785
William	1784	Glenn, Daniel	1787
Freil, John	1785	David	1789
Freel, Lewis	1784	Robert	1810
Fuller, Isaac	1785	William	1787
John	1785	Glover, Absalom	1839
John, Sr.	1785	Benjamin	1848
Joshua	1785	Jesse	1852
Fulton, Samuel	1785	Stephen	1784
Samuel, Jr.	1790	William	1787
Fuqua, Prater	1791	Godby, William	1786
Thomas	1784	Golden, John	1788
Furlow, William	1786	Goldsberry, Jonathan	1785

Goode, Edward	1787		Hadden, William	1785
Gordan, Benjamin	1815		Hagans, Edward	1784
Gordon, Ambrose	1785		Hoil, Edward	1785
Benjamin	1811		Haines, Nathan W.	1854
Gordsby, Cary	1785		Haley, Holliday	1808
Grant, Daniel	1787		Hall, Edward	1784
Peter	1785		James	1799
Thomas	1790		William H.	1860
Grantham, John	1797		Hamlin, Richard	1790
William	1801		Hamilton, Thomas	1785
Graves, Richard	1785		William	1786
Thomas	1787		Hammett, James	1784
Gray, Enoch	1821		William	1789
James	1786		Hammitt, Sitha	1786
John	1787		Hammock, Amelia	1795
Thomas	1785		Benedict	1784
Graybill, Henry	1788		John	1786
Grear, Robert	1785		Hammond, George	1785
Greazell, George	1784		Handley, George	1785
Green, Benjamin	1786		James	1789
Isaac	1785		Hannah, Thomas	1785
James	1785		Hanson, Michael	1848
John	1785		Harbuck, Michael	1797
Leonard	1787		Nicholas	1785
McKeen	1785		Hardee, Collins	—
Peleg	—		Isaac	1786
Thomas	1790		Hardie, William	1816
William Sr.	1784		Hardwick, William P.	1836
Greene, Benjamin	1787		Hargrove, Howell	1801
James	1791		Josiah	1797
William	1785		Harkins, Thomas	1785
Greer, Aaron	1785		Harper, George	1787
Gilbert	1787		Joseph	1785
Josiah	1797		Robert	1785
Thomas	1784		Samuel	1785
William	1786		William	1785
Grice, Fatha	1803		Harrell, Bailey	1787
Jesse	1801		Edward	1791
Griffin, Benjamin	1799		William	1800
Enoch	1834		Zachariah	1786
Farnafol	1792		Harrington, John	1787
John	1816		Thomas	1785
Lenn	1793		Harris, Archiles	1786
Major	1793		Buckner	1784
Mathew	1784		Daniel	1787
William	1787		David	1785
Griffith, Samuel	1784		Edmund	1787
Grimes, Nathan	1787		George	1792
Thomas	1786		James	1784
Grimsbey, John	1785		Jesse	1796
Griner, Phillip	1785		Mathew	1795
Groom, Heirs of Elijah	—		Nathan	1787
Jesse	1811		Tyre G.	1785
Grooms, Wiley	1812		Walton	1784
Groves, John	1795		Harrison, Benjamin	1795
Guthril, John	1796		Edward	1789

Harrison, Gabirel	1832		Herndon, George	1797
James U.	1851		Joseph	1829
Joseph	1836		Herren, Alexander	1797
William	1788		Herrill, William	1796
Hart, George	1784		Herring, William	1789
Joel	1787		Hewett, William	1784
Joseph	1843		Hewil, William	1850
Reuben	1810		Hewitt, William	1785
Robert	1796		Hickinbottom, Joseph	1784
Samuel	1798		Hickman, Joseph	1797
Harthorn, Thomas	1785		Theophilus	1789
Hartley, Henry	1785		William	1797
Burwell	1844		Hicks, John	1785
George	1859		James	1832
James	1815		Nathaniel	1788
Hartly, Raiford	1848		Nathaniel Jr.	1784
Hartsfield, George	1787		Samuel	1784
Harvel, Samuel	1787		Higdon, Charles	1798
Harvey, Blassingame	1789		HIckinbottom, Burrows	1784
Charles	1784		Hightower, Charnal	1814
Evans	1788		Hill, Edward	1786
James	1785		George	1791
Joel	1785		James	1785
John	1784		John	1788
Michael	1784		Joshua	1793
Thomas	1785		Moses	1785
Hatcher, Archibald	1784		William	1786
Henry	1793		Hillard, Abigail	1799
Jeremiah	1785		James	1785
John	1785		Hillary, Christopher	1785
Haughton, Joshua	1785		Hilliard, Major	1799
Thomas	1784		Hilyer, James	1796
Haul, George	1786		Hines, Churchwell	1835
Hawkins, Francis	1790		James	1790
Samuel	1789		Robert	1786
Hawthon, Thomas	1791		Hinsley, Thomas	1788
Hawthorn, Peter	1816		Hinson, William	1790
Hayman, Staunton	1791		Hinton, Job	1784
Hays, Andrew	1786		Hobbs, Jonathan	1787
Arthur	1787		Hobson, Briggs	1786
Haymon, Stephen	1784		Edward	1799
Headen, Louisa	1808		Griggs	1799
Headspeth, Charles	1788		Hodge, Robert	1785
Heard, Bernard	1786		Hodges, Redding	1841
Jesse	1788		Hoff, Samuel	1785
John	1786		Hoges, Lemuel	1818
John Sr.	1784		Hogg, James	1785
Joseph	1812		James Sr.	1785
Stephen	1784		William	1785
Heart, Samuel	1786		Holdness, James	1791
Hearthorn, William	1785		Hollaman, David	1807
Hearton, Thomas	1791		Holland, Demsey	1788
Helton, Joseph	1816		Holloman, Samuel	1784
Hemphill, William	1793		Hollenger, Titus	1784
Henderson, Zachariah	1784		Holliday, Ayers	1785
Hendley, John	1786		Holliman, David	1785

12

Holliman, Mark	1785	Hubert, Mathew	1793
Richard	1785	Huckaby, Isam	1788
Hollinger, William	1785	Hudson, Isaac	1791
Hollingsworth, Stephen	1793	James	1785
Holloway, Barnes	1787	Nathaniel	1784
Holly, Jacob	1794	Robert	1785
Jonathan	1792	William	1798
Nathaniel	1788	Hughes, James	1793
Thomas	1789	Nicholas	1784
Holmes, Robert	1785	Hughs, James	1789
Holms, John	1784	Nicholas	1785
Holt, Thomas	1811	Hull, William	1851
Holton, Francis	1784	Hunt, Daniel	1804
Samuel	1793	FitzMaurice	1802
Hood, Benjamin	1787	John	1790
Nathaniel	1793	William	1785
Willy	1803	Hunte, John	1810
Hooks, Thomas	1804	Hunter, Dalziel	1788
William	1791	Miles	1785
Hooper, Absalom	1792	Hunts, FitzMaurice	1790
Robert	1788	Hurd, William	1816
Hopkins, Lambert	1786	Hutchins, James	1795
William	1789	Hutchinson, James	1801
Hopson, Briggs	1786		
William	1825	Ikener, Michael	1787
Horn, Jacob	1790	Ingram, Richard	1793
Hornby, Philip	1784	Inman, Joshua	1784
Horne, John	1795	Shadrack--	
Horsey, Tarleton	1790	heirs of	1785
Horton, Daniel	1809	Irby, Edward	1787
Hoskins, Mariam	1790	Irvin, Alexander	1784
Houghs, Samuel	1787	Hugh	1784
Houghton, James	1788	Lawson I.	1784
Joshua	1786	William	1784
Thomas	1786	Irwin, Alexander	1787
William	1788	Hugh	1786
House, Joseph	1798	Jared	1784
Laurence	1785	John L.	1818
Housley, Weldon	1785	William	1788
Houston, James	1785	Islands, Absalom	1784
William	1785	John	1785
Houstoun, Henry	1791		
John	1785	Jack, Samuel	1784
Howard, Benjamin	1784	Jackson, Abraham	1791
Charles	1817	Absalom	1792
James	1787	Allen	1850
John R.	1837	Charles	1791
Joshua	1825	David	1796
Nancy	1805	Isaac	1785
Naughflight	1787	James	1784
Rhesa	1785	Job	1784
Samuel	1820	John	1785
Thomas	1787	Joseph	1786
Howell, David	1785	Peter	1784
Joseph	1797	Randal	1784
Nathaniel	1785	Reuben	1784
		Robert	1793

Jackson, Thomas	1786		Jones, H. P.	1853
Walter	1793		James	1785
Warren	1838		Jesse	1785
William	1784		John	1785
Jarrott, Robert	—		Jonathan	1785
Jarvis, Patrick	1784		Nathan	1785
Jenkins, Arthur	1785		Philip	1785
Benjamin	1784		Robert	1784
Daniel	1829		Seaborn	1784
Drury	1836		Thomas	1786
Evans	1817		William	1785
Francis	1793		Jordan, Asa	1804
Hezekiah	1839		Benjamin	1787
Lewis	1810		Britton	1811
Richard	1785		Cornelius	1838
Robert	1786		Dempsey	1787
Uriah	1839		Lewis	1786
Jennings, Sarah	1790		Thomas	1805
Jernigan, Lewis A.	1837		William	1790
Jerrett, Robert	1786		Jukns, Dempsey	1784
Jiles, Thomas	1792		Justice, Dempsey	1784
John, Zephaniah	1787		Isaac	1786
Johnson, Benjamin	1792			
Daniel	1785		Karr, Ezekiel	1797
David	1794		Keath, Samuel Jr.	1790
Elijah	1826		Keaton, John	1790
Equiny	1810		Kelly, Edward	1784
James	1785		Jacob	1786
James Jr.	1794		James	1784
James Sr.	1793		James B.	1846
Jared	1820		John	1789
John	1793		Thomas	1784
Sarah	1805		William	1785
Stephen	178-		Kemp, James	1786
William	1785		Thomas	1785
heirs of William	1786		William	1793
William	1854		Kendal, David	1795
Wilson	1798		Jeremiah	1784
Johnston, Caleb	1786		William	1795
Jesse	1786		Kendrick, Burrell	1793
John	1785		Hezekiah	1787
Malcolm	1787		James	1794
Samuel	1797		James Jr.	1796
Thomas	1784		Keniday, John	1788
William	1787		Kennedy, Andrew	1802
Joiles, William	1815		John	—
Joiner, Benjamin	1784		Joshua	1800
Edmund	1822		Samuel	1836
Elias	1855		Kerr, Henry	1785
Jones, Benjamin	1787		Kettle, Mary	1797
Charles	1787		Kilgore, John	1784
David	1784		Ralph	1784
Elias	1785		William	1785
Francis	1799		Kilpatrick -	1786
Frederick	1785		Kimbrough, Allen	—

Kimbrough, John	1785		Leapham, Moses	1785
William	1785		Ledbetter, Fred'k.	1787
Kimmea, William	1811		Isaac	1796
Kimmon, Kendrick	1836		John	1785
Kindrick, Nathaniel	1790		Lee, Bud	1833
King, Charles	1837		Cato	1817
John	1785		Elias	1814
Josiah T.	1841		Joshua	1787
Parks	1792		Sampson Sr.	1814
Kirk, John	1798		Leggett, Abner	1784
Kirkham, Joseph	1798		John	1785
Kirkland, John	1798		Lenair, Isaac	1787
Kitchen, Benjamin	1793		Leonard, John	1798
Kitts, John	1785		Lesley, Joseph	1784
Knight, Elijah	1844		Lester, Thomas	1785
Jess B.	1857		Lethgo, Robert	1807
Kilb, George	1788		Lethgore, Andrew	1785
Koonce, George	1799		Lett, Reuben	1787
			Leverett, Henry	1784
Lackey —	1788		John	1785
Lafever, John	1786		Lewis, heirs	
Lamar, John	1785		of Lewis	1787
Luke	1792		Thomas	1787
Samuel	1785		William	1851
Thomas	1784		Lightfoot, John	1793
William	1785		Lindsay, John	1792
Lamb, Abraham	1784		Dennis	1785
Jesse	1790		Lingo, Elijah	1818
Thomas	1785		Patrick	1791
Lamkins, Samuel	1790		Moses	1791
Land, Henry	1790		Linn, Charles	1787
John	1788		John	1785
Landers, Abraham	1786		Linsey, Dennis	1807
Jacob	1785		Linton, John	1793
Landrum, William	1798		Lipham, Aaron	1788
Lang, John	1785		Frederick	1788
Langford, James	1793		Lithgroe, Robert	1785
Langston, Benjamin	1785		Little, Frederick	1801
Samuel	1784		William Sr.	1789
Lankford, Josiah	1785		Lob, William	1786
Moses	1785		Lockhart, Benjamin	1785
Larimore, John	1784		Isaac	1801
Lasseter, Hansil	1790		Loftin, Elkanah	1788
Laughen, Noel	1822		Lofton, Margaret	1791
Lawhon, John	1829		Thomas	1797
Nathaniel	1819		Van	1790
Noel	1818		Logan, Benjamin	1833
Lawrence, John	1837		Phillip	1786
Sherwood	1853		Londay, Mathew	1812
Lawson, Andrew—			Long, Nicholas	1793
heirs of	1785		Nicholas Jr.	1791
John	1787		Robert	1784
Roger Jr.	1786		Longstreet, Daniel	1787
Thomas	1785		William	1796
Layton, Zilpha	1858		Lord, Lodwick	1804
Leapham, Aaron	1793		William	1796
Frederick	1788		Lott, Absalom	1787

15

Lott, Arthur	1787	Mathew, James	1785
John	1788	Mathews, Stephen	1810
John Jr.	1789	William	1786
Mark	1793	Matthews, John	1812
Love, David	1786	Mesheck	1785
Low, John	1787	Moses	1785
Lowe, Daniel	1785	Thomas	1802
Izaac	1786	William	1784
John	1787	Maxwell, Josiah	1785
Lowry, John	1795	Robert	1790
Simeon	1790	May, Edmund	1800
Loyd, Daniel	1817	James	1790
Lunday, Mathew	1795	John	1785
Lynch, John	1791	William	1784
Lynn, Curtis	1787	Mayo, Mark	1801
heirs of John	1787	Mays, Etheldred	1804
Lynzy, John	1850	Maze, John E.	1851
Nelson	1850		
		McCarcal, James	1790
Mackay, James	1785	McCartie, John	1785
Thomas	1790	McCaughy, John	1827
William	1806	McClendon, Wilson	1790
Madden, David	1785	Isaac	1785
Maddox, William	1784	Jacob	1786
Mahon, Archibald	1802	John	1795
Malpres, Hardy	1820	Joel	1790
Manadue, Henry	1787	Lewis	1799
Mann, John	1785	McCoan, Andrew	1786
Mannin, John	1785	McCondachies, John	1818
Manning, Adam	1785	McCord, David	1806
Mannon, Drury	1812	McCorkle, James	1796
John	1804	McCormack, Benjamin	1784
Robert	1784	James	1786
Marberry, Thomas	1786	McCormich, James	1786
Marbury, Thomas	1784	John	1786
Marcus, John	1801	Thomas	1785
Marlow, William	1785	McCrary, Jonathan	1805
Marshall, Rev. Abraham	1784	McCullen, Bryant	1791
Daniel	1784	McCullers, Bryant	1789
John	1787	Charles	1787
Joseph	1784	David	1787
Lachevous	1784	Drury & David.	1784
Levi	1787	Mary	1788
Mathew	1784	McCulloch, Patrick	1785
Moses	1787	Samuel	1785
Solomon	1784	McDaniel, Mary	1822
Martin, Henry	1838	McDonald, Charles	1786
James	1784	Thomas	1787
John	1788	McDouglad, Daniel	1838
John Jr.	1784	McDougall, Alexander	1785
Joseph	1790	McDowell, Thomas	1790
Levi	1816	William	1790
Richard	1810	McDuffie, Malcolm	1820
William	1790	McFarland, James	1784
Mason, George	1825	John Jr.	1784
Thomas	1798	McGarr, Owen	1784

16

McGary, Robert	1785		Messer, Thomas	1790
McGee, Lewis	1784		Metcalf, Anthony	1785
Shadrack	1795		Danza	1785
McGeehee, Thomas	1784		William	1786
McGehee, Samuel	1791		Metts, Levin	1830
Thomas	1786		Middleton, Holland	1785
William	1784		John	1815
McGill, John	1787		Robert	1785
McGilton, James	1785		Miles, John	1790
McGowan, David	1790		Moses	1802
Robert	1790		Millen, Nicholas	1786
McGregor, Alexander	1785		Miller, Alexander	1791
McGruder, Ninian	1786		Elisha	1790
Zadok	1786		Jesse	1787
McGwain, Patrick	1816		Jonathan	1789
McIntosh, John	1785		Joseph	1790
Lachlin	1785		Joshua	1784
McKaskill, Peter	1852		Lewis	1810
McKinney, Henry	1785		Nicholas	1786
William	1786		Millidous, George	1800
McLane, Daniel	1790		Millirons, Christopher	1818
McLean, John	1784		Mills, Elisha	1788
McLeod, Angus	1818		Stephen	1855
Neal	1819		Milner, John	1784
McMath—	1787		Milton, John	1785
McMillan, Mathers	1793		Mimms, Drury	1784
McMum, John	1794		Shadrack	1785
McMurphy, Daniel	1785		Mitchell, John	1785
McMurray, William	1790		Thomas	1784
McMurry, William	1786		Stephen	1785
McNabb, Rebot-heirs of	1788		William	1785
McNeely, Daniel	1792		Moats, Levi	1785
Mary	1787		Silas	1784
McNeil, Archibald	1784		Simon	1784
Daniel	1784		William	1784
Daniel Sr.	1784		Moffett, Gabriel	1807
James	1784		Monger, Sampson	1791
McNeil, Jess	1784		Moon, Samuel	1785
Michael	1784		Mooney, Joseph	1788
McNelly, Daniel	1784		Moore, Alexander	1785
McNiel, David	1785		Arthur	1787
McNully, Hugh	1784		Francis	1785
McQuathy, Thomas	1838		James	1784
McSwain, Patrick	1815		John	1785
McWilliams, John	1792		Jonas	1785
Thomas	1817		Josiah	1810
Meanly, John			Richard	1800
Meddow, John	1788		Thomas	1795
Meloan, John	1790		William	1785
Melton, Isaac	1786		Moorman, Charles	1801
Nathaniel	1794		Morgan, James	1790
Mercer, Asa	1785		Jesse	1784
John	1785		John	1785
Merchant, Isaac	1811		John M.	1799
John	1799		Philip	1785
Messer, Peter	1796		heirs of Robert	1787
	1787		Stephen	1787

17

Morgan, William	1784	Nobles, Lewis L.	1810
Morris, John	1786	Norgan, James	1790
William	1785	North, John	1786
Morganson, Asa	1784	Nowland, Phillip	1785
Moseley, Benjamain	1785	Numan, William	1790
Littleberry	1785	Nutt, John	1787
Robert	1785		
Thomas	1785	Oakham, William	1788
Thomas Jr.	1785	Oates, Jeremiah	1787
Mosley, William	1785	Oatlaw (Outlaw?),Edward	1799
Moss, Leonard	1784	Odom, Isaac	1795
Mott, Joseph	1786	Uriah	1787
William	1798	Offcutt, Ezekiel	1786
Motte, Joseph	1791	John	1785
Zepaniah	1785	Sampson	1815
Nathan	1790	Oliver, John	1784
William	1784	Martin	1816
Mullins, Clement	1787	O'Neal, Axom	1784
Murphy, Edward	1797	John	1784
William B.	1807	Oricks, James	1786
Murphry, Edward	1785	Orr, John	1820
Morris	1786	Osborn, Reuben	1853
		Outlaw, Edward	1790
Nail, Elisha	1792	Owen, Effingham	1788
Nall, Martin	1797	Owens, Robert	1785
Napier, Rene	1786		
Thomas	1786	Pace, Thomas	1785
Nash, heirs of Clement	1786	Padgett —	1788
Naylor, George	1788	Page, John	1844
Neal, David	1786	John D.	1851
Thomas	1785	Pain, Samuel	1784
Thomas Jr.	1785	Painter, Joseph	1787
Nealon, John	1786	Palls, James	1790
Neel, Elias	1800	Palmer, John	1785
William	1794	Jonathan	1786
Neeley, Thomas	1821	Solomon	1784
Julia	1846	Panill, Joseph	1784
Richard	1786	Parish, James	1819
Thomas	1797	William	1830
Neil, Thomas	1788	Parker, Aaron	1797
Neile, George	1784	Daniel	1787
Neiley, John	1789	Francis	1787
Neland, William	1797	John	1784
Nelson, William	1790	William	1796
New, Stephen F.	1848	Parkerson, Jacob	1786
Newberry, William	1785	Parks, John	1785
Newdigate, heirs of John	1786	Partain, Robert	1790
Newman, John	1786	Parum, Peter	1798
Newnham, John	1793	Patrick, Henry	1818
News, John	1842	Patterson, Gideon	1784
Newsom, Asa	1848	John	1784
Kinchen	1828	Robert	1785
Solomon	1786	William	1784
Nicholson, Benjamin	1791	Pavys, Dial	1788
Night, Jesse B.	1844	Paxton, William	1785
Nehemiah	1790	Payne, Samuel	1785

18

Payne, Samuel	1785	Pope, Wily M.	1843
Zachariah	1796	Porter, Benjamin	1785
Peacock, Archibald	1833	Thomas	1788
Asa P.	1835	Pothree, Francis	1790
John	1818	Pott, John	1765
Moalton	1829	Pounds, Rheuben	1785
Urian	1827	Powell, Alfred	1852
Peak, John	1785	Cader	1784
Peal, John	1784	Edward	1784
Pearrie, Nathaniel	1785	Jesse	1796
Peddy, Jeremiah	1796	Josiah	1786
Nehemiah	1799	Lewis	1785
Peeler, Frederick	1796	Moses	1784
Peevy, Dial	1785	Robert	1802
Pendleton, Solomon	1787	Stephen	1787
Pennington, Thomas	1784	William	1791
Penson, Isaac	1785	Prather, Edward	1784
Perison, John	1792	Price, Cabor (Cader?)	1792
Perkins, Abraham	1785	John	1785
Adam	1791	Littleberry	1840
John	1784	Moore	1838
Peter	1784	Rice	1811
William	1787	William	1790
Peret, Robert	1784	Prosser, Samuel C.	1853
Perrett, John	1785	Pugh, Elijah	1785
William	1790	Francis	1785
Perry, Isaac	1785	James	1786
John	1784	James Jr.	1785
Shadrack	1818	Jesse	1784
Petillo, John heirs of	1787	John	1785
Pevy, Peter	1784	Philophilus	1799
Pharas, William	1794	Pullen, Thomas	1792
Phenny, Lachlin	1785	Purnell, William F.	1853
Phillips, John	1793		
Lochariah	1792	Quarles, Roger	1784
Samuel	1793	Queens, John	1784
Zachariah	1784		
Dempsey	1787	Rachel, Zadok	1842
Isaac	1786	Miles	1789
John	1787	Rachels, John	1840
Joseph	1785	Rafforty, Michael	1784
Josiah	1785	Ragan, John	1784
William	1784	Nathaniel	1786
Pinkston, Daniel	1790	Ragland, Evan	1788
John	1790	William	1786
Zachariah	1802	Raiford, Morris	1792
Pittman, Phillip	1785	Raines, John	1784
Timothy	1784	Ramsey, Isaac	1784
Pitts, John D.	1826	John	1784
Polk, Charles	1787	Randol, Jr.	1784
John	1786	Randolph	1784
Pollard, James	1795	Samuel	1784
Robert	1785	Thomas	1785
William	1787	William	1784
Pool, Middleton	1797	Randolph, Isaac	1794
Pope, Willis	1788	Raney, John	1797

Raney, Thomas	1787	Robinson, Edward	1792
Ratcliff, Benjamin	1790	Israel	1793
Joseph	1789	John	1796
Rausaw, William	1790	John L.	1827
Rawls, John	1796	Samuel	1801
Ray, Ambrose	1817	William H.	1843
Charles	1799	Robison, Moses	1821
James	1797	Samuel	1810
William	1786	Robrick, James	1837
Zachariah	1798	Robuck, Rolly	1810
Rayfield, Spencer	1785	Rochel, James	1798
Rayley, Sarah	1793	Rochell, Miles	1790
Rayne, Joseph	1787	Rochels, Burwell	1820
Razar, Isaac	1784	Roe, Andrew	1786
Read, Thomas	1786	James	1793
John	1787	Roebuck, Rolly	1816
Reaves, Joseph	1793	Rogers, Andrew	1812
Red, James	1785	Britain	1785
Samuel	1785	Dread	1793
Reddick, William	1786	Drury	1786
Redding, George	1785	James	1854
Reddix, Abraham	1785	John	1787
Rees, Joel	1786	Nathan	1817
Reeves, John	1787	Peleg	1785
John L.	1833	Thomas	1795
Spencer	1785	Roquemore, Peter	1785
Thomas	1785	James	1785
Reiley, Joseph	1791	Rosebrough, George	1785
Renfroe, Enoch	1818	Ross, Moses	1793
Rentfrow, William	1792	Roughton, John	1788
Reyley, Edward	1796	Rountree, William	1790
Joseph	1789	Rousaw, William	1795
Reynolds, Absalom	1792	Rouse, Bartlett	1795
Rice, John	1784	Row, Hezekiah	1793
Richardson, Joseph	1784	Rowell, Edward	1784
Rickenson, Timothy	1785	Rowton, John	1791
Riddle, Anderson	1820	Rumley, Nathaniel	1788
William C.	1850	Runnells, George	1786
Ridon, Joseph S.	1785	Harmon	1796
Riley, Joseph	1785	Frederick	1785
Road, Charles	1795	Hannan	1789
Roan, Tudsdale	1792	Herman	1791
Roberts, Alvon	1793	Rushing, James	1816
John	1784	John	1788
Jonas	1785	Mathew	1784
Joshua	1789	Rutherford, John	1788
Richard	1798	Thomas B.	1816
Thomas	1785	William	1829
Robertson, David	1787	Ryan, James	1784
Edward	1798	Joseph	1793
Hugh	1795	Richard	1784
John Sr.	1790		
heirs of Jonathan	1787		
Joseph	1806	Saffold, Isham	1817
Robert	1794	Salisberry, Thomas	1788
William	1791	Sallis, John	1789

Sallisbury, Joseph	1789	Shelton, Henry	1795
Salter, James	1793	Shepard, Green L.	1857
Robert	1807	Shepherd, Thomas	1786
Thomas	1845	Sheppard, Andrew	1806
Salters, —	1784	David	1856
Sampson, Howell	1792	Francis	1843
Sanders, Jesse	1785	James	1817
Joshua	1784	John	1786
Mark	1784	Thomas	1790
Sanderlin, Robert	1799	William	1791
Sanford, Samuel	1790	Shepperd, James	1801
Sanson, James	1785	John	1787
Sapp, Dill	1785	Sherod, Joel	1798
Emanuel	1784	Shick, Frederick	1787
John	1784	Shield, Robert	1792
William	1785	Shields, Andrew	1784
Satterwhite, William	1785	Margaret	1805
Savage, Baker	17—	William	1791
Packer	1788	Shilton, Henry	1786
Robert	1785	Shipley, Robert	1791
Scarborough, Miles	1792	Show, Adam	1785
Moses	1800	Shuffle, William	1790
William	1786	Sikes, Daniel	1791
Scarbrough, Aaron	1799	heirs of Daniel	—
Ephriam	1797	William	1784
Scott, Abraham	1786	Simkins, Charles	1794
Benjamin	1787	Simmons, Charles	1784
Joseph	1786	James	1785
Peter	1785	John	1797
William	1785	Steve	1786
Scurry, Nicholas	1786	Simonson, Isaac	1785
Seals, William	1794	Simpkins, Charles	1791
Self, William	1800	Simpson, James	1784
Sessions, Joseph	1791	Samuel	1785
Shackleford, John	1786	Sims, James	1816
Shaddock, Thomas	1784	Mann	1784
Shaffer, David	1785	Sinquefield, Aaron	1794
Sharp, John	1785	Samuel	1787
John Sr.	1787	Sitten, heirs of John	1784
Joshua	1785	Sizemore, William	1785
Michael	1785	Skener, Michael	1787
Wiley	1793	Skinner, Isaac	1784
Shaw, David	1786	Skrine, Quintilian	1840
Thomas	1784	Slappey, Henry	1806
William	1798	Sled, Joshua	1790
Sheffell, Mark	1785	Smalley, Michael	1785
Sheffield, John	1785	Smart, Robert	1785
Robert	1790	Smith, Abraham	1788
William	1790	Bennett	1826
Sheffle, William	1786	Benajah	1807
Sheftall, Mordecai	1785	Charles	1785
Shelby, John	1793	Colbey	1816
Shelman, I.	1794	Cornelius	1785
John	1791	David	1785
Michael	1787	Eli	1850

Smith, Elijah	1856		Stewart, James	1785
George	1785		John	1785
Isaac	1839		Robert	1785
Jacob	1797		Stiff, William	1785
James F.	1849		Stinson, Nathan	1793
John	1785		Stocks, Bentley	1785
John C.	1787		Stokes, Drury	1818
Jordon	1815		John	1788
Joseph	1785		Nancy	1817
Lewis	1807		Samuel	1790
Nathaniel	1784		William	1844
Nehemiah	1788		Stone, Charles	1784
Nicholas	1804		William	1819
Peter	1829		Story, Edward	1785
Samuel	1787		Strahager, Rudolph	1785
Simon	1785		Straten, Joseph	1784
Thomas	1784		Strength, John	1786
William	1798		Stripling, Francis	1785
Smithson, Floristino	1786		Stroad, John	1796
Sneed, Charles	1794		Sturges, Andrew	1788
Dudley	1785		Sturgis, William	1787
Snell, Christopher	1790		Sullivan, William	1785
Snelson, Thomas	1784		Sutton, Jeremiah	1790
Solomon, David	1834		Phillip	1785
Spann, Francis	1790		Swain, Stephen	1790
Sparks, John	1797		Swanson, William	1796
Josiah	1790		Swearinger, John	1804
Samuel	1797		Swilla, Samuel	1798
Thomas	1842		Swint, Edward	1842
Spears, John	1787		Switzer, Leonard	1785
Speights, Jonathan	1837		Syllivant, William	1785
Spekes, Thomas	1790			
Spivey, James	1788		Talbot, Thomas	1786
Littleton	1787		Talor, Hodg	1817
Spurlock, heirs of Robert	1786		Tankersley, John	1786
Stallings, Ezekiel	1787		Tanner, Franklin	1850
James	1784		Joel	1786
Jesse	1785		Thomas	1842
Stamper, Howell	1792		Tannyhill, John	1791
Powell	1784		Tapley, John	1795
Stancock, George	1785		Tarver, Elijah	1816
Standley, Sands	1787		Tarbutton, Joseph	1837
Shadrack	1788		Benjamin	1841
Starnes, Ebeneezer	1790		Tate, Robert	1805
Station, Nathaniel	1796		Taylor, Drewry	1843
Statham, —	1794		Henry	1785
Steed, Phillip	1786		James	1802
Stephens, Benjamin	1794		James R.	1851
Jacob	1816		John	1784
John	1784		Joshua	1790
Steward, Jacob	1787		Josiah	1784
Stewart, Charles	1784		Thomas	1785
Clement	1784		William	1794
Isaac	1786		Wright	1793

Tennill, Benjamia	1794		Tunis, Nehemiah	1784
Francis	1785		Tunnell, Francis	1787
Terrell, Benjamin	1806		Turknett, Henry	1785
Joel	1787		Turner, Alfred	1808
Terrett, Robert	1786		William	1827
Tervin, George	1784		Tyson, Isaac	1799
Tharp, John	1842		John	1837
Thigpen, Randal	1831			
Thom, William	1787		Underwood, Benjamin	1791
Thomas, Etheldred	1787		Isum	1802
Gideon	1793		Josiah	1834
James	1785		Samuel	1784
Thompkins, Elizabeth	1794		Upton, Benjamin	1788
Thompson, Alexander	1788			
Benjamin	1785		Vann, William Westley	1842
Jesse	1785		Henry	1801
Joshua	1785		James	1787
Laban	1784		VanWinkle, John	1787
Robert	1817		Vasser, Micajah	1799
Samuel	1800		Veal, Edward	1818
William	1785		Thomas	1852
Thorn, David	1785		Verner, George	1788
Thornton, Elam	1793		Vickers, Abraham	1786
John	1801		Benjamin	1790
Samuel	1785		John	1790
Solomon	1785		Joshua	1786
William	1787		Robert	1789
Thrasher, George	1791		Thomas	1784
Thurman, Absolom	1785		Vinan, (Vivian)Thacker	1789
Tillmon, Littleberry	1790		Vinson, Levi	1817
Stephen	1789		Nathan	1819
Stephenson	1789			
Tindal, Joshua	1820		Wade, Nehemiah	1785
Tindall, William	1786		Wadkins, Mitchell	1804
Tine, Henry	1784		Wadsworth, James	1790
Tison, Frederick	1826		James Jr.	1790
Noah	1828		John	1832
Toler, Joel	1810		Wagner, George	1785
Tomlinson, David	1790		Henry	1784
Tomme, Joseph	1787		James	1785
Tooke, John	1836		Wagnon, Thomas	1786
Townsend, Henry	1785		Wainwright, George	1784
Thomas	1786		Walker, David	1785
Trapp, John	1785		Elisha	1790
Joseph	1804		James	1799
Travis, Gidion	1796		Jeremiah	1789
Trawick, Francis	1785		John	1820
Tray, John	1785		Joseph	1784
Mary	1791		Landers	1785
Trice, James	1790		Rev. Sanders	1784
Tripp, Henry	1785		Silvanus	1792
Tucker, Robert	1785		Thomas	1790
Thomas Jr.	1785		William	1798
Thomas Sr.	1784		Wall, Francis	1792
Tully, William	1787		John	1785

Wall, Joseph	1799	
Wallace, Charnal	1789	
Chathole	1788	
John	1794	
William	1784	
Wallacon, Daniel Jr.	1787	
Waller, William	1799	
Wallis, Charles	1791	
Charnel	1788	
Walton, George	1785	
Newell	1785	
Robert	1786	
Ward, John	1797	
John Jr.	1786	
Joshua	1784	
Moses	1792	
Ware, Nicholas	1785	
Warthon, Richard	1799	
Wash, William	1789	
Waters, Charles	1784	
Watson, Avaret	1802	
Benjamin	1797	
David	1790	
Elijah	1816	
Labon	1840	
Levi	1786	
Peter	1784	
Redick	1796	
Thomas	1784	
Watts, Jacob	1793	
John	1786	
Josiah	1811	
Thomas	1795	
Waudin, John	1785	
Weakly, Lewis	1787	
Weathers, Edward	1785	
Weaver, John	1799	
Webster, Abner	1785	
Samuel	1788	
Thomas	1785	
Welborn, Curtis	1799	
Welch, Benjamin	1784	
heirs of Joshua	1784	
Welcher, Jeremiah	1784	
William	1785	
Weldon, John	1788	
Wells, Benjamin	1785	
Benjamin Sr.	1784	
John	179-	
Joseph	1785	
Taverner	1806	
West, James	1785	
Sion	1790	
William	1786	
Wester, William	1784	

Westers, Elias	1799	
Westley, Lemon	1790	
Whatley, Jesse	1790	
John	1785	
Michael	1785	
Richard	1785	
Samuel	1784	
Wharton	1785	
Walton	1784	
Wheeler, Amos	1803	
Zachariah	1784	
Wheelis, Isham	1785	
Where, William	1784	
Whiddon, Green	1846	
White, Allen	1839	
Green B.	1850	
Isham	1839	
John	1785	
Samuel	1786	
Whitaker —	1785	
Whitfield, Robert	1838	
William	1820	
Whiteford, Jean	1788	
Whitehead, Amos	1790	
Jane	1790	
Thomas	1793	
William	1797	
Whitesides, John	1784	
Whitfield, Bryant	1835	
Reuben	1837	
Robert	1835	
Whitten, Oston	1787	
Whittle, John	1817	
Wicker, John	1823	
Nathaniel	1809	
Robert	1789	
William	1791	
Wiggins, Jesse	1787	
John	1784	
William	1785	
Welborne, Courtice	1787	
Wilbourn, Curtis	1792	
Wilder, Thompson	1784	
Wilds, Charles	1784	
Wilkins, Gabriel	1785	
William	1785	
Wilkinson, Reuben	1788	
Will, John	1785	
William	1784	
Williams, Charles	1784	
Daniel	1817	
Edward	1785	
Elijah	1786	
George	1786	
John	1785	

Williams, Joseph	1785	Wooten, James	1785
Joshua	1787	Nathan	1784
Paul	1810	Thomas	1785
Reuben	1795	Worthen, Richard	1799
William	1789	Thomas	1841
Williamson, Charles	1785	William	1799
Littleton	1786	Wright, Abednego	1785
Micajah	1786	Benjamin	1816
Robert	1797	Habucker	1785
William	—	Isaiah	1785
Willie, heirs of Wm.	1784	John	1785
Williford, Nathan	1794	John & Thomas	1830
Willie, Britton	1785	Thomas	1826
George	1787	William	1786
Isaiah	1785	Wingfield	1812
Wilson, Archibald	1842	Wyatt, Peyton	1735
John	1785	Wyche, Baille	1797
Samuel	1785	George	1786
Wimberly, David	1833		
Winfrey, Jesse	1785	Yankerfield, John	1786
Winne, John	1791	Yarborough, James	1786
Winsket, Samuel	1786	Littleton	1804
Wise, Sheridy	1791	Thomas	1786
Womack, Jesse	1787	Yearly, Henry	1796
Joseph	1786	Yorke, James	1785
William	1798	Young, Daniel	1784
Wood, Abraham	1790	Edward	1784
Balenger	1839	William	1785
David	1790	Youngblood, James	1784
Dempsey	1790	John	1786
Edward	1786	Jonathan	1784
George R.	1837	Younge, John	1785
Henry	1786	Younger, William	1785
James	1786		
John	1785	Zinn, Jacob	1785
Jonathan	1784		
Solomon	1789		
Thomas	1845		
William	1791		
Woodard, Warwick	1797		
Woodruff, Joseph	1784		
Woods, Nathaniel	1785		

(All names are written as they appear in the record).

LIST OF PERSONS LIVING WASHINGTON COUNTY
WHO REGISTERED FOR THE DRAWING - 1805
LOTTERY
────────────────────────────────

Persons entitled   Bachelor 21 years or over, one year
to draw   residence in Georgia, citizen of U.S.   1 Draw

                    Married man, with wife and/or child,
                    one year residence in Georgia and
                    citizen of U.S.   2 draws

                    Widow with minor child, one year
                    residence in Georgia.   2 draws

                    Minor orphan, or family of minor
                    orphans, with father dead and
                    mother dead or re-married.   1 draw

Land distributed in this lottery was the Districts 1 through
5 of Baldwin County; 1 through 3 of Wayne County; and one
through five of Wilkinson County. When the drawer received
land, the listing is "P"; when no land was received, the
listing is "B".

This list of those who registered to draw land for the 1805
Lottery has added significance because of the loss of the
1790, 1800, and 1810 census records of Georgia.

Abbu. Edward	BB	Andrews, Evans	BB
Acock, Benjamin	BB	Joseph	BB
Elias	P	Richard	BP
Adams, Hopewell	BB	Ard, James	B
William	BB	James	P
Adkins, Joseph	BB	Neil	B
Lewis	B	Reuben	BB
William	BB	Arline, John	BB
Akridge, Ezekiel	BB	Armstrong, Alexander	BB
William	BB	Jesse	BB
Alan, Bryan	BB	Avent, Ransom	BB
Mary	BB	Avera, Thomas	BB
William	P	Averett, Benjamin	BB
Albritton, William	BB	Henry	B
Alen, William	B	Avery, Jonathan	B
Allen, Charles	BB	Sanders	P
John	BB	William	BB
Allum, Edmund	BB	Ayers, Thomas	BB
Allums, Asa	BP		
John Sr.	BB	Baggs, Ezekiel	BB
John J.	BB	Baker, Francis	BB
Amison, Jesse	BB	John	BB
Josiah	BB	Jonathan	BB
Uriah	BB	Joseph	BB
Anderson, Elizabeth	BB	Thomas	BP
Willis	B	William	BB

26

Baley, David	BB		Betsill, Isaac	B
Harrison	BB		Bettis, Wyatt	BB
James Sr.	PB		Bishop, Seth	BB
John	B		Blackshear, Abraham	BB
William	B		David	BB
Ball, Anson	BB		Elijah	B
John	BP		Joseph	B
Richard	B		Moses	BB
Barber, Jacob	BB		Blakely, Blann	BB
Richard	BB		Blann, Elisha	LB
William	BP		Blount, James	PB
Barefield, Jesse	BB		Redding	LB
Richard	BB		Wilie	B
Bargainer, John	BB		Boggs, John	PB
William	B		Joseph Sr.	B
Barlow, Henry	BB		Boice, John	B
John	BB		Boon, Jacob	B
William	BB		James	BB
Barnes, John	BB		James Jr.	B
Joshua	BP		Joseph	PB
Barnett, Robert Sr.	BB		Bowen, Charles	BB
Robert, Jr.	BB		Harrod	B
Barron, Barney	B		John	BB
James	BB		Boyd, John	BB
Thomas	B		Boykin, Francis	BB
Barrow, Milly	BB		Sarah	BB
William	BB		William	BB
Basset, Richard	BB		Boys, Thomas	B
Bateman, David	BB		Bracken, James	BB
Jesse, Sr.	BP		William Sr.	BB
Theophilus	BB		William Jr.	B
William Sr.	PB		Bradley, Jesse	BB
William	B		Brantley, Benjamin	BP
Beasley, William	B		Harris	B
Beaty, James Sr.	B		James	B
Samuel	BB		Joseph	PB
William	BP		Solomon	BB
Beckcom, Laban	BB		Spencer	B
Russell	BB		Thomas	BB
Solomon	BB		Braswell, Mathew	B
William	PB		Reddick	B
Zachariah	BB		Richard	BB
Beddingfield, Alan	B		Sampson	BB
Joseph	BB		Sampson Sr.	B
Lewis	B		Wilie	B
Bedgood, John	BB		Bray, Peter	BB
John Jr.	B		Brazeal, Henry (orp.)	B
Richard	B		Bridges, Joseph	B
Bell, Hugh	B		Rebecca	BB
John Jr.	BB		Briges, Samuel	B
Reddick	BB		Bright, Levi	BB
Bennett, Levi	BB		Brinkley, Eli	BP
Rebecca	BB		John	BB
Benson, Nancy	BB		Britt, Jesse	BB
Berry, Lewis	B		John	BB

Brookins, Thomas	BB
Brooks, Edmund	BB
James	B
John	BB
William	BB
Brotton, John	BB
Brown, Alan Sr.	B
Asa	BB
Dempsey	BB
James	B
Jesse	BP
John Jr.	P
John Jr.	BB
Thomas	BB
William	BB
William	PB
Brumley, Micajah	BB
William	B
Brunson, Daniel	BB
Bryan, Augustus	P
Edward	BB
Bryant, David	BB
orphans of Lewis	B
Buck, William	B
Buk, William Sr.	BB
Bullard, Wilie	BB
Bullin, John	B
Bullock, Benjamin	BB
Carter	B
James	BB
Burgamy, William	BB
Burge, John	BB
Burk, Daniel	B
Elnathan	B
Nimrod	BB
Burnes, Joseph	BB
Burney, Arthur	BB
Elizabeth	BB
Ellis	B
Willis	BB
Bush, Levi	BB
Levi Jr.	BB
Busson, Jesse	BB
Butler, Bryant	B
Ford	B½
Bynum, William	BB
Cain, Nathaniel	BB
Calhoun, Ervin	B
James	B
James	B
James	BB
Philip	B
Campbell, George	P
John (Reverend)	B
John	BB
William	B

Cannon, Caleb	BB
Carlisle, Mathew	B
Micajah	B
William	B
Winnifred	BB
Carpenter, Peter	B
William	B
Carr, Isham	BB
Carter, George	B
Rachel	BB
Thomas	B
Cason, George	BP
Whitehouse	B
William	BB
Castelow, William	BB
Cavannah, Edward	B
Cavender, Mary	BB
Cawley, William	BB
Chalmers, Peter B.	B
Chandler, Edmund	BB
Chappel, John	BB
Wiley	B
Chastain, Blasingame	B
Peter	BB
William	BB
Cherrey, Samuel	P
Childers, Richard	BB
Childrey, Drury	B
Elizabeth	BB
Martha	BB
Childs, Isaac	BB
Moses	B
Chivers, Joel	B
Clark, Daniel	B
Clay, Chalender	
Orphans of	B
David	BP
Pierce	BB
Clemonds, Hosea	BB
Cloud, Jeremiah	BB
Cobb, Joshua	BB
Cobbs, Elizabeth	B
Jacob	BB
Cocks, Charles	B
Daniel	B
Henry	PB
James	BB
James Jr.	BB
John	B
Richard	BB
Thomas	BB
Cogburn, George	B
Coker, William	BB
Coleman, Elizabeth	BP
Menan	BB
Collins, Abhu	BB
Barbara	BB

Collins, John	BB
William	B
Colvin, John	BB
Comens, Eleazer	BB
Cone, Jesse	B
Coney, Aquilla	BB
Cook, Benjamin	BB
Deborah	BB
Julius	B
Lucy	BB
Orph. of Reuben	B
Thomas	BP
Cookson, Elizabeth	PB
Cooper, John	BB
Obediah	BB
Copeland, Elisha	BB
William	BB
Cordrey, Jonathan Jr.	BB
Jonathan	B
Cordry, Prudence	BB
Coventon, John	B
Crews, Etheldred	PB
Croby, George	BB
Crosby, Abraham	B
Lydia	BB
Spencer	B
Crumbley, Anthony	BB
Crumbly, John	BB
Cullens, Frederick	BB
Cullins, Alice	BB
Culpepper, Benjamin	BP
Charles	B
David	BB
Henry	PB
Joel	B
John Sr.	BB
John Jr.	BB
Malica	BB
Sampson Sr.	BB
Sampson Jr.	PB
Currey, Nicholas	BB
Samuel	B
Curry, Benjamin	BP
John	BB
Margaret	BB
Thompson	B
Cutts, Joseph	BB
Daniel, Aaron	BB
Abraham	BB
Amos	BB
Asa	BB
Charles	BB
Ezekiel	BB
Ezekiel Jr.	B
Orphans of Jos.	B
Jonas	BB

Daniel, Lewis	BB
Mathew	P
Moses	BB
Priscilla	BP
Stephen	BB
Wright	B
Darden, Francis	BB
Davis, Clement	BB
Diocliton	BB
Elijah	BB
Jesse	BB
John	B
Jonathan	PB
Joseph	BB
Mathew	BB
Davison, Caleb	B
Smithwick	B
Dawson, E. John	BB
Orph. of James	B
Dean, Frederick	BB
Micajah	P
Moses	BB
Dear, Richard	BB
Deason, Absalom	BB
Jonathan	BB
Decanter, Richard	B
Delk, David	P
Jacob	B
Joseph	BB
Samuel	B
Thomas	BB
Dennard, Abner	BB
Isaac	BB
Jacob	BB
James	B
John	BB
Shadrack	BB
Thomas	BB
William	BB
Dennis, John Sr.	B
Depriest, James	BB
Devenport, Joel	PB
Dew, Arthur	BB
Diamond, Reuben	P
William	BP
Dickson, Aaron	BB
B. John	B
James	B
Jeremiah Sr.	BB
Reubin	BB
William	B
William	BB
Orphans of Wm.	B
Dillard, George	BB
Nathan	B
Nicholas	BB
Phillip	BB
Sampson	B

29

Dinton, Edward	BB
Dixon, Anna	BB
L. John	BB
S. Tilman	B
Dominy, Frederick	BB
Dorch, Walter	B
Dorsey, John	B
Orphans of Leakin	B
Dubose, Jeptha	B
Duffill, Thomas	BB
Duggan, John	BB
Duggin, Cloana	BB
Edmond	B
Duncan, Thomas	BB
Dunn, Jacob	BB
Depree, Jeremiah	BB
Reid	BB
Durden, Lewis	B
Durham, Mary	BB
Samuel	B.
Dyer, John	B
Eady, John Sr.	BB
John Jr.	B
Eakins, Alexander	BB
James	B
Early, Jesse	B
Earp, Cullin	BB
Eastwood, Elijah	BB
Ecols, Joel	BB
Edmonds, David	B
Edmondson, John	BB
Edwards, Andrew	B
Elizabeth	BB
John	BB
Thomas	BB
William Sr.	BB
William Jr.	B
Elliott, William	BB
Ellis, Ephriam	BB
Elmore, Stephen	B
Elton, Abraham	BB
English, John	BB
Joseph	BB
Robert	BB
Thomas	BB
Esom, Mezzak	P
Ethridge, Abel	BB
Calley	BB
Merit	B
Evans, Burwell	B
James	B
Jehu	BB
John	B
William	B
Exum, Benjamin	BB

Fagan, Aaron	BB
Fairchilds, Lofton	B
T. John	B
Farmer, John	BP
Finney, Arthur	B
Fisher, John	P
Fletcher, James	BB
John	BB
Joseph	B
Wiley	PB
Fluker, Baldwin	BB
David	BB
orphan of David	B
Gemimah	BB
Flukaway, R. Randolph	BP
Fdk, Henry	BB
John	BB
Joseph	B
Lucretia	BB
Mark	B
William	B
Forehand, Amos	PB
Forgerson, Robert	PB
Fort, Thomas	BB
Fouler, John	BB
Franklin, George	BB
Thomas	BB
Frazier, John	B
William	B
William	BB
Frederick, Delilah	BB
Friday, David	B
Frizzle—orphans of	
Bryant	B
Ellisshaba	BB
Gale	BB
Thomas	B
Fulgham, Jesse	B
Micajah	PP
Fuller, Isaac	B
John	BB
Gainer, Samuel	BB
William	BB
Gardner, Aaron	B
Ashel	BB
B. Jesse	PB
G. Jason	B
Jacob	B
Mark	B
Thomas	B
Garner, Jacob	BB
Reddick	B
Garrett, Samuel	BB
Gates, Samuel	BP
George, Daniel	B

Germany, William	BB	Grindstone, John	B
William	P	Grinsteed, William	B
Gibson, James	B	Groom, Catherine	BB
William	PB	Jesse	BP
Gilbert, Drury	B	Wiley	BB
Hilkiah	B	Guilder, Jacob	B
Jeptha	B	Sinnet	B
Jesse	BB		
John	BP	Hail, Edward	BB
Thomas Sr.	BB	Hailey, Holliday	PB
William	BB	Haines, Ezekiel	PB
Gilmore, George	BB	Leven	B
James Sr.	BB	Nathan	BB
James	BB	Hall, James	B3
John Sr.	BB	John	B
John Jr.	P	John	BB
Sarah	BB	Samuel	B
William	P	Orph. of Tho.	P
Gladden, James	BB	William	BB
Glenn, Ann	BB	Hambleton, Duncan	BB
Robert Jr.	B	Hammock, Daniel	B
John	BB	John Sr.	PP
Robert Sr.	B	Hampton, Edward	P
Glover, Stephen (orph.)	B	Thomas	B
Golden, Benjamin	B	William	BB
John	BB	Hancock, Elisha	B
Golightly, James	BB	William	B
Good, McKerness	BB	Handley, Jesse	BB
Gordon, Allen	B	Hardaman, Elizabeth	BB
Kenneth	B	Hardee, Thomas	BB
Richard	B	Harden, Adam	BB
Goza, Elijah	B	John	PB
John	BB	Nicholas	BB
Joshua	BB	Hardison, Thomas	B
Graham, Samuel	BB	Hardy, Alan	BB
Green, Ephriam	BB	Alan Jr.	B
Jesse	BB	James	B
John	B	John	BB
John	B	Harper, John	BB
Leonard Jr.	B	Harrel, Bailey	BB
Greene, Leonard	BB	James	BB
William	B	Jesse	BB
Greyer, Elizabeth	BP	Joseph	BB
George	BB	Harrell, Henry	BB
Richard	B	Solcmon	B
Grice, Jesse	PB	William	BB
Richard	BB	Harris, Alsey	BB
Griffin, Allen	B	Benjamin	B
Evington	B	Churchwell	BB
Joseph	BB	Daniel	B
Len	BB	David	B
Major	BB	Harrison	BB
Miller	B	Orph. of James	B.
William	PB	Mary	BB
William	B	Mathew (Rev)	BB
Griffin, Comfort	BB	Sarah	BB
		William	B

Hart, Henry	B	Hogan, Edmond	BP
Reuben	BB	Griffin	BB
Samuel	BP	John Jr.	BB
Samuel Sr.	BB	R. John	BB
Harthhorn, John	BB	Holeman, David	BB
Thomas	BB	Holland, Margaret	BB
Hartsfield, Andrew	B	Hollen, James	B
Harvey, Benjamin	B	Suel	BB
James	BB	Holley, Henry	B
John	BB	Isaac	B
Thomas	B	Thomas	B
Thomas	B	William	PB
Thomas	BP	William Jr.	P
Harville, John	B	Hollin, William	B
Hatcher, John	BB	Holliway, David	B
Hatley, John	B	Holt, Tapley	B
Head, James	PB	Thaddeus	PB
Richard	BB	Thomas	BB
Heath, Benjamin	B	Holton, Salathel	BB
Elizabeth	PB	Homes, David	BB
John	B	G. Nathan	B
William	B	J. William	B
Helton, James	BB	James	B
William	B	Hood, Alan	B
Hemphill, Andrew	B	Edward	BB
Henington, Jonathan	B	Wiley	BB
Henry, Isaac	BB	William Sr.	BB
Henson, Caleb	PB	William Jr.	BB
Herndon, George	B	Hooks, Thomas	BP
George Jr.	B	William	BB
James	B	Hopson, Briggs	B
Joseph	BB	Edmond	B
Lewis	BB	Edward Sr.	BP
Stephen	BB	Hardy	BB
William	BB	William	B
Hickman, James	BB	Horn, Elizabeth	BP
Hidleberg, John	BB	John	BP
Higgs, Elisha	BB	Horton, Levi	BB
Hill, Daniel	BB	Howard, Ann	BB
Hilliard, Major	B	Benjamin	BB
Hilson, John	BB	Isaac	P
Hilton, Abraham	BB	Isaac	BB
Hinson, John	B	James	B
Hitt, John	BB	James	B
William	B	James	B
Hobbs, Drury	BP	John	BB
Hobs, Sarah	BB	John	PB
Hodge, Mathew	B	Lemuel	B
Hodges, Benjamin	BB	Samuel	BB
Charles & James,	B	Samuel	BB
orphans		Solomon	BP
Edward	BB	Howell, Elizabeth	BB
Foreman	BB	Jehu	B
John	B	John	BB
Robert	B	Hunt, Thomas	BB
Samuel	B		

32

Hutchins, Zachariah	BB
Hutson, Benjamin	B
Samuel	BB
Zadok	B
Ightner, Michael	BB
Ingram, Charles	BB
Irwin, Alex.'s orphs.	B
Jared	BB
John Jr.	B
Nancy	BB
Samson John Sr.	BB
William	BB
Jackson, Benjamin Jr.	B
Benjamin Sr.	PB
Charles	BB
Jacob	B
Jeremiah	BB
Julius	BB
Levi	BB
Thomas	BB
James, John	B
Jenkins, John	B
Jewell, Thomas	B
Jinkins, Allen	BP
Wiley	BB
Johnson, Abby	BB
Benjamin	B
Clary	BB
David	B
Henry	B
Isaac	BB
Sampson	B
Simon	BB
Whitmill	B
Wilson	BB
Joice, Edward	B
Joines, Edmond	BB
Ezekiel	B
Joel	BB
John	BB
Joseph	BB
Jones, Amos	B
Benjamin	B
Elizabeth	BB
James	BP
James	B
James Jr.	BB
Joel	B
John	BB
John	BB
John	BB
Jonathan	BB
Joshua Sr.	BB
Joshua Jr.	PB

Jones, Leonard Sr.	BP
Leonard Jr.	BB
Wiley	BB
William	PB
Jourdan, Asa	DB
Baxter	BB
Burwell	BB
Levi	B
Thomas	BB
Joy, Turner	B
Keaton, Benjamin	BB
Cader	BB
Charles	BB
Jesse	B
Kellam, Seth	BB
Kelley, William	B
Edward	B
George	BB
Kelly, Michael	B
Kemp, Benjamin	BB
Lucy	BB
Reubin	B
Thomas	BB
William	BB
William Jr.	P
Kendall, Susannah	BB
Kendrick, Benjamin's	
5 orphans	B
Jones	BB
Martha	BB
Martin	BB
Tabithy	BB
William	BP
Kennedy, William	BB
John	BB
Sarah	BB
Kent, John	BB
Levi	B
Killingsworth, John	B
Kimbro, John	BP
Kimmy, William	BB
King, Anna	BB
Chloe	BB
David	BB
Ephriam's orphans	B
James	P
John	BB
Joshua	B
Kinman, William	BB
Kinney, John	BB
Kitchen, Laurence	BB
Knight, Silvanus	BB
Kolb, George	B
Koonce, George	BB

Langston, Benjamin	BB		Lyon, James	P
James	BB		Nathan	B.
Lard, Lodowick	B		Richard	P
Sarah	BB			
Lassiter, Brinkley	B		McCarley, Samuel	B
Laurence, Devereaux	B		McClendon, Lewis	BB
Henry	BB		Mason	BB
John	BB		Willis	BB
John	BB		Wilson	BB
Lawhorn, Nathaniel	B		McCord, David	B
Noel	BB		McCreary, Isaac	BB
Lawson, Charles	B		McCullers, Thomas	BB
Hugh's orphans	B		McDade, Charles	B
John	BB		James	BB
John Jr.	PB		William	BB
Reubin	B		McDaniel, John	BB
Roger	BP		McDonald, Hugh's	
Sarah	BP		orphans	B
Leath, James	PB		Mathews	BB
Peter	BB		McDougal, Andrew	B
Ledbetter, Ephriam	B		Robert	B
Samuel	B		McDowell, John	P
Lee, Iry	B		Thomas	BB
Leneves, Samuel	B		McKee, John	B
Leonard, John	B		McKey, Mike	BB
Levingston, John	BB		William	BB
Lewis, Daniel	BB		McKigney, George	P
George	B		McKinney, Tabitha	BB
John	B		McKinvale, James	BP
John	BP		McKinzee, Aaron	BB
Licett, David	BB		Rachel	BB
Liles, Sherwood	B		McKissick, Mack	BB
Lindsey, Henry	BB		McMath, Philip	BB
John	BP		McMillen, Angus	BB
Lingo, John	BB		Archibald	B
Moses	PP		McMurray, John	BB
Linton, John	BB		William	B
Lithgo, Robert	PB		McNatt, Benjamin	B
Little, Nancy	BB		McNeel, Turguil	BB
Locky, Sarah	PP		McNiel, Niel	BB
Loftin, Ezekiel	BB		McVey, David	BB
Logan, Philip	BB		McWhirter, Moses	BB
Long, Arthur	B		McWilliams, Gracy	BP
Davis	BB			
James	BB		Mallet, Isaac	BP
Lord, John	BB		Jesse	BB
Solomon	BB		Mann, Mary	BB
William	BB		Manning, Benjamin	BB
Lowe, John	B		Isaac	B
Stephen	BB		John	P
Loyd, Daniel	BB		John	PB
Lundy, Mathew	BB		Mares, Alexander	B
Lyles, John	BB		Marshall, William	B
Lynch, John	BB		Martin, Charles	BB
Lynum, William	B		David	PB
			James	PB

Martin, James	BP	
John	BB	
John	BB	
John Jr.	P	
Julius	B	
Levi	BB	
Richard	BB	
Thomas	BB	
William	B	
Zachariah	BB	
Mason, James	BB	
Turner	PB	
Mathews, Daniel	B	
Isaac	BB	
Isham	BB	
Jacob	P	
John	BB	
John	BB	
Reubin's orphans	B	
Temperance	BB	
Mathis, John Sr.	B	
William	BB	
Mattocks, Lewis	BB	
May, Dread	BB	
Edmond	BB	
Francis	B	
Hardy	PB	
William	BB	
Megehee, Solomon	BB	
Megrogary, Dempsey	BB	
Melone, William	BB	
Mercer, Peter	BP	
Miller, John	PB	
John	BB	
Lewis	BB	
Nathaniel	B	
Millirons, Christopher	BB	
Mills, James	P	
John	BB	
Moses	P	
Rolley's orphans	B	
William	BB	
Mims, David	BB	
Drury	BB	
John Sr.	PB	
John	BB	
Mathew	B	
William Sr.	BB	
William Jr.	BB	
Wright	B	
Minter, M. Anthony	B	
Morgan	BB	
Robert	P	
Mires, Elijah	BB	
Mitchell, Andrew	B	
Benjamin	P	
Uriah	B	

Mitchell, Thomas	BB	
William	BB	
Moffatt, Gabriel	BB	
Craven	B	
Moffutt, Solomon	B	
Moncrief, Mathew	BB	
Montgomery, Lewis	B	
Moody, Daniel	BB	
Moor, Casen	B	
Moore, Josiah	B	
Levi's orphans	B	
Luke	BP	
Shadrack	PB	
Shadrack	B	
Moreman, Charles	BB	
Morris, Israel	BB	
Nimrod	B	
William	BB	
William	BB	
Morrison, Angus	B	
Morton, John	BB	
Moses, John	BB	
Joshua	BB	
Robert	B	
Samuel	B	
Moss, Howell	P	
Motley, Robert	BB	
Wilson	BB	
Mott, Lovelace	B	
Nathan	BB	
Mullowney, Laughlin	B	
Mumford, Jeffry	BB	
John	BB	
Joseph	B	
Thomas	B	
Munford, Robert	B	
Murkerson, John	BB	
Murphy, William	BB	
Cornelius	BB	
Daniel	BB	
Drury	BP	
James	BB	
Napier, Polly	BB	
Neel, John	BB	
Thomas	BB	
Neeland, James	BB	
John Sr.	B	
O. David	BB	
Neeley, Thomas	B	
Nellson, Ambrose	BP	
Newman, Francis	BB	
Newsom, Agnes	BB	
Hardy	B	
Nicholson, Harris	BB	
Night, Kinman	BP	
Nipper, Benj. orphans	B	

35

Norton, William	B	Peacock, Samuel Sr.	B
Nunn, Edmond	B	Samuel	BB
James' orphans	B	Peddy, Beverly	B
Samuel	B	Bradford	B
William Jr.	BB	Jeremiah	BB
Nutt, John	B	Nehemiah	BB
		Rachel	BB
Oats, Jane	BB	Pennington, Henry	B
Obanion, Dawson	B	Perkins, Benjamin	B
Ruth	BB	Joseph	B
Obar, John	B	Perrey, James	BB
O'Daniel, William	PB	Joseph	B
Offcutt, J. William	BB	Joseph	BB
John	BB	Perrit, James	B
Sampson	BB	Perry, Ambrose	B
Oneal, William	BP	Arthur	B
Oneel, James	BB	Thornton	B
Jesse	B	William	B
John	B	Phillips, Dawson	B
Orr, Jane	BB	Isham	BP
		John	BB
Pace, Mildred	BB	Joseph John	B
Nathaniel	B	Sarah	BB
Thomas	BB	Sherwood	B
Padgett, Elisha	BP	Solomon	B
Page, Solomon	BB	Pierson, Jonathan	BB
Thomas	BB	William	BB
Wilson	BB	Pinkston, Bazil	BB
Pain, Isham	BB	Daniel	BB
John	BB	John Sr.	BB
Joseph	BB	Pinson, Benjamin	B
Palmer, John	B	Isaac	BB
Parham, Hadden	BB	Joab	B
James	BB	Pitman, John	BB
Paris, James	BB	Pollard, William	BB
Parker, Cader	B	Pool, James	B
Jonathan	BB	Middleton Sr.	BP
Joseph	BB	Middleton Jr.	BB
Mary	BB	Pope, John	B
Wm.'s orphans	B	Wiley	BB
Parmer, Samuel	BB	Porter, Frederick	BB
Parrish, Benjamin	B	Joel	PB
Pasmore, John	BB	Nobles	B
Patridge, Henry	PB	Posey, H. John	P
Patten, James	BB	Powel, Henry	BP
Patterson, Drury	PB	Powell, Charles	PB
Gidion	BB	James	BB
Paul, Brice	B	Jesse	BB
James	B	Osborn	BB
John	P	Sampson	BP
Peacock, John	BB	Price, Edmond	B
Jonathan	B	Edmond	BB
Levi	PB	Richard	BB
Michael	BB	Zachariah	B
Pierson	B	Prichet, Thomas	BB

36

Prince, George	BB	Roberson, Elizabeth	BB
Hamelton	BP	George	PB
Proctor, Joshua	B	Henry	B
William	BB	Joel	B
Pugh, D. Guilford	B	John	BB
Mary	BP	John	BB
Pullen, Henry	B	John	BB
William	B	John	BB
Pullin, Thomas	BB	John Jr.	BB
		Joseph	PB
(No Q's)		William Sr.	B
		William	BB
Rachels, James	B	Robertson, George	BB
Miles	BB	Robinson, Allen	PB
Raley, Charles	BB	Benjamin	BB
Raney, Benjamin	BB	John	B
John	BB	Rachel	BB
Ray, Ambrose	B	Samuel	BB
Charles	P	Samuel	BB
Charles	BB	Robison, William Jr.	B
Francis	B	Robuck, Rolley	BB
Gabriel	BB	Rogers, Mary	BB
John	BB	Roughton, John	BP
William	BB	Rountree, Arthur	BB
William Jr.	B	Rowell, Robert	BB
Redding, Anderson	BP	Rozer, David	BB
Arthur	BB	Rushing, James	BB
Charles	PB	William	BB
William	B	Rutherford, B. Thomas	BB
Reeves, Greene	B	John	BB
Simon	BB	Robert	BB
Renfro, David	B		
Edward	P	Saffold, Ishal	B
Elisha	B	Reuben Jr.	P
Elizabeth	BB	Samuel	BB
Joel	BB	William Sr.	BB
John	BB	William Jr.	BB
William	BB	Salter, James	BB
Renfroe, Nathan	BB	John	BB
Rhodes, Charles	BB	Robert	B
James	B	Simon	BB
Smith	B	Sanford, Abner	B
William	B	William	B
Richardson, John	PB	Sannor, Elizabeth	BB
Jonathan	B	Saunders, Lewis	BB
Silas	B	Savage, Mary	BB
Richmond, Samuel	B	Saxton, Henry	BB
Ridley, Robert	B	Scarborough, William	BB
Riggins, Robinson	BB	Scarbrough, Amos	B
Rigins, Richard	PB	David	B
Riley, Edward	BB	Elias	B
John	BB	Ephriam	BB
Joseph	BB	Scarcy, William	B
Rivers, Jones	BB	Scott, Elizabeth	BP
Roberson, Ann	BB	Scrogging, Josiah	BB
Bailey	BB	See, Jesse	BB

Sessions, Daniel	B		Smith, Mary	BB
Delilah	BB		Mary	BB
Frederick	BP		Miles	B
Joseph	BB		Milly	P
Sexton, William	B		Needham	BB
Sheke, Daniel	PB		Phillip	B
Shelby, John	BB		Powel	B
Shepherd, Andrew	PB		Rebecca	PB
Charles	BB		Reddick	B
James	B		Richard	BB
John	PB		Richard Sr.	BP
John Sr.	BP		Samuel	B
John Jr.	B		Sarah	BB
Mary	BB		Thomas Sr.	BB
Thomas	P		William	BP
William	B		William	BP
Sherry, Isaiah	BB		William	B
Sherwood, Benjamin	B		William	BB
Sikes, Willoughby	BB		William	BB
Simms, James	BB		William	BB
Sims, M. John	B		William	PB
Sinquefield, Moses	BP		William Jr.	B
Samuel	B		Sneed, Anderson	P
Samuel	BB		Ansil	BB
Skrine, Benjamin	BP		Spann, George	BB
Slade, Jethro	BB		Sparks, John	BB
Slappy, Henry	BB		Samuel	BP
Smiley, Elizabeth	PB		Spencer, Thomas	B
William	B		Spiller, Jeremiah	P
Smith, Alexander	BB		Phillip	BB
Alexander	PB		Spivey, John	BP
Britton	B		Mary	BB
Caleb	BB		Moses	PB
Charles	BB		William	BB
Dempsey	B		Spurlin, John	BB
Francis	BB		Spurlock, David	BB
Harbert	BP		John	BB
Hardy	BB		Robert	BB
Henry	BB		Stanford, Richard	BB
Isaac	PB		Statum, William	BB
James	BB		Stavley, Robert	PB
Jeremiah	BB		Stegall, Benjamin	B
Jesse's orphans	B		John	BB
John	BB		Stephens, Thomas	BB
John	BB		Stinson, John	P
John	BB		Stokes, Allen	B
John	P		Ann	BB
John	BP		Burwell	B
John	B		Henry	BB
John Jr.	B		Henry Sr.	P
John Jr.	BB		John Sr.	BB
Jordan	BB		John Jr.	P
Joshua	B		Samuel	BB
Lewis	B		Silvanus	BB
Lydia	BB		William	BB

38

Story, Thomas	PB		Tooke, Allen	B
Stricklin, Sion	BP		Arthur	B
Sturdivant, Peterson	B		H. Harlow	B
Summerville, George	B		James	B
Hugh	B		John	BB
Sursfield, Mathew	B		William	P
Sutton, Absolom	BB		Trammell, Jared	BB
William	PB		Traywick, Moses	BB
Swint, John	B		Trotman, Winnefred	BB
			Truelock, Sutton	BB
Taff, George	BP		Tucker, Benjamin	BB
James	B		Reubin	BB
Talbert, Edmond	BB		Tufts, Francis	B
Tanner, Thomas	BB		Turner, Jonathan	B
Tanton, Henry	PB		Samuel	PB
Nathan	BB		William	BB
Tarver, Frederick	BB		Tyson, Moses	BB
Jacob	B			
Tatom, John	P		Underwood, Benjamin	BB
Taylor, George	B.		Daniel	P
Henry's orphs.	B		George	BB
Hodge	BP		Isham	B
Isaac	PP		John	B
James Jr.	BB		Josiah	BB
James	PB		Reubin	B
James	PB		Thomas	B
John's orphans	P		Urquart, John	B
Joshua	BB		Neel	B
Josiah	BB			
Kinchin	BB		Vance, Davis	BP
M. James	BB		Vann, Samuel	BB
Thomas's orphs.	B		Vasser, Josiah	BB
Tennill, Benjamin	BB		Micajah	BB
Francis	BB		Verden, William	BB
Tetterton, John	BP		Vickers, Abraham	B
Tharp, Charnick	BB		Abraham Jr.	BB
Thigpen, Jonathan	BP		Benjamin	B
Thomas, Darius	B		Bryant	B
William	BP		Elisha	B
Thompkins, Partin	B		Jacob	B
Samuel	BB		Jesse	P
Thompson, Charles	BB		Joshua	BB
Isham	BB		Nancy	BB
James	BB		Wiley	B
Jeremiah	BP		William Sr.	BB
Jesse	PB		Vincen, George	BB
William	PP		Vincent, Jethro	BB
Thrift, Robert	B		John	B
Tillet, Geo.'s orphs.	B			
Tiner, Lewis	BB		Wade, Isaac	BB
Toler, Joel	B		Thomas	PB
Tomlin, Thomas	BB		Wadkins, Levin	BB
Tomlinson, Benjamin	BP		Mitchell	PB
John	BB		Wadsworth, John	BB
Tompkins, Burwell	B		Walker, Elizabeth	BB

Walker, James	B
James	B
James Sr.	PB
William	BB
William	BB
Wall, Ezekiel Jr.	BP
Ezekiel Sr.	BB
Jesse	PB
Joseph	BB
Shadrack	B
Waller, Priscilla	BB
William Sr.	BB
Silliam Jr.	B
Ward, E. Thomas	B
Francis	B
Jesse	P
John	BB
John Jr.	B
Moses	BB
Watson, David	BB
David Jr.	B
Elijah	B
Everett	BB
Ezekiel	BB
Isaiah	B
Laban	BB
Phillip	B
Reddick	BB
Silas	BB
William	B
Watts, Jacob	BB
James	B
Tabitha	PB
Weaver, John	P
Othinal	BB
Webb, Jesse	BB
John	B
Josiah's orphans	B
Kinchin	BB
Saml.'s orphans	B
Susannah	PB
Welcher, Nathaniel	B
Wells, Elijah	BB
Taverner	PB
West, Charles	BB
Hamlin	B
Isham	P
Westly, Lemans	BB
Wheeler, Amos	PB
Reuben	PB
Whitaker, Elizabeth	BB
Hutsons's orphans	P
J. Jordan	B
Richard	B
Simon	B
White, John	BP
Whitehead, Charles	P

Whitfield, Robert	BB
William	B
William	BB
Wicker, Julius	BB
Nathaniel	BB
Robert	B
Robert	BB
Wiggins, John	B
Wilbon, Robert	B
Wilkinson, Reuben's orphans	B
Williams, Darkes	BB
Drury	B
Elisha's orphans	P
John	B
John	B
Paul	BB
Reubin	BB
Samuel	B
Winnifred	BB
Wilson	BB
Williamson, Francis Sr.	BB
Francis Jr.	BB
Wiley	B
Willis, James	B
Mary	BP
Willson, Daniel	B
Wilson, Alexdr.'s orph.	B
Robert	PB
Wimberly, D. Fredericks's orphans	P
Ezekiel Sr.	P
John	BB
Mary	BB
Noah	B
Thomas	P
William	BB
Wingate, Martin	B
Winn, Robert	BP
Thomas	B
William	BB
Wood, Abraham	BB
James	B
Misel	BB
Peter	BB
Robert	B
Thomas	P
Willis	BP
Works, James	BB
Worthen, Elijah	BB
Richard	B
William	BB
Wright, Benjamin	B
Benjamin	PB
Elijah	BP
Elizabeth	BB
M. John	B
William	

Wright, Winfield	BB
Yarbrough, Ambrose	B
Joseph	BB
Young, Elizabeth	BB
R. John	BP
Jacob	BB
Mills	BP
Youngblood, Henry	BB
Jacob	BP
James	B
John's orphans	P
Jonathan	BB

RESIDENTS WASHINGTON COUNTY WHO DREW LAND LOTTERY 1832

The Lottery of 1832 covered land in the following counties:

Cass (Bartow)   Gilmer
Cherokee   Lumpkin
Cobb   Murray
Floyd   Paulding
Forsyth   Union

Key to designations:

WRS—Widow of Revolutionary Soldier   RS—Revolutionary Soldier
W—widow
Orp—Orphan
SLW—Soldier late war
Sol—Soldier
F A—Father absent
Orps.—orphans

* *

Achord, John
Adams, Benjamin
Adkins, John
Albritton, Elizabeth
    Peter
Ard, Margaret—orp.
Arnold, Elizabeth—W

Bagley, Benjamin, F A
Bailey, Burrell
    Keziah—WRS
Baker, Thomas H.
Barber, William
Barge, Abraham
Barnes, Colman
    Dempsey
    John Sr.—SLW
Barnett, Anabella—orp.
    John—SLW
    Tillman
Barrington, William
Bartlett, Thomas
Beddingfield, John H.
Bedgood, James M.
Bivins, Samuel
Blair, Elizabeth
    John D.
    Thomas R.
Blesard, Levi
Bond, Robert
Bradley, Charles
Brantley, Green
    Harris
    John F.
    Joseph
    William

Brantley, Wm.
    William Jr.
    William Sr.
Bray, Sarah—W
Brett, Henry—SLW
Brown, John D.
    John
    M.
    Sarah—orp.
    Sarah—W
Buck, James A.
Bullard, Lewis
Buckhannon, Betsy
Burgamy, Tobias
    William J.
    William Sr.
Buris, Hanford

Cain, Wm. T.—orp.
Calhoun, James M.
Canada, James—orps.
Canter, Sarah—W
Carter, Kindrell—orps
Cason, Dennis
Caston, Thomas
    William
Cherry, Spencer
Clay, John
    William
Clements, Ezekiel
Coleman, David
Collins, Thos. J.
Conyers, Jacob
Cook, Starling
Cordrey, Jonathan P.
Coseys, Alfred

Coston, Thomas
Coward, Polly—W
Cox, James
Craft, Jno.—orps.
Crafton, William
Cumming, I.—WRS
Currey, Ldsley—W

Daily, Vines
Daniel, Amos
    Kenneth
    Mary—WRS
    Moses
    Zachariah
Davis, Lewis—orps.
Dean, Joel—orps.
Dillard, Bathsheba-
Dixon, Thomas
Dudley, Eden
Dupree, James
Durden, Francis
Dickerson, Henry-RS

Eastwood, James
    Marium—W
Echols, Patience—W
Edwards, Leroy
Elder, Robt. B.
Ellis, Mayor
Elton, Eliz.—W

Farmer, Thomas
Fisher, Wm.
Fluker, Milton B.
Foose, Moses
Forshe, John

42

Fort, Owen H.
Fountain, Wm.
Frasier, Stephen
   William
Fuller, I. minors-Fa

Garess, George
   John
Garner, M. Sr.-Sol.
Giles, Celia--W
Gilmore, James-RS
Glenn, William B.
Golightly, James
   S. - WRS
Goodgame, George-orp.
Goodson, Edwin
Guiton, Tabitha Ann-orp.
Greene, Gideon
   Thomas
Greiner, Charles A.
Gregory, William

Hamilton, William
Hassard, David
Harrell, David
   Jesse
Harrison, Wm. D.
Hart, Barnabas
Haines, Nathan Jr.
   Leonard
   Bethel
Hamilton, Calvin-orps.
Haines, Nathan W.
Hardwick, Robt. A.
Hart, Jonathan-orps.
Harrell, Solomon
Hart, Nancy--W
Harris, Chruchwell-orps.
Harrison, Gabriel
Harris, William
Haines, Albin O.
Herndon, Charlotte-W
Helton, Richard
Hearndon, Charles
Hightower, G. D.
Hicks, William
Hicklin, R. N. - orps.
Hill, Theophilus
Holley, John
Hood, Larkin
   Wiley
Hodges, Wiley T.
   Elbert
Holt, Susannah-W
Holt, John-orps.

Horton, Howell
   Fred K.-orps
Holton, Steph.-orps.
Horton, Daniel
Hodges, Sarah-W
   Henry
Hotton, E.-W
Hudson, Henry-orp.

Ikener, Sampson
Irwin, Alexander
   Nancy-W
Jenkins, Lewis-RS
   S. D.
Johnson, Hartwell
   Isaac-orps.
   Jason
Joiner, Abraham
Joins, Edward W.
Joines, James
   Jared
   William
Jones, James
Jordan, Asa-Sol.
Jordon, W.-WRS
   Winnafred-W

Keaton, Benjamin
   Jesse
Kemp, Reuben-orps.
Kenman, Austin
Kenneday, S.
Killingsworth,
   Randall
Kilpatrick, Austin
King, Joel
   John-orps.
   William R.
Knight, Jesse B.
   Lewis

Landcaster, James A.
Laton, John
Laurence, John-orp.
Lee, Milly
   William Jr.
Lewis, Redding R.
Lightfoot, Martha-W
   Philip
   Robert
   William D.
Linsey, John
Lingo, Peter
Little, James
Lofley, Daniel

Love, Robert
Loym(?), Wm.
Lyman, Charles

McDougald, Dugald
McRae, John
McCanless, Wm-orps.
McDonald, Lovett
McCoy, William
McAfee, Arthur

Martin, Lemuel
Moye, Benajah A.
Martin, Henry
Meeks, Wiley
Malone, Chas. J.
Mills, Daniel
Massey, Sampson--
   orps.
More, Underhill H.
Moore, Shadrack
Mays, Jemima-W
May, Wm. Sr.
Murkison, Green
Miller, Lee R.
Morris, Benj.
May, Wm. Jr.
Martin, George
Musslewhite, G.B.
Miher, Wm.-orps.
Murphy, William
May, Edmund, Jr.
Mimms, Joseph
Miller, Bright
Martin, John
Miller, Elizur-W
Martin, Bird
Mathis, John-orps.

Newsom, Kinchen
   Seaborn
Northington, Jesse
   E.

Odam, Rebeccah-W
Offutt, Nath'l-RS
Oliver, Eady-W
   Isaiah
   John
   Sirass B.
Orr, William
   William J.

Quick, Zachariah

Pace, Nath'l. G.
Page, John

Page, Solomon Jr.
Parker, Mason S.
Partridge, Payton
Payne, James
Pittman, Malachi
    Zilpha-orp.
Phillips, Jane-W
Parker, Hardy
Powell, Ambrose
    Henry
    John Jr.
Price, James
    Pledge
Pusser, James

Register, Benjamin
Renfroe, Bryan
    James M.
    Jared-orps.
    Nath'l.
    Peter-orps.
Riddle, Marthy-W
Robinson children-FA
    Robert
    Samuel
    William
Roughton, William
Rushing, Sarah-WRS
Ryal, Eliza-orp.

Scott, Hiram
Sessions, Joseph
Shepherd, David
    Lewis
Shepperd, David
    Lewis
Shepperd, David
Shinnon, Kendrick
Shiney, Benjamin
Shirey, Silas
Simmons, Joseph T.
Slade, William
Smith, Colsbey-RS
    Gideon
    Jordan R.
    Lewis
    Samuel
    Wm. F.-orps.
Sparks, Morgan-orps.
Spears, Lewis
Sperlock, Cleton D.
Stokes, Georgiana-orp.
    James K.
Strange, Gideon
Swint, Edmund

Taylor, John-minors-FA

Taylor, Jared
Tarver, Starling-orps.
Taylor, Isaiah
Tarver, Stephen-Sol.
    Benjamin
Taunton, William
Taylor, John
Tanner, Thos. J.
Tennell, W. A.
Tillman, Malaki
Tennelle, Alex St.C.
Titman, Alfred
Thomas, John H.
Tompkins, James
    Elkin
Tomlinson, Harris
Tomalson, Wm.-RS
Tyson, Stephen
Tucker, Henry C.
Turlington, T.
Tuter, Shadrack
Tucker, Anna
Took, John A.-orp.
Tompkins, Rukin(?)
Tucker, John R.

Vann, James
Veal, Richard H.
Vickers, Ann-W
    Joshua
Vinson, George
Vincent, Powell

Wesson, Sarah-WRS
Webb, Giles-orps
Williams, Wm. K.
Warthon, Wm.-orp.
Whitaker, Willis
Wheddon, Demp.-orps.
Whitaker, John B.
Wise, John-orps.
Wamack, Sarah-W
Wilson, John
Wood, Henry
Whiddon, Green
Wiggins, James A.
Whitehurst, Josiah
Wood, Mary-W.
Wamble, Wm. F.
Wood, Thomas
    Jared
Williams, Freeman
Waller, John H.
White, Isham
    Elijah

Wilson, Augustus
Whiddon, William
Wamack, William
Williams, Ann-hus
Watson, Elijah
Wicker, Eliz.-W
Waters, Simon
Wamblem,Lucretia-
Walker, Wm. H.
Wesson, Sarah-WRS

Yeates, Mary-W
    James-orps.
Young, David
    Green

Eady, John-orp.
Watkins, Mitchell-
Cook, Deborah-WRS
Walker, Eliz.-WRS
Metts, Fred. RS

1820 HEADS OF FAMILIES

From National Archives - Microfilm No. 33 Roll 9

p. 126
Rawlings, William
Perry, Shadrack
Rogers, William
Barwick, Benjamin
McDougall, Daniel
Mathis, Tempe
Hopkins, Jesse
Kelly, George
Jordan, Jacob
Crowell, Henry
Robinson, Lewellen
Watkins, Ansel L.
McDougal, Alexander
Coleman, Robert
Williamson, Charles
Rutherford, Abner M.
Williams, Syllatus
Holton, William
Sneed, Sarah
Avera, John
Vickers, William
Lightfoot, Richard

p. 127
Langston, Dorcas
Perry, James
Lingo, Moses
Heethe, Sarah
Brinkley, Eli
Murphy, William
Potridge, Henry
Tennille, Mary
Taylor, Henry S.
Skrine, Sarah
Greenle, Eliza
Mobly, Wiley
Walker, Solomon
Partridge, William
Manning, Benjamin
Whiddon, William
Carmichael, James
Daniel, Littleton
Williams, John
Shelsee, A. B.
Knight, Charles
Mathis, Sally
Manning, Reuben
Bentley, John
Mills, William Jr.
Hooks, Sally
Chivers, Nancy
McMillan, A.

Parker, Joseph
Little, Edmund
Parham, Haden

p. 128
Miller, John
Edwards, John
Moore, Mathew
Tennille, Wm. A.
Price, John
Manning, Benj. Jr.
Tison, Stephen
Jordan, William
Hardee, Theophilus
Hardeen, James
Newman, Walter
Perkins, Joseph
Hardee, Whitt
Jordan, Thomas
Adams, Hopewell
Howard, Solomon
Renfroe, Enoch
Renfroe, Nathan
Salter, Simon
Brown, Turner
Cook, Benjamin
Pinkston, Basil
Havetey, Robert
Watkins, Mitchell
Wicker, Nathaniel
Bennett, William
Norris, Robert
Howard, James
Griffin, James

p. 129
Joice, William
Barrow, Barney
Bright, Levi
Crook, Robert
Hardison, Frederick
Knight, Sylvanus
Frzier (Frazier),
   Jemima
Gray, Joseph
Parker, Isac
Whitten, Dempsey
Brown, William
Hurst, Hardy
Gardner, John E.
Mills, James
Garrett, Samuel

Salter, John
Wall, Jesse
Helton, Abraham
Griffin, William
McDaniel, Thomas
Townsley, Victor Sikes
Townsley, Job
Curry, Benjamin
Sessions, Joseph
Brown, Morgan
Sneed, Ansel
Avera, Samuel
Malpus, Maurice
Wicker, William

p. 130
Malpus, Hardy
Worthy, Elison
Robinson, Moses
Fizzle, Jane
Thrift, Robert
Mills, Jesse
Walker, John
Miller, Benjamin
Womble, Elisha
Walker, Dorset
Mills, John
Cook, Abraham
Cook, Allen
Cook, Mike
Garner, Henry
Baker, Blake
Hurst, James
Coleman, Ishum
Johnson, Willis
Garner, Stephen
Johnson, Daniel
Long, William
Davis, Vincen
Butcher, Thomas
Davis, Edmund
Pasmore, Housman
Garrett, Asa
Yates, James
Wilkie, Betsy
Armstrong, Alex.
Armstrong, Edward

p. 131
Armstrong, Alex. Jr.
Duggan, John
Duggan, John H.

45

Duggan, William
Hamilton, Samuel
McLean, Laughlin
Worthy, Peggy
Collins, Thomas
Powell, William
Baker, John
Cone, James
Bailey, John
Comens, Robert
Comens, William
Mathis, John
Frzier (Fryer or
   Frazer), Wm.
Cone, Archelaus
Summerville, Sally
Gardner, Licia
Dunevent, Nancy
Bullock, Carter
Rachaels, William
Jordan, Asa
Tanton, William
Jordan, Benjamin
Amison, Eli
Amison, Abram
Hateway, David
Amison, Cullin
Cato, Francis

p. 132
Amison, Warren
Henington, Betsey
Long, James
Williams, William
Lucas, Samuel
Coursey, Alfred
Holliman, Thomas
Smith, Caty
Massey, Abraham
Johnson, Thomas
Ubanks, Daniel
Hampton, Mary
Tait, Sally
Key, James
Bustle, John
Bustle, Priscilla
Barnadore, Nancy
Bustle, Isaac
Cogburn, Cyprus
Bustle, Solomon
Bustle, Nancy
Pilcher, Lewis
Guthrie, William
Cofield, John

Mott, Nathan
Davis, Elijah
Manning, Caser
David, Richard W.

p. 133
Beckom, John
Worthen, William
Worthen, Elijah Jr.
Chambliss, Samuel
Worthen, Elijah Sr.
Beckom, Daniel
Beckom, Abel
Singleton, James
Miles, Abraham
Amison, Jesse
Ridgen, Sarah
Burgamy, William
Burgamy, Drury
Amison, William
Ryland, Benoni
Canter, Richard D.
Hodges, William
Tanton, Henry
Amison, Josiah
Tanton, Newsom
Amison, William
Comens, Eli
Sanders, Elizabeth
Sanders, Burril
Newsom, Kinchin
Jordan, Rolin
Windham, Benjamin
May, Edmund
May, Jethro

p. 134
Collins, John
McDowell, Thomas
Akridge, John
Comens, David
Barnes, John
Harrison, Joseph
Stubbs, John
Barnes, William
Middleton, John
Sparks, Sarah
Gray, Enoch
Sparks, John
McNiel, Mary
Collins, Joshua
DeYumpert, Alsey
Fenn, Eli
Campbell, Burrel

Neeland, Polly
Price, Richard
Hilton, James
Brown, Hezekiah
Sterling, John
McDaniel, Thomas
Daniel, Amos
Daniel, Rufus
McDaniel, Susannah
Curry, John
Curry, John Jr.

p. 135
Curry, Margaret
Rogers, Harvey
Brown, William
Harris, James
Hilton, Richard
Bynam, William
Roughton, Martha
Roughton, Enoch
Welch, Asa
Horn, Judy
Bowen, Malachi
Wiggins, William
Taylor, Drury
Rogers, Stephen
Haynes, Nathan
Bulger, John
McNeil, Archiblad
Odum, Dempsey
Perkins, William
Hudson, Benjamin
Smith, Wm. F.
Elliott, Benjamin
Brookin, Nancy
Hanford (or Sanford)
   Betsey
Franklin, Vashti
Franklin, James
Ivins, Ezekiel
May, Tempe

p. 136
Howard, Samuel
Howard, Lemuel
Howard, James Sr.
Ramsey, William
Hines, Richard
Holmes, Nathaniel
Pope, Wylly
Mathis, Lewis
Barrow, William
Whittle, Burrel

Pope, Fereby.
Gardner, Ezekiel
Gilmore, John
Gilmore, James
Cook, Deborah
Barrow, James
Barrow, Barney
Jordan, William
Jones, William
Gordon, Richard
Collins, Frederick
Cook, John
Parker, Keder
Rogers, Charles
Frizzle, Thomas
Allen, Charles
Freeman, Fanny
Pervis, Isaac

p. 137
English, Sampson
Bentley, Jerry
Parker, James
Howard, Nauflight
Jones, Henry
May, John
Oliver, Martin
Robertson, William
Green, William
Barwick, William
Peddy, Julius C.
Edwards, Britton
Peddy, Betsy
Cox, Darius
Renfroe, Peter
Myers, Thomas
Blue (Buie?), Betsy
Arrenton, Isaac
West, Charles
Tanner, Joseph
Loro (Lord?), Solomon
McLeod, Daniel
Joins, Edmund
Osteen, Caleb
Lanier, Sarah
Cone, Lewis
Ely, John
Hill, Enoch

p. 138
Hopson, William
Jordan, John
Barber, Frederick
Rogers, Eliza
Rogers, Nathan
Howard, Solomon Jr.

Shehe, Allafair
Shehe, John
Shehe, Thomas
Smith, Thomas
Tyler, Elisha
Morris, Jacob
Price, Joshua
Tanner, Becky
Mayo, William
Woodham, Edward
Hudson, Evan
Barwick, John
Register, Jesse
Williamson, Malachi
Register, William
Tindall, Jacob
Tindall, Joshua
Pernell, Scarbro
Haynes, Ezekiel
Register, John
Bailey, James

p. 139
Daniel, Stephen
Tennille, John P.
Prince, George
Laurence, Susan
Dorch, David
Brady, Druscilla
Rowell, Humphrey
Lord, John
Bailey, David
Sheppard, Charles
Odum, John Jr.
Odum, John Sr.
Odum, Jacob Jr.
Davis, Lewis
Gainer, James
Hand, Abraham
Haynes, Levin
Odum, Jacob Sr.
Odum, William
Hodge, John
Wall, Ezekiel
Wall, Mary
Cordry, Jonathan
Mathis, John
Laurence, John
Brookins, Benjamin
Knight, Robert
Montgomery, Lewis
Moor, Cason
McDaniel, Daniel

p. 140
Davis, Lewis Sr.

Dubose, Reuben
Curry, Nicholas
Harris, Samuel
Darby, Armistead
Abbott, Thomas
Hodges, George C.
Hayley, Holiday
Curry, Solzy (?)
Brantley, Aron
Moye, Devran
Ballard, Winnifred
Goodgame, Alexander
Sinquefield, Wm.
Gillum, Miles
McDaniel, Ennis
Key, Henry
Riddle, Cato,
Riddle, Anderson,
Hardison, William
Sinquefield, Moses
Kellums, Russel
Davis, Sally
Lathrope, Eliza
Jordan, John
Jordan, Burrel

p. 141
Davis, Deoclesion
Davis, Baldwin
Davis, Goodrum
Lyon, Jonathan
Page, Solomon Sr.
Moore, John
Joiner, Abraham
Mercer, Dennis
Griffin, David
Cross, Edward
McVay, John
McVay, David
Davis, John
Lee, Elias
Holly, Henry
Williams, Paul
Loyd, Daniel
Bailey, William
Hartley, James Sr.
Hartley, Burrel
Hartley, Hillery
Layton, John
Brantley, Zachariah
Peacock, William
Wimberly, David
Dudley, Elam
Tibbett, William
Tarver, James
Dunst (?), Moses

47

p. 142
McAnless, William
Holms, Lewis
Hunt, Thomas
Duke, William
Robinson, Samuel
Williams, Thomas
Elton, Charles
Brantley, Spencer
McLendon, Mason
Jacobs, Shadrack
Elton, John
Robinson, Thomas
Cannon, William
Malone, Madison
Arnold, William
Waters, Richard
Brantley, Edward
Daniel, John
Logan, Benjamin
Tarver, Sterling
Berrien, Thomas M.
Coker, William
Boatright, George
Cook, Savary
Chasteen, Raney
Hurst, Henry
Dupree, James
Renfroe, John

p. 143
Hood, William
Thompson, Robert
Womble, Egbert
Avera, Sally
Harrill, George
Ethridge, Enoch
Mills, Thomas
Wood, Misuel
Metts, Frederick
Dean, Joel
Lowe, John
Moore, Josiah
Chasteen, Peter
Hall, William
Hall, Lydia
Bullard, Lydia
Brown, John
Bateman, David
Mashburn, Daniel
Jones, Isaiah
Jenkins, Uriah
Fleming, John
Handley, James
Dudley, Elam
Joiner, Malichi
Joiner, Hardy

Dudley, Eden
Lee, Bud
Howard, Charles

p. 144
Howard, Joshua
Howard, Henry
Beasley, John
Jenkins, Moses
Jones, Benjamin
Jenkins, Lewis
Jenkins, Hezekiah
Cotten, John
Kendrick, James
Sheppard, James
Moye, George
Chasteen, Blas
Hunsham (?), Thomas
Page, James
Lee, Sampson
Hartley, James Jr.
Page, Solomon Sr.
Whitfield, Ruben
Whitfield, Jemima
Whitfield, Robert
Pate, John
Whitfield, Bryan
Whitfield, William
Maxfield, Feliz
Moore, Shadrach
Davis, Goodrum Sr.
King, John
Curry, John

p. 145
Salter, Zadock
Salter, Charles
Gainer, William
Gainer, Martha
Jordan, Henry
Bryant, Jason
Godwin, Elias
Godwin, Alan
Whiting, John
Page, Alan
Long, Charity
Francis, Cordel
Huggins, Daniel
Britt, Jesse
Britt, James
Blount, Sarah
Bell, Olive
Ubanks, Mary
Sutton, Abel
White, Elisha
Smith, Jordan

Turlington, Thomas
Moore, Donaldson
Smith, Alan
Gordon, Benjamin
Dickinson, Charles
Brock, John
Burney, Ellis
Brooks, James
Spier, John

p. 146
Farmer, John
Franklin, Josiah
Harrison, Joseph
Holt, Thomas
Sheppard, Thomas
Sheppard, John
Jackson, Kinchin
Bedgood, John Sr.
Bedgood, Samuel
Manning, Isaac
Joiner, Elisha
Farmer, William
Joiner, Abraham
Burney, (Silas?)
Burney, Elizabeth
Burney, Willis
Burney, Harris
Furgurson, Daniel
Scott, James
Rolandson, Robert
Dawkins, Frances
Smith, Mary
Carter, Ezekiel
Carter, Silas
Carter, Silas Sr.
Price, Rice
Price, Berry
Price, James
Bedgood, John

p. 147
Joiner, Edmund
Brantley, Green
Gardner, Ishum
Bedgood, Richard
Turner, William
Daniel, Joseph
Britt, John
Lindsay, David
Daniel, Janus
Sheppard, David
Motley, Benjamin
Howard, Harmon
Sessions, Lewis
Thigpen, James

Cook, John
Speights, Jonathan
Fort, John
Robertson, Isaac
Whitaker, Oran
Rieves, Thomas
Gilmore, Thomas
Peacock, John
Carter, Giles
Forbs, Benjamin
Forehand, Jerry
Peacock, Pilson
Crawford, Thomas
Brantley, Harris

p. 148
Ellis, Major
Cole, Benjamin
Peacock, Right
Peacock, Jonathan
Peacock, Archibald
Smith, Cooper John
Peacock, Tinker John
Powell, William
Peacock, Washington
Peacock, Molton
Sherlin, James
Cohonn, Sarah
Barlowe, Edith
Brantley, Patsey
Hays, Quinny
Barlowe, Henry
Brantley, James
Young, Elizabeth
Young, William
Brantley, John
Brantley, Abbie
Brantley, Spencer
Brantley, Thomas
Smith, Micajah
Smith, Colesby
Smith, George
Smith, Isaac
Smith, John
Young, Pierson

p. 149
Jackson, Warren
Smith, Thomas
Chester, Absolom
Irwin, William
McWilliams, Thomas
Orr, John
Bridges, William
Neely, Thomas Sr.
Johnson, John
Collins, Lewis
Collins, William

Chambers, Peter
Johnson, Willis
Powell, George
Collins, Creed
Kimmy, John
Williams, David
Quick, William
Townshind, Henry
Quick, Zachariah
Kirk, Thomas
Oliver, Rowan
Jackson, Charles
Murray, John
Vasser, Micajah
Forehand, Jordan
Daniel, Ezekiel Jr.
Daniel, Ezekiel Sr.
Vickers, Elijah
Crab, Robert

p. 150
McLeod, Angus
Cutts, Crecy
Newton, Daniel
Ennis, James
Acols (?), Zelpha
Watson, Ezekiel
Watson, Fereby
Smith, Samuel T.
Raines, Winny
Johnson, Quincey
Johnson, Jared
Vann, Samuel
Johnson, Israel
Cohoon, Adam
Cohoon, William
Cohoon, Alan
Young, Jesse
Hylliard, Major
Alexander, William
Shirly, James
Johnson, John
Johnson, Elijah
Havard, John
Forehand, David
Vickers, Bryant
Singleton, Hansel
Jenkins, Owen
Jenkins, Evan
Cutts, Joseph
Radcliff, Polly
Hilliard, Nancy

p. 151
Cutts, Elisha
Curl, Wilson
Watson, Elijah
Hilliard, Martin

Musslewhite, William
Tucker, William
Smith, Job
Smith, Samuel R.
McDuffie, Malcolm
Stone, William
McCorquedale, Daniel
McLeod, Niel
McQueen, John
Hart, Barney
McCorquedale, Malcom
Hart, Jonathan
Lamborn, Noel
Mason, George
Lee, Ira
Rains, John
Smith, Lewis
Leeper, John
Stone, John R.
Kemp, Elitha
Young, William
Bridges, William F.
Covington, John
Berryhill, James
Webb, John

p. 152
Montzingo, Lewis
Fisher, Charles
Foster, John
Webb, Giles
—(illeg.), Louisa
Swilly, Lewis
Bray, Peter
Bray, Benjamin
Grady, Frederick
Williams, Robert
Cox, Betsy
Parrymore, Sarah
Parrymore, James
Webb, Samuel
Oliver, Asa
Willson, Daniel
Wright, John M. and
    Thomas
Horn, John
Tootle, Fereby
Sheffield, John C.
Jackson, Edward
Bryant, David
Allcock, Seddy
Watters, Lodowick
Underwood, Ruben
Martin, Richard
Cox, Williamson
Sheppard, Henry
Heath, Daniel

Dupree, Jesse
Cason, William
Cason, Henry
Upchurch, Benjamin
Smith, Needham
Rains, Allan
Smith, William
Smith, Richard
Rains, Washington
Messicks, George

p. 159
Dean, Rachel
Albritton, Zachariah
Hardin, James
Holt, Arrington
Hern, Stephen
Hern, Wyatt
Barnett, Sarah
Dillard, Mary
Langhurn, Richard
Arnold, Ambrose
Harden, John
Kitchens, Sarah
Moore, John
Williamson, Benjamin
Cox, Aaron
Pace, Samuel
Schiry, Isaiah
Smith, James
Cannon, Elisha
Massey, Abel
Smith, Hardy
Killingsworth, Wm.
Rutherford, Benj. H.
Moye, George
Adkins, Joseph
Pace, Thomas
Mimms, William
Ryland, Alan
Ryland, John
Foose, Jesse

p. 160
Hawkins, William
Blow, George
Gregory, William
Fisher, Metcalf
Adams, Abner
Barge, Richmond
Glenn, Thomas
King, Ann
Glenn, John
Hern, Joseph
Bailey, John
Cohoon, James
Taylor, Isaac
West, John

Bridges, Joseph
Blount, Phillip
Hardy, Thomas Sr.
Hardy, Thomas Jr.
Daniel, Peter
Todd, Hardy
Newman, James
Corbett, Groove
Fowler, Jeremiah
Jenkins, Drury
Phillips, John
Wood, Jared
Wood, George
Smith, Ladden

p. 161
Yarborough, Benj.
Neely, Thomas
Irwin, John L.
Irwin, Jared
Hardeson, Elizabeth
Hardeman, Thomas
Robison, John
Sessions, Benjamin
Sessions, Joseph
Rushing, Sarah
Rushing, Eli
Rushing, William
Swint, Edward
Cawill, William
Durden, Frances
Bateman, Claibourne
Mills, Thomas
Freeman, John
Bateman, William
Harris, Churchwell
Miller, Francis
Bateman, Theophilus
Bateman, John
Ray, Gabriel
Ray, Hardy
Brookins, Charles V.
Gladdin, James
Renfroe, William
Renfroe, Enoch
Osteen, Thomas
Jiles, Jacob

p. 162
Jiles, William
Jiles, Alexander
Ray, Ambrose Sr.
McDuffie, John
Morrison, John
Dublain, George W.
Hood, Lucy
Renfroe, Averett
Avera, Patience

Avera, Lander
Trawick, Moses
Mitchell, A. G. C.
Clay, Pierce
Barnett, John
Hall, William
Hall, Lydia
Blair, Thomas
Parker, Henry
Harris, James
Trawick, Elizabeth
Gainer, Michael
Vincent, George
Vincent, Josias
Groom, Major
Groom, Emmry
Vincent, Alsey
Sehlvy, Moses
Oquin, John
Horn, Sherod H.
Pool, Middleton

p. 163
Anderson, James
Anderson, Robert
Holton, Stephen
Sneder, Jacob
Goodrum, Lydia
Butler, William
Eastwood, Elijah
Allen, Susan
Carter, David
Anderson, Shadrach
Hicklin, Rubin
Liptrot, Aquilla
Veal, Nathan Sr.
Veal, Nathan Jr.
Veal, George
Griffin, Sally
Deason, Absolom
Deason, Sheppard
Wood, Peter
Veall, Edward
Lewis, Ira
Lewis, Samuel
Lewis, Asa
Daniel, Keneth
Daniel, Frances
Daniel, Thomas
McGab——, Daniel
Fason, William
Groom, Wylly
Manning, Sophia

p. 164
Simpson, Ezekiel
Groom, Jesse
Cone, Levi

51

Swilley, Elijah
Parish, James
Griffin, Enoch
Mobley, Abner
Prosser, Elly
Stephens, John
Cone, John
Vincen, Nathan
McDaniel, Mary
Fuller, Chloe
Hardy, Collins
Colvin, John
Armstrong, James
Hardy, William
Wadsworth, John
Hardy, John
Rogers, Mesheck
Rogers, Daniel
Davis, Joel
Pitts, John
Horton, Daniel
Cox, James
Cone, Mary
Whitaker, William
Pace, Bryan
Stock, Turner
Hutchinson, William

p. 165
Cox, Moses
Furguson, Benjamin
Avent, Isaiah
Bigham, Joshua
Albritton, Elijah
Pitts, Jane
Bray, Joseph
Arnold, William
Castelow, William
Castelow, James
Pace, Nathaniel
Avent, Ransom
Stephens, Jacob
Armstrong, Jesse
Greer, George
Greer, David
Lawson, Thompson
Powell, Henry
Hasteen, William
Mathis, John
Stewart, Nathaniel
Lingo, Pinkston
Smith, William
Hurst, Humphrey
Taylor, William
Hutchinson, Richard
Hutchinson, Nathaniel

p. 166
Sanders, William
Bennett, Jerry
Brown, Jesse D.
Jackson, Alsey
Tooten, Sarah
Dixon, Alla
Horton, Howell
Albritton, Asa
Albritton, Peter
Whittle, Ambrose
Strange, Gideon
Stokes, Joel
Conyers, William
Brantram, John
Brooks, Sarah
Hardison, John
Crumbley, Anthony
Mathis, John
Bland, Elisha
Smith, Jesse
Conyers, Henry
Conyers, Rachel
McKinley, Joseph
Griffin, Mary
Rogers, Zachariah
Crafton, Malton

p. 167
Hodges, Foreman
Dean, Thomas
Achard, John
Cannon, Richard
Branham, Susan
Crumbley, George
Crumbley, Anthony Sr.
Rawls, Dempsey
Blachly, Eliza
Williams, Daniel
Achords, John Sr.
Kennedy, Jane
Youngblood, Isaac
Arnold, James
Hodge, Henry
Griffin, Lewis
Miller, Lewis
Ikener, Michael
King, Thomas
Blount, Richard A.
Turner, I. D.
Safold, Ishum H.
Irwin, John
Jells, Francis
Whitaker, Willis
Elton, Robert
Elton, Abram

p. 168
Horn, ——
Dixon, Tilman
Buck, William
Motley, Robert
Glen, Otway
Jodun, Jane
Rutherford,
    Thomas B.
Williams, John

52

National Archives Film 19 Roll 21

p. 239
Brown, Morgan
Soullard, Edward
Goodson, Thomas
Jenkins, S. D.
Barnes, David H.
Ainsworth, James
Biggs, Jesse
Slade, William
Harris, N. F.
Rogers, Charles
McBeth, James
Solomon, David
Gregory, William
Haynes, Wm. P.
Northington, Jesse E.
Hill, James J.
Paurnelle, Wm. F.
Schley, P. T.
Sessions, Sherrod
Franklin, George
Jenkins, Thomas N.
Jernigan, L. A.
Williams, David
Elton, Charles
Tooke, Jesse B.
McDaniel, Edward
Chester, A.

p. 240
Smith, John
Holley, Henry
Fish, Joseph
Lloyd, David
Forbes, Benjamin
Peacock, William
Bridges, Sialas
Brantley, James
Peacock, John
Peacock, Asa
Barlow, Henry
Brassel, Arthur
King, Charles C.
Crabb, Robert
Peacock, Uriah
Bonson, Lewis
Brantley, Spencer
Brantley, John
Burris, Alfred
Brantley, Edw.
Allen, David
Peacock, A.

Jenkins, Evins
Brantley, Harris
Williams, George
Brantley, John F.
Irwin, Thomas A.

p. 241
Jenkins, Uriah
Peacock, William
Daniel, John
Powel, William
Brantley, Aaron
Burns, James
Smith, Micajah
Williamson, P. G.
Oliver, James
Womack, William
Bowen, Herrod
Brown, Samuel
Tison, Stephen
Tison, Fred.
Lawhon, John
Hartley, Hardy
Tison, Noah
Thigpen, James
Young, William
Hart, Nancy
Speirs, A.
Sessions, Jos. Jr.
Northington, Wm.
Tarver, Ben(or Bryan)
Night, Jesse
Watkins, Daniel
Barwick, Samuel

p. 242
McVey, David
Townsley, V. S.
Davis, Goodrum
Johnson, Isaac
Brown, Solomon
Cordry, Jonathan
Collins, M. D.
Rawlings, William
Price, Joshua
Boatright, George
Boatright, James
Purkins, William
Duke, William
Hust, Henry
Cannon, William

Hodges, Seth
Simmons, William
Barnes, Jacob
Ketrell, Noah
Martin, John
Lyon, Jonathan
Cook, Sterling
Tarbutton, Wm. Sr.
Tompkins, John Y.
Griffin, Larkin
Massey, Bennett
Boyd, John

p. 243
Brown, Handley
Miller, James
Edwards, John
Parker, Hardy
Tarbutton, Benj.
Massey, John B.
Tarver, Robert
Kelly, John
Patridge, Henry
Hopson, William
Wimberly, David
Horton, F. K.
Harrell, David
Wilson, Augustine
Cox, Denous(?)
Tennille, F. G.
Robinson, Samuel
Coston, Thomas
Horton, George W.
Chevers, Larkin
McCoy, Daniel
Daniel, Keneth
Kennida, Samuel
Jones, Howel
Pool, Middleton
Finney, Mrs. E.
Purkins, Stephen

p. 244
Adams, John W.
Sessions, Joseph
Johnson, John
Avery, Mrs. Sarah
Barrentine, Wm.
Alford, Bias
Whitfield, Reuben
Smith, Samuel

Pierce, W. A.
Carter, Silas
Dudley, Edam
Sheppard, John
Taylor, Kinchin
Webb, John
Ikner, Solomon
Blann, Simeon
Blann, Micajah
Davis, William
Shiry, Benjamin
Williams, Daniel
Martin, James
Allen, Joseph
Tompkins, Rukin
Tanner, Joseph
Posey, Henry
Pridgen, Edwin
Holton, Thial

p. 245
Summer, Jethro
King, John C.
Hodges, John
Hodges, Wiley T.
Hodges, Redding
Stansel, Wm. R.
Strang, Gideon
Thompkins, Burwell
Brooks, Robert
Miller, John
Cain, Lidda
Hood, Sean
Joines, Jabaze
Gilmore, Hugh
Achord, John
Moore, Mathew
Cox, James
Farwick, Benjamin
Cook, James
Sims, James
Love, Robert
Braddy, Charles
Harrell, Solomon
Harrell, Jesse
Renfroe, Samuel
Webb, James
Jones, James

p. 246
Waller, John H.
Blann, Elisha
Webster, Lewis
Trotman, Blount
Ellis, Major
Dillard, Mrs. B.

Vincent, Benjamin
Vincent, Josiah
Vincent, George
Martin, Bird
Clifton, Nathan
Lord, John
Brookins, Haywood
Barwick, John
Gendol (Tendol), Jacob
Stokes, Wm.
Reves, Lee
Brantley, Z.
Paine, James
Pope, Daniel
Buck, William
Boatright, Rolly
Tucker, Harper
Harrison, Joseph
Hartley, Barwell
Lord, Wheatley
Pate, Redding

p. 247
Williamson, Wm.
Boatright, John
Hunt, John
Johnson, Wm.
Arnold, Arnet
Arnold, Harrell
O'Quinn, Allen
Fowler, John
Wright, John M.
Sessions, Benj.
Darby, James
Avent, J. B.
Tarbutton, Joseph
Cox, John
Smith, Matilda
Daniel, Joseph
Lee, Elias
Cason, Henry
Orr, Henry
Molssass (?), Morris
Tarver, Stephen
Mayo, William
Barrett, Thomas
Tennille, Wm. A.
Sessions, Levi
Cason, William
Brown, Emanuel

p. 248
Irwin, Alexander
Fisher, Metcalf
Glenn, John
Dorch, David

Hardwick, W. P.
Gainer, James
Drew, Jesse B.
Terlington, Thomas
Whitfield, Robt.
Brantley, Green
McMellon, Malcom
Harris, Daniel
Hardison, Wm. L.
Newsom, Jordy
Dupree, James
Tedder, Zachariah
Barwick, William
Smith, Allen
Dudley, Elam
Bates, William
Lane, Bryant
Page, Solomon
Newsom, Asa
Jackson, L. B. A.
Davis, Joel A.
Daniel, Alexander

p. 249
Folker, Joseph
Johnson, Henry
Whitaker, Willis
Brown, Hezekiah
Laton, John
Renfroe, Enoch
Williams, John
Cullens, W. W.
Hood, William
Clay, William
Jones, Benjamin
Hill, Theophilus
May, George
Foster, John H.
Murphy, William
Cherry, William
Avent, R. D.
Phelps, Augustus
Jordan, Wm. D.
Harden, John
Armstrong, Jesse
Howard, Polly
Drake, Francis
Robinson, Moses
Bridges, Joseph
Langham, Richard
Whidoon, Kody

p. 250
Roughton, Enoch
Tanner, Vincent
Martin, William

54

Page, John
Crafton, Mathew
Crafton, William
Moody, Daniel
Williamson, Benjamin
Killingsworth, Randal
Killingsworth, Wm.
Lasler, Hardy
Love, Thomas
Jenkins, Hezekiah
Renfroe, John
Tanner, Rebecca
Pope, Wiley
Watkins, Redding
Floyd, Silas
Watkins, Jonas
Miller, John
Skrine, William A.
Tennille, Robert
Hodges, Abel
Cummings, Robert
Golightly, Susannah
Thomas, Euphama
Thomas, Robert F.

p. 251
Sheler (?), Ellafair
Finn, Eli
Collins, John S.
May, Jethro
Coffield, John
Rogers, Harvy
Sterling, John
Williams, Lewis
Peddy, Juslous (?)
Newsom, Rauzy
Hynes, G. W.
Jordan, James
Curry, George
Sanders, Burwell
Bynam, G (or T)arner
Helton, Richard
Lenier, James
Long, John J.
Collins, Joshua
Brantley, William
Kendrick, James
Miller, J. F.
Curry, John
Gorden, Benjamin
Smith, E. B.
Key, Henry
Smith, Patrick

p. 252
Salter, Zedoc

Britt, James
Smith, Jordan
Pate, John W.
White, John
Smith, William
Brookins, Benj.
Whiting, John
Hunt, William
Bryant, Jason
Moore, Shadrick
Moy, Duran
Moy, George
Moy, John
Goff, Sarah
Joiner, Mary
Paradis, William
Whitfield, Myles
Page, John
Whitfield, Bryant
Kelly, Lidia
Whiddon, William
Cook, Edward
Salter, John
Sneed, William
Wood, George R.
Baker, John Jr.

p. 253
Howard, James M.
Dickins, Gillum
Smith, Samuel G.
Page, Solomon Jr.
King, Mary
Haynes, Bythol
Page, Joseph H.
Hynes, Churchwell
Pournelle, John
Spears, Frances
Holland, Margaret
Dorch, John
Moy, Thomas
Pitts, William C.
Pitts, John D.
Gladdin, Solomon
Tucker, John R.
Rutherford, Franklin
Brown, John
Sparks, Thomas
Conyers, Rachel
Hooks, Sarah
Mathis, Littleton
Cook, James S.
Page, Mary

Bailey, William
Dudney, Arthur

p. 254
Smith, Gideon
Massey, Elizabeth
Worthen, Wm. B.
Brown, William
Giles, John
Wicker, Thomas
Duggan, John H.
Fentress, J. C.
Armstrong, Edward
Stubbs, John
Brown, Turner F.
Jordan, Jacob
Yates, John
Tanton, William
Phillips, James
Giles, William
Hattiway, Daniel
Mott, Joseph
Harrison, Gabriel
Hawkins, Drewry
Rachels, Myles
Cato, James
Johnson, Wm. C.
Amison, Warren
Duggan, John
Cummings, Eli
Baker, Jonath. Sr.

p. 255
Worthen, Thomas J.
Wicker, John
Griffin, William
Watkins, Mitchell
Sherman, Robert
Amison, Nathan
Bateman, David
Keen, William
Bedgood, John
Miller, Lewis
Blann, John
White, Allen
Glenn, Patience
Tison, John
Robinson, Wm.
Green, William
Brantley, Edward
Miller, Joshua
Swint, Edmond
Herndon, Wiatt

55

Hartley, Hillery
Hanson, Michael
Webb, John
Smith, P. P.
Joines, James
Amison, John
Outlaw, Morgan

p. 256
Horton, Frederick G.
Long, William
Cox, David
Webster, Richard
Sneed, Sarah
Jordan, Benjamin
Bray, John
Twilly, William
Dixon, Thomas
Brantley, Harris
Nowel, Isham
Garner, Henry
Webb, William
Peabody, John
Brooks, James
Wood, Harrod
Prince, George
Wicker, Benjamin
Wicker, Alfred
Albritton, Joel
Walker, John
Cox, Henry
Dillard, Allen
Fish, William
Tanton, Newsom
Mills, Mathew
Sheppard, John Jr.

p. 257
King, Charles
Sheppard, Charles
Tanner, William
King, John Jr.
Elton, John
Tucker, Henry C.
Shirling, James
Perser (?), James
Worthen, Green H.
Jordan, John
Cook, Samuel
Lightfoot, Robert
Purkins, Joseph
Parker, Jonathan
Rains, Washington
Daniel, Ezekiel
Jordan, Mrs. W.
Curry, David
Linzey, David

Cordry, Daniel
Myors, Thomas
Nowel, Elisha
Taylor, H. S.
Miller, Jordan
Linzey, Nelson
Baily, John
Underwood, Reuben

p. 258
Atkins, John
Martin, Green
Whitaker, Samuel
Martin, James
Thigpen, William
Todd, Susan
McAfee, Arthur
Tucker, William
Alexander, William
Carlile, Mathew
Kennida, Elizabeth
Shery (Shiry), Jno. M.
Lord, Levin
Lord, Mary
Joiner, Ezekiel
Franklin, Vasnty
Smith, Sarah
Lawrence, John
Moore, Cason
Sinquefield, Moses
Batts, Nathan
Joines, William
Stanford, Elizabeth
Elliott, Benjamin
Sinquefield, Wm.
Townsley, Lott
Maxwell, Felix

p. 259
Davis, Nancy
Flemming, Oliver
Rauzey, William
Wise, Nancy
Odem, Dempsey
Haynes, Emulia
Wiggins, Joshua
Odem, Elizabeth
Jordan, William
Grier, David
Arnold, Thomas
Dixon, Shadrack
Coston, John
Wood, Henry
Ely, John
Adams, Hopewell
Francis, Cordial
Moore, A. D.

Blount, James
Pinson, Elizabeth
Worthy, Robert
Hodges, Sarah
Lightfoot, Martha
Carter, David
Scott, Hiram
Miller, H. B.
Whittle, Sebron

p. 260
Shiry, Samuel
Cason, Dennis
Deen, Joel
Dillard, Dempsey
Dupree, Lewis
Mathis, Mrs. P.
Smith, Richard
Dupree, T. R.
Sanders, Daniel
Goodson, Edwin
Smith, Allen
Ivy, Owin
Whittle, Ambrose
Deen, James
Phillips, Jane
Bartlett, Lainda
King, Elisha
Ivy, James
Kennida, David
Wilson, Barbary
Mills, Thomas
Harris, Trecy
Smith, Thomas
Register, John
Register, Abel
Massey, Cordy
Bell, Tandy

p. 261
Stone, William
Vincent, Casie
Gorden, Richard
Sheppard, Lewis
Derdan, Stephen
BAker, Thomas H.
Croom, Emmara
Ford, Hillery
Hall, William
Thompson, Sarah
O'Quinn, John
Renfroe, Eliaha
McCoy, Robert
Leaptrot, Bolin
Kilpatrick, David
Horton, Laborn
O'Quinn, Bryant

56

Ford, Anna
Veal, Edward
Horton, Howel
Forshee, John
Parrish, William
Wodsworth, John
Leaptrot, A.
Giles, Alexander
Griffin, Sarah
Wood, Polly

p. 262
McCoy, Nancy
Cone, Levi
Cone, Thomas
Croom, Major
Rogers, Hezekiah
Parrish, James
Gilis, William
Cone, Abel
Prosser, Oty
Bond, Robert
Dardin, Stephen
Jones, Henry
Murkinson, Wm. M.
Britt, Obed
Williams, Shadrack
Wilson, Daniel
Tomlinson, Harris
White, Abijah
Welker, Dorsett
Britt, Henry
Jordan, Margaret
Cole, Benjamin
Ikner, Michael
Peacock, Willis
Edwards, William
Chambers, Simeon P.
Avent, L. S.

p. 263
Youngblood, I. R.
Hocklin, R. N.
Barnett, John
Glover, A.
New, Daniel
Womble, Elizabeth
Adams, James
Riddle, Anderson
Tanner, Thomas
Spaight, Jonathan
Mills, Stephen
Herndon, Joseph
Maguher (?), Nathan
Fluker, Robert

Oliver, Roan
Coleman, David
Jackson, William
Moore, Josiah
Cummings, David
Mills, John
Womble, Thomas
Martin, Richard
Orr, John
Heeth, Daniel
Daniel, Zachariah
Jordan, Asa
Thomason, William

p. 264
Oliver, Odin
Barron, Barnabas
Lord, Leandy
Williams, Robert
Trotman, Thomas
Traywick, Moses
Newsom, Kinchin
Miller, Benjamin
Barron, William
Gardner, John E.
Haynes, Nathan
Cook, McKeen
Wallace, William
Gilbert, William
Walker, David
Osborn, Ruben
Early, Jesse
King, Thomas
Watson, Elijah
Goodson, Abram
Johnson, Elijah
Godwin, Elias
Childers, Richard
Nowel, Henry
Tompkins, Samuel
Green, McKeen
McRae, Charity

p. 265
Miller, Francis
Matthews, Lodowick
Posey, Richard
Barnes, John
Watkins, Richard
Towson, Henry
Morrison, John Sr.
Joines, Edmond
Garner, James
Bateman, Jason
Covington, Cloe

Jenkins, Drewry
Rains, Allen
Young, Elizabeth
Holton, William
Avera, Samuel
Bray, Jarrod
Mathews, John
Walters, Richard
Price, Rice
Stewart, Nath'l.
Dupree, James
Pittman, Nimrod
Tull, Isaac
Eastwood, Marium
Eastwood, John
Smith, Isaac

p. 266
Rains, John
Mayo, Benjamin
Cox, Cullen
Phillips, John
Atkins, Randal
Johnson, Israel
McCorkdale, Daniel
Berryhill, James
Messer, George
Hardee, Thomas
Metts, Leven
Powell, John
Swilly, Senos (?)
McAfee, James
Hamilton, Duncan
Johnson, Willis
Evens, Peter
Sheppard, Frances
Foose, Moses
Powell, Henry
Jones, Bassel
Wood, Miesels (?)
Anderson, Evan
Fowler, John
Deen, Jesse
Martin, John
Vann, William W.

p. 267
Vann, Samuel
Arline, James
Mims, John
Sheppard, David
Young, James
Metts, Wright
Oliver, Asa
Cutts, Elijah

Brown, George
Brown, Turner
Corssey, Alfred
Mott, Hiram
Bynam, Henry
Curry, John
Collins, John G.
Armstrong, Alex
Worthen, Richard
Night, Lewis
Meakes, Benjamin
Night, Sylvanus
Walker, William H.
Perry, Henry
Armstrong, Alex Jr.
Cone, Archilas
Cone, James
Duggan, Asa
Harrison, Joseph

p. 268
Jordan, Thomas
Rachel, William
Jordan, Cornelius
Massey, Abraham
May, Edmond
Potent, Robert
Dickins, James
Amison, Josiah
Burgamy, William
Hooks, Hillary
Cone, John D.
Heeth, Sarah
Cook, Benjamin
Adams, Arnold
Fizzel, Jane
Frasure, Wilkinson
Little, Edmond
Renfroe, Nathan
Holmes, John J.
Hodges, Henry
Neely, Thomas
Davis, John
Fontain, William
Sterling, John G.
Gilmore, John
Gilmore, James
Howard, Elizabeth

p. 269
Howard, Solomon
Bright, Meley
Simpson, Ezekiel
Lenier, Lewis
Gray, Enoch

Stubbs, Gabriel
Sterling, David H.
Hamilton, Samuel
Blount, Richard A.
Holt, Ellis
Lloyd, Daniel
Lloyd, John
Carter, William
Barron, James
Jenkins, Lewis
Garros, Amos
Sheppard, Thomas
Jackson, Warren
Bedgood, Samuel
Frost, James
Page, Britton
Price, Littleberry
Bedgood, Richard
Holt, Susannah
Ellis, John
Price, Bridgers
Night, Mathew

p. 270
Moore, Burwell
Moore, Winnaford
Renfroe, Enoch
Hood, Sherrod
Everett, David
Traywick, William
Horton, Jesse
Newman, Eliorll
Renfore, James
Derdan, Frances
Horton, Wiley B.
Miller, John
Etheridge, Enoch
Grier, George
Porter, William
Mills, Charles
Veal, George
Cox, John
Haywood, Archibald
Pittman, Isham
Wilson, John
Pittman, Malichi
Giles, John
Spann, John
Mills, Daniel
Clay, John
Ray, Ambros

p. 271
Clay, Pirce
Anderson, Mariah

Craft, Selia
Parker, Joshua
Lumby, Thomas
Holton, Elizabeth
McDuffee, Christia
Rushing, Sarah
Wise, John
Albritton, Peter
Mathews, John
Fisher, William
Atkins, Joseph
Massey, Abel
Camby, Leroy
Brown, Mary D.
Robinson, Nancy
Corbet, Sarah
Cox, Aaron
Mims, William
Calhoun, James
Oliver, John M.
Eason, Isaac
Powell, George
Smith, Lewis
Powell, Wright
Lewis, Redding R.

p. 272
Low, Elizabeth
Welch, Asa
Mills, Asaph
Blair, James
Burgamy, Tobias
Blair, George
Murphy, Samuel
Worthen, Rebecca
Brantley, Thomas
Tucker, Daniel R.
Smith, English
Davis, E. A.
Giles, Nathan
Mathis, John
Cox, William
Osborn, William
Griffin, Thomas
Williams, Phillip
Veal, Richard H.
Renfroe, William
Cone, Archibald
Dickins, Joseph
Dickins, Isaac
Dickins, John
Rachel, Zedoc
Coe, Joseph
Achord, L. H.

King, John Sr.
Blakley, Elizabeth
Snider, Jacob
Stokes, Joel
Whittle, John
King, Thomas H.
Williams, Daniel
Cox, Moses
Ikner, Phillip
Owens, Milly
Achord, John F.
Bray, Joseph
Hodges, Jordan
Fuller, Peggy
Giles, Mary
Derdan, Mathew
Croom, Jennet
Mathews, John
Rutherford, Mary
Manning, Cassandra
Attiway, Susan
Dixon, Thomas
Beckham, Abel
Beckham, Osborn
Mott, Nathan
Cato, Ailcy
Amison, Henry

p. 274
Harrington, John
Amison, Cullen
Blair, Nancy
Blair, John D.
Garner, Jacob
Johnson, Nancy
Cook, Allen
Smith, George
Howard, Nancy
Brown, William
Morris, Jacob
Thigpen, Randal
Davidson, Asa
Wiggins, William
Roughton, Wm.
Jones, William
Taylor, Sofiah
Perry, John
Sanders, Elizabeth
Dickins, Robert
Canter, Richard
Tanton, Henry
Harrell, John
Andrews, Green

Taylor, Drewry
Garrott, Asa
Duggan, A. C.

p. 275
Tarver, Penny
Hartley, Pherraby
Joiner, Malichi
Williamson, Malichi
Ade, James R.
Thompson, John H.
Parmer, Isabella
Daniel, Mary
Outlaw, Nancy
Wells, E. H.
Hodges, Elbert
Webb, Hollan
Vann, Henry
Camp, Mary
Carter, William
Metts, Frederick
Hightower, Rolly
Ellington, John
Metts, Lewis
Martin, John
Jackson, Rosannah
Tuttle, Pherraby
Johnson, Chimia
Young, Jesse
Calhoun, Samuel
Calhoun, William
Echols, Zelphia

p. 276
Stewart, Mary
Lee, Milley
Rains, Winnifred
Mason, George
Tharp, John
Walker, Henry
Hay, Ruben
Braddy, John
Crawford, Thomas
Cunningham, Thomas
Vickers, Elijah
Cullins, Ferd
Calhoun, Allen
Coker, Daniel
Howard, John R.
Logan, Benjamin
Phillips, Cloe
Frazure, Margaret
Tison, Frederick

Traywick, Lunsford
Hardin, John F.
Williams, Paul
Johnson, Jason
Johnson, Queny
Hays, Queny
Womack, Sarah
Veal, Nathan

59

WASHINGTON COUNTY--1840 Census

96th GMD

page 194
Giles, John
Armstrong, Alexdr.
Armstrong, Edw.
Watkins, Isaac H.
Long, Clarissa
Garner, Patience
Frarser (?), Wilkins
Amerson, Josiah
Meeks, Wiley
Garner, Henry
Cone, Archd.
Garner, Joshua
Garner, John
Brown, Sarah
Coleman, David
Thigpen, James
Cook, Allen
Cook, James L.
Womble, Martha
Garrett, Asa
Walker, Clarissa
Yates, Mary
Barron, Frances
Duggan, Asa
Fonkee (?), Elisha
Duggan, John
Bright, Nelly
Herrington, John

page 195
Cummin, Eli
Thigpen, Ivey
Brown, John D.
Meeks, Howel
Cone, Archilles
Baker, Jonathan Sr.
Cone, James
Meeks, Benj.
Cone, Jesse B.
Rachels, Zacock
Baker, Jonathan Jr.
Osborn, Wm.
Amerson, Charles
Amerson, Uriah
Amerson, Nathan
Cofield, John
Amerson, Cutten
Harrison, James
Taunton, Wm.
Downs, Silas
Nichols, Wm.
Dickens, Isaac

Dickens, Joseph
Jordan, Mary
Lewis, W. B.
Moll, Hiram
Holton, Mary
Thompson, John P.
Christy, Allen
Hawkins, Henry
Coursey, Alfred

page 196
Pilcher, Lewis
Griffin, Thos.
Warthen, I. M.
Redfern, Bransen
Beckham, Mary
Lingo, Peter
Williams, William
Jordan, Benj.
Harrison, John L.
Johnson, Wm. C.
Bergamy, Wm.
Dickens, Sarah
Hattaway, Davis
Hawkins, Drury
Cato, James
Amerson, Jonah
Hattaway, Baton
Burgamy, Tobias
Decanter, Sarah
Decanter, W. R. L.
Brazel, Elias
Sprague, Riley
Macaoni, Sarah
Ferrell, Jane
Staveley, Elizabeth
Cook, Nancy
Morrison, Margaret
Cummins, Robert
Harrison, Wm.
Warthen, Richard

page 197
Bell, John
Walker, Allen A.
Gatlen, Feriby

95th GMD

page 198
Warthen, Green H.
Adams, Arnold L.

Wiggins, George
Shehee, Ellafaw
Robison, Wm.
Collins, Mary
Roughton, Enoch
Barwick, William
Perry, Henry
Lord, William
Collins, Thos. J.
Newsom, Kinchin
Jones, William
Lord, Leonerda (?)
Brantley, Harris
Curry, John
Brown, Wm. L.
Brown, Sophia
Finny, Ezekiel
Howard, Penelope
Welch, Emanuel
Ingram, Gilford
Bynum, Turner L.
Brown, Sarah
Sheppard, Benj.
Newsom, Seaborn
Martin, Elizabeth
Knight, Lewis
May, Jethro
Brown, Uriah
May, William Jr.

page 199
Thigpen, Randall
Curry, Wm. W.
Jordan, Cornelius
Greene, Tilman
Collins, James
Fenn, Eli
Sparks, Thomas
Welch, Washington
Curry, David
Jordan, Thomas Sr.
Jordan, Elisha
Jordan, Thomas Jr.
May, William 3r.
Tolbert, Patrick
May, Edmund
Parker, Elizabeth
Johnson, Ellis
Cummins, David
Knight, Silvanus
Walker, David
Barnes, John Sr.

60

Barnes, David H.
Harrison, Joseph
Harrison, James G.
Watkins, Mitchell
Brown, William
Griffin, William
Osborn, Reuben
Adams, Benj.
Howard, Sally
Collins, Jackson

page 200
Gray, Wm.
Miller, Samuel
Gray, Enoch
Thompson, Sarah
Stubbs, Ann
Stubbs, Gabriel
Wicker, Thomas
Gilmore, John
Gilmore, Mary
Jones, Henry
Buckhanner, Eliz.
Finny, Eupherna(?)
Allen, Caroline J.
Cofield, Chas. A.

100th GMD

page 201
Ethridge, Enoch
Mills, Thos.
Harris, John
Durden, Stephen
White, James L.
Jordan, E. D.
McCoy, Robert
Hust, Henry
Thompson, Sarah
Renfroe, Nathl.
Durden, Frances
Hooks, Hillary
Walker, John
Walker, Wm. H.
Mills, John
Mills, Stephen
Newman, Elwell
Bailey, Elizabeth
Rives, Lee
Ray, Ambrose
Ray, James
Hood, William
Harris, Tracy
Gladen, Solomon

Wamble, Wm.
Mills, Daniel
McDaniel, Anna
Andrews, Greene
Hair, Winnefred
Weaver, James

page 202
Holmes, John
Hood, Sherrod
McDuffie, Mary
Betha, Phillip P.
Miller, Francis
Miller, Eli
Miller, William
Clay, William
Holton, Selathul(?)
Renfroe, James
Wise, John
Rushin, Sarah
Hitchcock,
    Turner P. (R.?)
Pittman, J. D.
Renfroe, Anna
Anderson, Anariah
Swint, Edmund
Barnett, Nancy
Haygood, Archd.
Taylor, John
Pool, Middleton
Pittman, Nimrod
Renfroe, James M.
Renfroe, John
Hall, James
Hall, Wm. Sr.
Griffin, Rebecca
Hust, Barbara
Brooks, Johnson
McSwane, Catherine

page 203
Lawhorn, Bryant
Wamble, Elizabeth

93rd GMD

page 204
Adams, Sarah
Brown, Sarah
Sheppard, John
Brown, Handley
Johns, Mary E.
Salter, Ephram
Roberson, Robert

Lord, Mary
Tanner, Thomas J.
Walden, Ira
Tanner, Wm.
Newcom, Ellafair
Casson, Rebecca
Tanner, Richard
Tanner, Vincent
Salter, John
Saber (?), Thos.
Kelly, Lydia
Sanders, Burnide(?)
Tanner, Rebecca
Smith, Sarah
West, Jacob
Price, Nancy
Mayo, William
Whiddon, William
Morrell, Enoch
King, Henry
Moore, James
Sheppard, Chas.
Brown, Emanuel
Howard, James W.

page 205
Dorch, John
Regester, Nole
Northington, Jesse E.
Prince, Rebecca
Wall, James
Dorch, David
Wise, Nancy
Odom, Elizabeth
Davis, Nancy
Pierce, Abraham
Walker, Willis
Riddle, Anderson
Tomston, William
Love, Robert
Sellers, Anna
May, John E.
Harmon, William M.
Mayo, Benj.
Mayo, Reuben
King, Charles
Dudley, Elam
Brantley, Edward
Dorch, Russel
Brown, Hezekiah
Sheppard, John Jr.
Barwick, John

Tanner, Thos.
Regester, Benj.
Register, John
Williamson, Sarah
Mayo, Howell

page 206
Watkins, Mitchell
Venters, Francis
Dorch, Walter
Kelly, James
Shearling, James
Whiddon, Rhoda
Franklin, Geo. F.
Bailey, William
Bailey, David
Whiddon, Greene
Wicker, James
Corday, John
Long, John J.
Brantley, Greene
Stone, Wm. H.
Smallden, Peter

99th GMD

page 207
Field, William
Giles, Alexander
Leverett, Joel P.
Veal, John T.
Cone, Seaborn
Tompkins, Samuel
Buck, William
Crooms, Major
Hall, Wm.
Crooms, Jennett
McCoy, William
Vinson, George
Giles, Nathaniel
Johnson, Wm.
Parrish, James
Horton, James
Oguin(?), Bryant
Bullington, Reuben
Salmons, James J.
Durdin, Mathas
Chambers, Ira
Christian, James
Cone, Nancy
Parker, Lewis
Strange, Geo.
Leaptrot, Milbra
Johnson, Joseph
Horton, Labon

Eastwood, Mary A.
Eastwood, John

page 208
Childers, John A.
Tomerson, Wm.
Snider, Jacob
Tompkins, John Y.
Muse, Eli
Veal, Edward
Garner, Piercy
Leaptrot, Bolin
Veal, Nathan
Veal, Geo.
Crooms, Penny A.
Durden, Lewis
Brackins, Benj.
Wright, Geo.
Grooks, John
Rener, Michael I.
Oguin, John
Giles, William
Parrish, William
White, Robert
Wood, Mary
Avent, Ransom
Renfroe, James B.

98th GMD

page 209
Hinson, William
Tucker, John R.
Bland, John
Bland, Agnes
Hodges, Henry
Youngblood, Isaac R.
Daniel, Jesse
Rener, Philiip I.
Buck, S.W. & J.J.
Avent, J. B.
Wood, Greene
Davis, Wm.
Cox, John
Armstrong, Ancarl(?)
Pace, Nathl. C.
Hodges, Abel
Lawson, Roger
Gilmore, James H.
Achord, John F.
Achord, John
Cullens, Frederick
Cullens, F. B.
Avent, John F.
Dupree, T. R.
Elkins, Wm.

Darby, James
Cox, Wm.
Hall, Reuben
Roberson, H. D.
Tull, Isaac
Moy, Isaac

page 210
Strange, Gideon
Smith, English
Posey, Henry
Congres, Rachal
Bland, Simeon
Mitler, L. R.
Bland, Micajah
Cox, Henry
Rogers, Mary
Hodges, W. T.
Greer, David
Adams, Frances
Blenot (?), R.A.

136 GMD

page 211
Perkins, Jackson
Jordan, John
Brown, Morgan
Wicker, Elizabeth
Edge, Daniel
Duggan, John H.
Mills, Charles
Wicker, Benj.
Howard, Mary
Gardner, Celia
Mills, Asaph (?)
Edge, Jonathan
Baker, T. H.
Miller, John
Pridgen, Edwin
Heath, Henry
Taylor, Henry S.
Murphy, Wm.
Jones, Howell
Murphy, Cullen
Moore, Mathas
Robison, Moses
Malpass, Nancy
Taylor, Drury
Bailey, Mary Ann
Mills, James
Jordan, Wm.
Salter, Prescilla
Cherry, Riley
Gilmore, Wm. M.

Adams, James

page 212
Adams, Hopewell
Tanner, Wm.
Hooks, Hopewell
Mills, Mathew
Mathis, Littleton
Hooks, Sarah
Street, Mary
Pournell, Wm.
Smith, Thomas
Tennelle, Robert
Barrow, Barma
Brantley, Jack
Tennelle, Francis T.
Chivers, Jacob

91st GMD

page 213
Steel, Wm.
Peacock, Asa P.
Laton, Hillary
Bridges, Permila
Gregory, William
Jernigan, J. R.
Tarbutton, Wm.
Jenkins, Drury
Franklin, Elizabeth
Boatright, Geo.
Peacock, Archibald
Hill, Theophilas
Peacock, John Sr.
Poobs, Benjamin
Benson, Sarah
Chester, Asolona
Williams, George
Brantley, James Jr.
Brantly, Benj.
Massey, K. W.
Daniel, John
Brantly, Harns
Brantly, Wm.
Williams, Lemuel
Peacock, Uriah
Bazel, Arthur
Wilson, Barbary
Peacock, John Jr.
Love, Levey
Cobb, Amos
Love, Caleb

page 214
Powell, Wright

Jones, Celia
Burns, Ansford
Hays, Qunny
Gay, John
Tison, Fredrick
Jones, John
Sumner, I. B.
Boatright, Rolly
Brantley, Spencer
Smith, John Jr.
Smith, John C.
Wood, Thomas
Brantly, Spencer
Smith, John Jr.
Smith, John C.
Wood, Thomas
Brantly, Thomas
Young, Wm.
Smith, Joseph
Wood, James
Peacock, Wm.
Brantley, Celia
Hart, Nancy
Smith, Isaac
Brantley, Edwin
Smith, Micajah
Johnson, Rebecca
Brantley, Edw.
Brantley, John F.
Brantley, Aggy
Morris, Wm.
Boatright, John
Sheppard, Francis
Laton, James

page 215
Loyd, Daniel Sr.
Loyd, Daniel Jr.
Scott, Mary
Sheppard, Lewis
Elton, John Sr.
Joiner, Malachi
Joiner, John
Hartley, Burwell
Barron, James
Brock, Jesse
Peacock, Molton
Costin, Lott
Brantley, James Sr.
Griffin, Sheppard
Watkins, Reddin
Kendrick, James
Jenkins, Uriah
Tooke, Allen
Oudly, Eden
Costin, John

Dudly, John
Jackson, Lewis
Jenkins, Hezekiah
Sheppard, David
Tribble, Morris
Hartley, Hardy
Linsey, Nelson
Hannl(?), Michael
Bird, Charles
Reddin, Thos.
Banks, Joseph

94th GMD

page 216
Hines, Churchwell T.
Newsom, Nancy
Welch, Asa
Wiggins, Elizabeth
Wiggins, Wm.
Hanes, Nathan
Newsom, Davis R.
Walden, Morris
Sessions, M. L. W.
Lord, Wheetley
Milber, Wm. B.
Newsom, Solomon
Moy, Thomas E.
Newsom, Asa
Laurance, John
Moore, Lason
Miller, Charles
Brantly, Aaron
Elliott, Benj.
Hanes, Nathan W.
Davis, Enos A.
Pope, Owen C.
Pope, Celia
Cowart, Penny D.
Rhodes, Joseph T.
Davis, Joel A.
Fullford, Bryant
Batts, Jesse
Moy, Geo.
Bates, Wm.
Joines, James

page 217
Hardwick, Wm. P.
Harris, Daniel
Wade, John M.
Jordan, John
Gainor, James
Smith, J. R.

90th GMD

page 218
Robison, Samuel
Mims, Joseph
Robison, Wm. H.
Shira, Samuel
King, Elisha
Barnes, Jacob
Kenman, Kendrick
Killingsworth, Jane
Ivey, James
Wood, Jared
Wood, George R.
Scott, Hiram
Elkins, John
Deckins, Lewis
Daniel, Mores
IVey, John
Roberts, James M.
Kenneda, Thos.
Phillips, John
Cason, Dennis
Wood, Henry
Sneed, Wm.
Speight, Jonathan
Barge, Benj. F.
Edwards, Leroy
Tarver, Robt.
Pate, Elizabeth
Donaldson, Robert
Ketrale, Noah
Sessions, Benj.
McAfee, Jesse

page 219
Massey, Abel
Smith, Matilda
Shira, Margarette
Smith, Gideon
McAfee, Arthur
Smith, Allen
Horton, Harrell
Blakely, Geo. W.
Ellis, Major
Taylor, Kinchen
Williams, Moses
Massey, Bennett
Cox, Robert
Ranes, W. W. (?)
Williams, Jordan
Roberts, Wm. B.
Cox, Moses Jr.
Hodges, Reddin
Cox, Aaron
Aslomes, Huel

Dean, Elizabeth
Powell, Nancy
Shira, John M.
Keen, Wm.
Crafton, Martha
Arnold, Elizabeth
Arnold, Arnette
Smith, Richard
Avent, Joseph
Holt, Lewis A.

page 220
Neely, Julia
Irwin, Alexander
Fish, William
Carlisle, Matthew
Taylor, P. T.
Key, Warren
McIntyre, Thomas
Kenneda, David
Glenn, Patience
Cook, Samuel
Tarbutton, Joseph
Ranes, Needham
Deen, Jesse
Arnold, Harrel
Collins, Wm.

89th GMD

page 221
Webb, John
Wright, John B.
Young, Jesse
Jones, Isaac
Parker, John
Parker, Jonathan
Walker, Henry
Vann, Elzy
Ranes, John
Watson, Elijah
Moy, George
Vann, William W.
Davis, Irwin
Mason, George
Walker, Jeremiah
Wilson, Archibald
Crabb, Robt.
Hamilton, Morris R.
Jenkins, Evan
Dailey, Vines
Johnson, James
Wilson, John Jr.

Hamilton, Sherrod
Vann, James
Bateman, Jason
Smith, Elizabeth
Calhoun, Orra
Crawford, Thomas
Smith, George
Webb, Crawford

page 222
Daniel, Ezekiel
Braddy, John
Olliver, James
Page, John
Smith, Samuel
Brown, Samuel
Burnes, James
Walker, Lott
Waters, Richard
Daniel, Mary
Underwood, Reuben
Olliver, Asa
Calhoun, Allen
Smith, Hamilton
Johnson, Chany
Williams, Freeman
Williams, Samuel
Williams, Shads
Johnson, Elijah
Vann, Sarah
Watson, Labon
Hust, William
Johnson, Israel
Wright, Thomas
Toolle, Enoch
Price, Harriet
Mathis, Lovey
Martin, Pressilla
Tucker, Wm.
Hightower, F. C.

page 223
Underwood, Elizabet
Olliver, John L.
Jackson, Wm.
Martin, Lemuel
Martin, James
Johnson, Willis
Tison, Gideon
Tucker, T. H.
Heeth, Daniel
Parker, Jeremiah
Vickers, Joel
Tharp, John

Wilson, John
Logan, Benj.
Smith, Lewis
Wamack, Wm.
Logan, Dawson
Cunningham, Thomas

88th GMD

page 224
Goff, William
Love, Thomas
Orr, John
Paradis, Mary
Palmer, Isabella
Salter, William
McAfee, James Jr.
McAfee, John
McAfee, James
Fowler, John
Daniel, Joseph
Thigpen, John
Hardee, Diana
Williamson, Daniel
Wood, Henry H.
Messeck, George
Bailey, Burwell
Cox, Bryant
Bailey, John
Mims, Wm.
Mims, John
Dupree, Jacob
Greene, Edmund
Crafton, Wm.
Calhoun, Nancy
Calhoun, Wm. G.
Fisher, Metcalf
Herendine, Charlotte
Greenwood, Benj. L.
Barge, Hannah

page 225
Stone, William
Gilbert, William
Gilbert, Nathan
Powell, John
Clance, Martin S.
Eason, Isaac
Young, Martha
Dickens, Gillum
Williams, Robert
Adkins, Randal
Wood, R. T.
Fowler, J. D.

Blackburn, Wm.
Adkins, Joseph
Adkins, John
Moody, John
Bell, Tanoy
Underwood, James
Metts, Wright
Cochran, John
Martin, Greene
Metts, Lewis
Martin, John
Whitaker, Mary
Powell, Alfred
Berryhill, James
Bedgood, Sias
Bowen, Herrod
Martin, Nancy
Vann, Henry
Scoggins, Joriah

page 226
Olliver, Oden
Horton, William
Peacock, Greene B.
Gilbert, Drury
Turner, George J.
Martin, John
Fluker, Robert F.
Anderson, Evan

92nd GMD

page 227
Jackson, Allen
Page, John
Bedgood, Mary
Glover, Mary
Spurlock, Samuel
Wood, Balinger
Bedgood, Richard
Frost, Allen
Ross, James
Eli, Rhoda
Price, Littleberry
Sutton, Rachel
New, Ezra
Bird, Celia
Price, Nathan
Price, Moor
Gelber, D. E.
Price, Rice
Price, Cullen
Page, Britton
Bedgood, Saml.

New, Daniel
Hull, William
Hull, Daniel
White, Allen
Jackson, Warren
Brett, Henry
King, Josiah
Glover, Benj.
Knight, Eli
King, Calvin

page 228
Harrison, Joseph
Tanner, Isaac
King, Mary
Whitfield, R.
Brown, R. S.
Salter, Zadlock
Holt, Willis
Darek, John
Whitfield, Bryant
Holt, Mary
Smith, Mary
Turlington, Thos.
Pate, John W.
Maxwell, Felix
Johnson, Henry
Page, Solemon
Smith, Wm.
Hunt, Wm.
Whiting, Lovey
Frances, Nancy
Hardison, Wm. L.
Brantley, Wm.
Lewis, James
Moore, Shadrick
Bryant, Jason
Moore, Winnifred
Smith, Allen
Smith, John
Moore, Catherin
Smith, P. P.
Donaldson, Wm.

page 229
Pope, Wiley M.
Barefield, James
Hicks, Henry
Myers, Mary
Scott, James
Fort, Owen
Knight, J. B.
Whitfield, Robert
Page, John
Page, J. H.

Moy, Duran
Smith, Samuel

97th GMD

page 230
Chives, Abner
Malone, Charles I.
Perry, John H.
Anesworth, James
Biggs, Jesse
Williams, John
Davis, Goodwin
Boatright, James
Hall, M. M.
Soulard, E. A.
Jernigan, L. A.
Pournell, John
Waller, John
Warthin, Wm. B.
Renfroe, Wm.
Howard, Elizabeth
King, Clarissa
Davison, J. H.
Joines, Wm.
Salmons, James B.
Brown, Morgan
Hardin, John
Brooks, Aaron
Franklin, Samuel O.
Harris, N. F.
Boatright, Edmd.
Solomon, David
Barnes, D. H.
Thomas, Euphema (?)
Barwick, Benj.
Lyons, Jonathan

page 231
Kelly, E. W.
Joiner, Moses
Hall, Sarah
Hutson, Sarah
Skrine (?), Benj.
Northington, J. F.
Smith, J. R.
Scarborough, Myles
Ware, A. G.
Massey, J. B.
Owens, Keziah
Bateman, David
Saffold, J. H.
Tennelle, A. S.
Waugh, W. H.
Arrington, Hardy
Jones, S. A. H.
Glenn, John
Hodges, Wm.
Renfroe, Nathan
Skrine, Q
Whitaker, Willis
Webster, William
Hodges, Seth
Brookins, H.
Flournoy, R. W.
Norris, T. W.
Lightfoot, Martha
Bailey, Wm.
Carter, Susan

page 232
Jones, Isaac
Griffin, Wm.
Brown, Nancy
Hodges, Henry
Tompkins, Rukin
Odom, John A.
Webster, Lewis

Barwick, Jesse
Williams, Franklin
Massey, Elizabeth
Patridge, Peyton
Brantley, Jephtha
Odom, John A. Sr.
Drake, Richard
Slade, William
Tarbutton, Benj.
Tanner, Joseph
Lord, Levin
Robison, James
Mathis, Logan
Martin, John O.
Joines, Edmund W.
Armstrong, Burton
Tompkins, Burwell
Jones, Jobey
McColester, Richard
Sheppard, John
Sheppard, David
Brooks, Robert G.
Hall, Wm. C.

page 333
Mathis, Lorinzo
Tompkins, C. C.
Floyd, Silas
Rawlings, Wm.
Webster, Richard
Jones, James
Drake, F. B.
Dolittle, Wm.
Crumly, Ephraim
Tompkins, James M.
Morrel, Fanny
Warthen, F. J.
Hodges, John
Kelly, John
Lowe, Samuel
Mathis, Isaac

PENSIONERS FOR REVOLUTIONARY OR MILITARY SERVICES IN 1840 CENSUS

Name	Age	Page
Jones, Isaac	79	232
Cox, Moses	86	219
Peacock, Uriah	88	213
Love, Thomas	90	213
Howard, George F.	27	199
Thompson, Lustatia	74	198
Williams, William	86	196

This index is printed through the courtesy of Mrs. Mildred Watkins who publishes the genealogical column "Ancestor Hunting" in the Shreveport Journal (Shreveport, La.) and of Miss Gloria Monk.

The names of the heads of households are listed in the order in which they appear on the census; persons of other names residing in the household are listed immediately below the name of the head of the house.

1 E. S. Langmade
2 Zachariah Brantly
3 Augustua A. Cullins
4 Freeman W. Johnson
5 John R. Prescot
  James S. Hook
  Wiley Harris
  Henry Butcher
  Yeoman Haines
  Isham H. Saffold
  W. L. Holifield
6 R. L. Fulton
  James R. Hunt
  Mary Peumell (?)
  Mathew Carswell
7 E. C. Williamson
8 Thomas Mills
9 Arnold L. Adams
10 James R. Smith
  Bennet Crafton
11 William G. Brown
  Ezekiel Loyd
12 E. B. Aisina (?)
13 Richard Worthen
  John Walker
  Benj. Wcker
  Franklin Howard
  William Cone
  James Trawick
  William Rushing
  Frank Smith
14 H. N. Huntington
  Lewis Benson
  Michael L. Wit
15 Eli B. Whiddon
16 Walter Dorch
17 Robert W. Flournoy
  Mary Rawlings
  Asabel Beach
18 William P. Haynes
  Tabitha G. Brown
19 Reuben Mayo
20 Mark Newman

21 Morris Lazeron
22 Uriah Peacock
23 William Joiner
  Mary Hodge
24 Wright W. Buck
  William Hinson
  C. W. Stuart
  Moses Agins (?)
25 Edward Rowley
  Hughrea Lawson
26 Clark O. McConnel
27 John W. Rudisill
28 Isham H. Saffold
  William Beal
  Samuel Field
29 William Hodges
  Uriah G. Buckner
  Jonathan G. Baker
30 Littleton Mathis
31 G. W. Young
  Larkin Hood
  Joseph Chambers
32 Haywood Brookins
  Elizabeth Crews
33 Samuel M. Law
34 Joseph Tarbutton
35 William Mills
36 James L. Jenkins
  Thomas Took
  Riley M. Hartley
37 William B. Harmon
  John R. Brown
38 Lewis Bullard
  Edwin Bridges
39 Michael Hanson
40 John Kitrill
41 James Ainsworth
42 John B. Massey
43 Moses Joiner
44 Robert Tennille
45 William Pournell
46 Thomas W. H. Baker
47 George W. Massey
  Wilas Jones
  Augustus Martin

48	George E. Boatright		87	Benjamin Tarbutton
	Washington Renals		88	Eliza E. Langmade
49	Ann Harris		89	John Sheppard
	Andrew McConley		90	Joseph H. Page
50	John Swint		91	Gideon Smith
51	Henry S. Taylor		92	Archibald Jordan
52	Ellen Scarbrough		93	Hardy B. Thompson
53	Lewis A. Gernigan			Sarah A. Durden
54	O. P. Brasington		94	Francis D. Tennille
	Catherine R. Spears		95	Levin Lord
	Owen P. Elkins		96	Raford Hartley
55	Sarah Hudson		97	Samuel Robison
	Elizabeth Cannon			H. W. Raford
56	James Wicker		98	Jacob P. Welch
57	David H. Barnes			Mary Whitaker
58	Mathew Moore		99	William Snead
	Augustus McMurry		100	Homer Lawrance
59	Alvin O. Haines		101	James Baron
	Susan J. McCullers		102	Henry Heath
	James E. Barwick			Josephus Trussel
60	Howel Mayo		103	William Smith
61	Nathaniel Renfro		104	William H. Armstrong
62	William F. Pournell		105	John Cordry
63	James B. Kelly		106	John Bland
64	Clarisa King			William Griffin
65	Sarah Hall		107	Jarred Newsom
66	Owen Dolen		108	Milton C. Smith
67	Asa Peacock		109	Elbert D. Taylor
68	James Robison			Paten Jackson
	Joseph Daniel		110	Paten Patridge
69	Euphemy Thomas			Sarah Rocket
70	K. F. Malpas		111	Nelson Linsey
71	Elefair Slade			Henry Gregory
72	William Doolittle		112	Lewis Knight
73	George Strange		113	William B. Werthen
74	Lemuel W. H. Strange		114	Richard Lightfoot
	Martha Johnson		115	Isiah B. Avant
75	Richard Drake		116	Thomas J. Jordan
76	George Wiggins		117	Leroy Edwards
77	James Joiner			Delany Myres
78	John Pournell		118	Jeptha Prantley
	Amanda Davis		119	Green Whiddon
	Jincy Riddle		120	Dempsy C. Whiddon
79	Robert Whitfield		121	Mathew Mills
	Sarah Rogers			William Griffin
	G. A. Runhart		122	John W. Graybill
	L. H. Jordan		123	William C. Riddle
80	Sarah Perry			Mary Paridise
81	Thomas W. Norris			Mary Took
	Robert Donaldson			Francis Gilmore
82	Jesse Northington			A. Acman Hardison
83	Reuben A. Mathews			Jane Prescot
84	Lewis Peacock		124	George B. Peacock
85	Jesse A. Northington		125	William Bailey
86	James H. Hall		126	Moulton Peacock

127 James M. Collins	168 John B. Pitman
128 Samuel O. Franklin	169 Thomas C. Strange
129 James F. Rogers	170 John Daniel
Mc E Boatright	Julia F. Mills
Martha A. Boyd	171 John Josey
Daniel Johnson	172 Hardy Hartley
129 Kaleb Weeks	173 Thomas J. Worthen
130 John E. Moy	174 Timoth Brosiel (?)
John M. R. Page	175 Thomas Sparks
131 Mary Swint	176 Isaac Smith
132 William H. Tanner	177 John B. Williams
133 Benjamin Bell	178 James Brantley
134 William W. Mayo	179 John Morris
135 Middleton Jordan	180 William Brantley
136 John Barwick	181 John F. Brantley
137 John Sheppard	Calvin Morris
Hardaman Smith	182 Theophilus Hill
138 James N. Wood	183 Mitchell Taner
139 Thomas Barber	184 Spencer Brantley
140 Robert Brooks	185 Sherrod Hamilton
141 John A. Odum	186 John W. Cox Hamilton
142 Allen A. Walker	187 James H. Priget
Sheppard Green	William Hill
143 Edward Brantley	Malcolm McMillon
Sarah Thomas	188 James Sanders
144 Ivy Fountain	189 John M. Walden
145 Aiden M. Vining	190 Edmund Boatright
146 Green Roberts	John Perkins
147 John W. Roberts	191 Zilpha Boatright
148 Abel J. Barwick	192 John H. Waller
Mary Cox	193 Enweh (?) Roughton
Dolly Brooks	Louisa Forbes
Charles Tompkins	Jackson Brock
William Barwick	194 Solomon Tanner
149 William L. Smith	James Ellis
150 F. Y. Tompkins	195 James Barwick
151 Robert Fluker	196 Unity Brock
152 Jordan R. Smith	197 Henry C. Long
Ebenezer Brown	John Massey
153 James M. Robert	198 Lucy Cheeves
Watson Foley	199 Janathan Lyon
154 James Wood	Alvin Dison
155 John Elkins	200 William Tompkins
156 Anderson Riddle	201 John R. Achord
157 Jonathan Speight	202 John Sheppard
158 Zachariah Gray	203 David Sheppard
159 Randol Thigpen	Charles B. R?ellin
160 John E. Thompson	204 Richard McAlister
161 James J. Renfro	205 Rukin Tompkins
162 Allen H. Knight	206 Robert Tompkins
163 Jonathan Baker	207 James Tompkins
164 James W. Mills	208 Burwell Tompkins
166 Cullen C. Tompkins	209 James Brooks
Sarah Chastain	210 John R. Tucker
167 James Barnes	Tully Graybill
	Sally McLaughlin

211 John Wise	253 John Powel
212 E. D. Jordan	Mary Clance
213. Richard Webster	254 John Thigpen
214 John Sheppard	255 Ally Anderson
Elizabeth Tompkins	256 John Moody
Pitman Ellis	257 Jefferson C. Moody
215 William Webster	258 Seaborn Jones
Francis Griffin	259 Cato Riddle
216 John Williams	260 Washington Gilbert
217 John Harris	261 William Rheny
218 Elizabeth Tompkins	262 M. C. Williamson
Francis Hicklen	Adison E. Dudley
219 William Taylor	B. R. Smith
220 Elizabeth Massey	263 Nancy Martin
221 Moses Williams	264 John Martin
Joseph Martin	265 Drury Gilbert
222 Noah Kittrell	266 Freeman Orr
223 Richard Rains	267 Rebeca Williamson
224 Martha R. Roberts	268 Stephen Blackburn
Thomas Lyon	Diannah Hardy
225 John Robison	269 William L. Salter
226 Redding Hodges	270 Sarah Oliver
Budd Massey	271 James Martin
227 Moses Cox	272 H. L. Orr
228 Martha Crafton	273 L. A. Orr
229 Arthur Watkins	274 George F. Orr
230 Martha Cox	275 Jesse E. Williams
231 Hull A. Joiner	James Womble
Simon Martin	276 William Gregory
232 Aaron Cox	277 John F. Ashly
Martha Pearce	278 Patience Glenn
233 Wiley Cox Pearce	279 Westly Van
234 L. N. Vining	280 Isabella Parmer
235 John Roland	Jane Johnson
236 William Pitman	281 Lemuel Martin
James Kenedy	282 Richard Brown
237 Clark Brown	Sarah J. Pittman
238 Penelopy Adkins	283 John L. Oliver
239 Henry Posey	284 Robert Williams
240 Samuel M. Parmer	285 John Anderson
241 Bailey Bell	286 William Jackson
242 James F. Northington	287 R. L. Josey
243 William H. Robison	288 Henry C. Walker
244 Sins Bedgood	289 Lott Walker
245 John Fisher	290 Elizabeth Chester
246 William G. McBride	291 C. D. Bray
John L. Youngblood	292 John Webb
247 M. F. Fisher	293 John Webb
Green Young	294 Allen Page
Henry Mann	295 William A. Webb
248 John W. Josey	296 Lina Williams
249 Sherrod Jones	297 William A. Smith
250 Freeman Killingsworth	298 Samuel Williams
251 Charles D. Powel	299 Thomas Wright
252 James B. Sherrer	300 Osborn O. Martin
Caroline Cooler	301 Frances Mathews

302 Mary Whitaker	349 Lewis Webster
303 Pricilla Martin	Joshua Robison
304 Green Martin	James N. Trussell
305 William Gilbert	350 Isabella Carter
306 James Underwood	Elizabeth Spears
307 John B. Wright	Richard Rocket
308 William Martin	351 Thomas B. Harrison
309 Robin Cooler	352 Jeptha K. Jernigan
310 Rebecca Cooler	353 Nathan J. Hains
311 Richard Cooler	Nathan M. Bowen
312 Harriet Price	354 David Canada
313 Richard Waters	Jane Key
314 Nathan Gilbert	355 Sarah Kenedy
315 James J. Page	356 Nathan Renfro
316 Hannah Barge	Lewis Brown
317 William Blackburn	357 William Renfro
318 Mathew C. Killingsworth	358 Harrel Horton
319 John A. Woodburn	359 Margaret Shiry
320 Elizabeth N. Daniel	360 Alexander Smith
321 James B. Everitt	361 William Robison
Benjamin Hudson	362 Thomas S. Smith
Sarah Groves	363 Abel Massey
Coleman Keen	364 Samuel Shiry
322 Silas Daniel	Elizabeth Williams
323 John Evans	365 Liby Smith
324 Martha Fowler	Levi M. Kinman
325 Thomas S. Fowler	366 Isian B. Shiry
Jasper J. Evans	367 Isaac Moye
326 Courtney Darby	368 William L. Hardison
327 James J. Massey	Nancy Willingham
328 Drury May	369 Charles Miller
329 William A. Irwin	370 Noah Kitril
330 William Wood	371 Matilda Smith
331 Dennis Cason	372 John R. Hodges
332 Thomas E. Moye	373 Sarah Smith
333 John Baily	Elizabeth Albritton
Jane Barret	374 William Crafton
334 Jesse McAfee	Sarah Forbes
335 Bryan Cox	375 Elizabeth Dean
Elizabeth Martin	376 Rodiska Cook
336 Lewis H. Holt	377 Willis Walker
337 William G. Calhoun	378 Abram Pearce
Charles Lynam	379 William M. Wadley
338 Allen Smith	Eason McAfee
339 William G. Chester	380 James R. Avent
340 Rebeca Barber	381 Henry Wood
341 Henry H. Wood	382 Winfield Scott
342 Bird Baily	Mary McAfee
343 Benjamin Woods	383 Jane Killingsworth
344 Barbary Avant	Kendrick Kinman
345 Elizabeth Fowler	384 William Keen
346 Joseph Bell	385 Wiley McVey
347 John Smith Jr.	386 Samuel Cook
348 J. W. Watson	387 Gideon Brantley
Delia G. Reiley	388 James McAfee
	Penny Hardy

389	Arthur McAfee	424	Green E. Cummings
390	Jordan McAfee	425	Robert Cummings
391	William L. Smith	426	John L. Harrison
392	Dickson Forbs	427	Henry Cheely
393	Isaac Whitaker		Jourdan Tood
	Betty Glenn (?)	428	Angus Morrison
394	Mary Jordan	429	Henry Holton
395	Elizabeth Horn	430	Silas Dowhs
	Redding H. Pate	431	Allen Chrisba
396	John Martin	432	William Brassil
397	Benjamin Sessions	433	Lucius Jourdan
	Mary W. Blount	434	Henry Blunt
398	E. N. Ennis	435	Zadoc Rachaels
399	Jabes Joiner	436	David H. Barnes
	Catherine J. Ecoles	437	Charles A. Cofield
400	John Jones	438	Jacob D. Fulgam
	Matthew Brasiel	439	James M. Pinkston
401	Goodrum Davis	440	Isaac Dickins
402	Reding Hodges	441	Hiram Mott
403	James Castin		Moody Beckham
	John J. Newsom		William Holton
404	Margaret M. Irwin	442	Lewis Piltcher
	Phasin Whitehead	443	Alfred Courney
405	Owen Vining	444	James M. Worthen
	Joseph Ivy	445	Baten Hattaway
406	Julia Neely	446	John Hattaway
	Rebecca Stanton	447	Henry Hawkins
407	Joseph Harrison	448	Nathaniel B. Giles
	Elizabeth Ennett	449	Penelope L. Hattaway
408	Thomas G. Davis	450	Thomas Davis
409	Benjamin T. Ingram	451	Burwell Rachaels
410	Thomas Blackburn	452	Joseph Williams
	William B. H. Jones	453	Asa Griffin
411	Margaret S. Wicker	454	Sherrod Green
412	Mitchel Watkins	455	George D. Boatright
	Mary Cherry	456	Jane Hains
413	Virginia Skrine		William Alfred
	Jane Davis		Mary Bowen
414	Sarah Brown	457	Ansel W. Wicker
	Seaborn Osburn	458	John Gilmore
	Lovinzy Cordry	459	Thomas Ingram
415	Riley Sprague	460	Joseph Harrison
	Mary Williams	461	James Fulgam
	Matilda McAvin	462	John Barns
416	Nathaniel Wicker		W. J. Worthen
	William H. Daniel	463	Green Amerson
417	Archibald Cone		William Worthen
	Asa Taunton		William H. Lewis
	Lawson Beckum		Robert H. Wicker
418	James S. Cook	464	William May
419	Benjamin L. Wooford		Sarah Bickham
420	Francis Darden	465	Pledge Price
421	Mathew Fulgam	466	William A. D. Canter
422	John G. Fulgam	467	Sarah Canter
423	Eli Cummings	468	Tobias Burganny

469	Sarah Hurst
	John H. Arington
470	James Cato (Arington?)
471	James Stavely
472	John Cofield
473	John Williams
474	Charles Conaway
475	David Cummings
	Sarah H. Barge
476	Abigail Bridges
	Lewis H. C. Barge
477	Elbert L. Edzil
478	Edmond May
	Elizabeth Parker
479	Josiah Jones
480	Catherine Jourden
	Nancy Robinson
481	Elijah J. Perry
	David E. Cummings
482	James G. Armstrong
	John Wicker
	John Johnson
483	Ashley A. Howell
	Debro Simmons
484	Emeline Collins
475	William H. Walker
486	Ellis Johnson
487	David Walker
488	Gabriel W. Stubbs
489	Lewis Sheppard
490	A. C. Moltrie
491	John Amerson
	Sarah J. Hawkins
492	William Gray
493	Thomas Griffin
494	William Ramsay
	E. Buckhanan
495	Henry Jones
496	Abel Jones
497	J. J. Howard
	Martha May
498	Reuben Osburn
499	Sarah Adams
500	Bryant Watkins
501	Harris Brantley
	John C. Fennill (T?)
	John H. Tripp
502	Henry J. Oliver
503	William W. Curry
504	Martha Newsom
505	William H. Howard
506	John Davis
507	Amanda Hopson
	Elizabeth Curry
	Joseph Pinkston
	John B. Turner
	James F. Walker

508	William May
509	Cornelius Jordan
510	Morgan W. Bright
	Aggy Osborn
	Robert Salter
511	Neely Bright
512	Hessy Ann Bynum
	Elizabeth Neeland
513	Sarah W. Brown
	Wiley Hutchins
514	Emily Wiggins
515	Washington Hilton
516	John Bell
	Christopher Lyons
	Ann Little
517	Miles Turner
518	Asa Welch
	John Jones
519	Emanuel Welch
520	Elizabeth Welch
	William Wiggins
521	William L. Brown
522	Leah Brown
523	Albert G. Curry
524	Elizabeth Howard
525	Hopewell Hooks
526	Charles McDanil
527	John P. Tompson
528	William Danil
	Henry Weeks
529	Brabazin (?) Talbot
530	Thomas Jourdan
531	Charles H. Shepherd
532	Wheatley Lord
	Franklin W. Killey-worth
533	C. T. Shivers
534	Francis Orr
535	John J. Long
536	Jesse Pounds
	Wiley J. Coston
537	Abner M. Kelly
538	Allen Jones
539	C. T. Hines
540	Susanna Dudley
541	John Curry
542	Candass Lyons
543	Nathan Hattaway
544	William Jones
545	Seaborn Howard
546	E. Green
547	William M. Brantley
548	Green Brantley
549	Stephen Darden
	Wiley W. Yost
550	Leander Lord

551	Euphemia Finney
	John Alfred
552	James /all
553	William Tanner
554	Mary Lord
	Rebecca Shepherd
555	William Tanner Sr.
556	Thomas Tanner
557	Ira Walden
558	J. B. Willis
	William O. Brown
559	John B. Smith
	Dennis Thigpen
560	Edmond D. Brown
561	David Vincent
562	James E. Yates
563	James Thigpen
	Sidney H. Salter
	Hubbard Horton
564	James R. Thigpen
565	John D. Brown
566	Elizabeth Coleman
567	Morgan M. Sparks
	Viny Collins
568	William Garner
	John Bridges
569	Moses Garner Sr.
570	Henry Garner
571	Archelias C. Duggan
572	Asa Duggan
573	Joshua J. Garner
574	Cullen Murphy
575	Howell Jones
576	Edward Pridgen
577	Jesse J. Duggan
578	Redding Jones
579	James Ainsworth Jr.
580	Barnabus Barrow
	Virgil H. Perkins
581	Virgil T. Perkins
582	Nancy Salter
583	William Cook
584	Celia Gardner
585	Barsheba Newman
586	Daniel Mills
587	John M. Duggan
588	John H. Duggan
589	Hopewell Adams
590	Jourdan Adams
591	Sarah Adams
591	Sarah Hooks (two ⁊591)
592	Elizabeth Garrett
593	Alexander Armstrong
	Daniel A. White
	William B. Cook
	William T. Reynolds

594	Edward Armstrong
595	Edward F. Armstrong
	Elisha Womble
596	John Duggan
597	Margaret Morrison
	Margaret Floyd
598	Robert Norris
599	William M. Gilmore
600	Turner T. Brown
601	William D. Harrison
602	William W. Walker
603	Jonathan B. Cone
604	Washington Welch
605	Jesse B. Cone
	Clara B. Hopkins
606	Jesse W. Cone
607	Luamber J. May
608	Benjamin Amerson
609	James C. Harrison
	Hilsey Taunton
*610	Nancy Meeks
612	James Cone
	Mary Baker
613	Sarah Osborn
	Hilsey Cates
614	Newsom Taunton
615	Branson Redfeard
616	Samuel Murphy
	Richard Hargrove
617	Elizabeth Taunton
618	Howell Meeks
619	William P. Taylor
	Rebecca Lewis
620	Ezra New
	Ezra Martin
	Arthur Roundtree
621	Quincy Lamb
	Elizabeth Whiten
622	Isaac G. Sanford
623	Nancy McGowen
624	John P. Gibson
625	John Barefield
	Catherine Thigpen
	Felix Maxwell
626	Moore Price
627	Shellman Whitefield
628	Bryan Whitefield
629	William Vealle
	James Holder
630	Mary Josey
631	Samuel Josey
632	Henry A. Josey
	James Fagan
	Edward Lazeron
* 611	Washington Meeks

633	Benjamin G. Smith	679	W. P. Hardwick
	Simon Thomas		Aaron Lewis
634	Thomas Turlington	680	William Gainer
	Lovey Whiting	681	Thomas J. Hardwick
635	William Hunt	682	Rachel Sutton
637	Penelope Bryan	683	John Harrison
636	William G. Bryan	684	Kincey Chambers
	John Y. Smith	685	Jesse Glover
638	James S. Bryan	686	G. Bedgood
639	James Barfield	687	Mary Bedgood
640	Elijah L. Knight	688	Alfred Turner
641	Charles P. W. Whitefield	689	Nancy Page
642	Elbert W. West	690	Warren Price
643	Matthew K. West	691	David Atkins
644	Eaton Shepherd	692	Berry Price
	Mary Price		Ruben Frost
645	Morning Price	693	Isaac Jones
646	Celia Bird	694	Archibald Wilson
647	Alfred Granway	695	John Tharp
	Caty Coleman	696	Henry Mason
648	Nathan Price	697	-
649	William Hull	698	John Brady
650	Britain Page	699	A. J. Braddy
651	James Frost	700	Green Watson
652	Lewis J. Harrison	701	Oliver B. Braddy
	William King	702	Jordan Outlaw
653	Rachel New	703	Thomas Cunningham
654	Noel Jackson	704	John Wilson
655	John New	705	James Wilson
656	John W. Barber	706	Sarah Vann
657	Daniel Hull	707	Lydia Crabb
658	James M. Donaldson	708	Riland Crab
659	Josiah T. King	709	George W. Hamock
660	John King	710	Jackson Heard
661	Ruben Whitefield	711	Elsey Smith
662	John D. Paradise	712	Jacob Shivers
	John Fountain	713	Mary Chivers
663	Cordy Francis	714	Larkin Chivers
664	Owen C. Pope	715	John Page
665	Thomas L. Davis	716	Thomas Wood
666	Jacob Davis	717	George Smith
667	Joseph T. Rhodes	718	John Smith
668	Daniel Inman	719	Lewis Smith
669	Joel A. Davis	720	Jonathan Smith
	Bryan B. Fulford	721	James Smith
670	Sarah Fulford	722	Lewis Jackson
671	Augustus Newsom	723	Erwim Jackson
672	Josiah Jackson	724	James Logan
673	Daniel Harris	725	Lewis Sheppard
674	George Batts	726	Samuel Smith
675	Ezekiel Finney	727	John Bedgood
	Wiley Wyat	728	Mathew Logan
676	Sarah Moore	729	William Young
677	John Jordan	730	Sarah Warmack
	Joshua R. Price	731	Margaret Warmack
678	Samuel B. Palmer	732	Ezekiel Daniel

733	John Mungin		781	W. T. Odam
734	John Johnson		782	H. H. Newsom
	Moley Wilson		783	John J. Wise
735	Isard Johnson		784	James Gainer
736	James Johnson		785	James J. Gainer
737	J. F. Smith		786	James R. Taylor
738	David Allen			George Brett
739	William S. Hart		787	Henry Turlington
740	Nancy Hart			David Shepperd
	Anna Vicus		788	Allen Jackson
741	L. Williams			Mary Dortch
742	Richard Williams		789	Aaron Brantley
743	Edwin Brantley		790	Corda Gaskins
744	William Peacock		791	Henry Brett
745	Celia Brantley		792	Francis Shepperd
746	Benjamin Logan		793	David Sheppeard
747	William Young		794	Hardy Hartley
	Elizabeth Craig		795	Burrill Hartley
748	William Young Jr.			Emily Francis
749	Thomas Brantley			— Edge
750	Joseph D. Smith		796	David E. Clark
751	Frederick Tyson		797	Benjamin Brantley
752	James Jackson		798	George Williams
753	Thomas B. Smith		799	Sarah Joiner
754	John J. Page		800	Benjamin Forbes
755	Jesse B. Knight		801	John Lindsey
756	Repsey Keyton		802	Elias Joiner
	Cherry Moore		803	Zachariah Peacock
757	Henry Hicks			Huldy Logan
758	Green B. Thigpen		804	George F. Brantley
759	Isaac Tanner		805	William Morris
	Isham White		806	Thomas B. Smith
760	Owen H. Fort		807	James Brantley
761	Duren G. Moy		808	James L. Brantley
762	John E. Moye		809	Maning Thomas
763	W. A. Myers		810	Edward Brantley
764	William Myers		811	Sampson Daniel
765	Patrick J. Pate		812	S. P. Williams
766	Wiley M. Pope		813	William E. Goff
767	William J. Sellers		814	S. B. Pierce
	James A. Holder		815	Amos Goff
768	Anna Sellers		816	G. G. Webb
769	Rebecca Matthew		817	Eldridge Hatcher
770	Mary Paradise		818	Isiah Jackson
771	James Ross		819	James Scott
772	Etheldred Smith		820	Jeremiah Parker
773	Mary Byrn			— Morgan
774	Joseph Hewlin		821	Martin Jenkins
775	N. B. Whitefield			Henry Vann
776	Nancy Francis			Erwin Hamilton
	Robert E. Carr		822	William H. Crawford
777	Hillary Laten		823	John Jenkins
778	Mary Brown		824	William G. Young
779	W. P. McCliven		825	James-Hutchinson
	Elizabeth Sheppeard		826	Joshua Hutchinson
780	David J. Dortch		827	Ephriam Hightower

828	John Rains
	James Ennis
829	Nancy Tucker
830	Green Spell
831	Jonathan Parker
832	J. D. Dailey
	Melviria Echols
833	Jesse Young
	Hansell Johnson
834	William Brantley
835	Mary Hamilton
836	Laban Watson
	M. Lee
837	Elijah Johnson
838	Asa Oliver
839	Caty Cernigin
840	John Page
841	Samuel Bedgood
842	William Hust
843	Kinchen W. Massey
	William Erwin
844	Benjamin Brantley
845	Isaac L. Smith
846	Berrill Chester
847	William Chester
848	Rebecca Chester
	Mary Barber
849	Elizabeth Chester
850	Sherod Hamilton
851	Harris Brantley
852	Allen White
853	Charles King
	David Jenkins
854	John Hunt
855	Daniel Loyd
856	Drewry Loyd
	James Bentley
857	Hezekiah Jenkins
858	Benjamin Brantley
859	James F. Boatright
860	John Caston
861	John Boatright
862	Leonard Laton
863	Hardy Hartley
864	Cornelius Blackburn
865	James Layton
866	William Duggan
867	Jesse H. Franklin
868	James Saunders
869	Robert Maxwell
870	M. Joiner
	Robert Tuke
871	John D. Cordry
872	Rebecca Kelly
	Moses Daniel

873	Redden Watkins
874	James Sherlin
875	James H. Sherlin
876	John Elton
877	Homer M. Lawrence
878	Augustus G. W. Hodges
	William W. Cox
879	Robert Y. Rogers
880	Rebecca Green
881	John C. Pace
	Benjamin Johnson
882	Charlotte Hodges
883	Elisha W. Jordan
884	Elexander E. Lawson
	Lewis S. Achord
	Franklin Cox
885	Franklin B. Cullins
	Alexander H. Giles
886	Elias Brassel
887	William A. Lingould
888	Edward G. Lewis
889	Richard B. Strange
	Robert F. Cox
890	Rebecca Tootle
891	James Langford
	Mary E. Hale
892	Abner Mims
	Nancy A. E. Tull
	William Thomas
893	Harmon D. Roberson
	Eliza Hall
894	Young A. Cox
895	George T. Franklin
	Richard Cox
896	Gideon Strange
	Green Elkins
897	John J. Strange
	Joseph G. Davis
898	Reuben G. Strange
899	John F. Avant
900	John T. Achord
901	English Smith
	William J. Chasteen
902	William Elkins
903	William J. Jones
904	Jacob Cunyers
	Francis M. Hall
905	Agnes Bland
906	Simeon Bland
907	Seaborn Cone
908	Richard Croom
	Martha Durden
910	Micajah Bland
911	Henry Cox
912	Joseph Forbes
	Calvin Cook

913 Daniel M. Leveritt	956 Calvin Blizzard
914 Constantine Carvello	Larkin Hood
915 Sampson Likner	957 Nancy Cone
916 John Hodges	958 Edward Vealle
917 Philip Likner	Hardion K. Chambers
918 John R. Tucker	William Cone
919 Lemuel W. H. Moore	959 Jordan F. Vealle
920 William W. Giles	960 Richard H. Vealle
921 Pheury Pittman	961 John Cato
922 William Davis	962 William H. Hall
923 John Cox	963 John T. Vealle
924 Willis Whitaker	Nancy Blakely
925 Middleton Haygood	964 William Fields
926 John Oquin	965 Jacob Stephens
927 Milbra Leaptrot	966 Green Wood
928 Daniel O'Quin	967 Robert Cox
Nancy A. Butler	968 James H. Gilmore
929 William Johnson	969 William Giles
930 Laban Horten	Anderson Wood
931 William Buck	970 William Watkins
932 William P, Hicklin	971 Randol Duckworth
933 Jacob Snider	Nancy Stephens
934 Bryant Oquin	972 George W. Leveritt
935 Calvin Giles	973 Joseph Johnson
Jackson Cone	974 Doctor F. Jones
936 Elijah Eastwood	975 Archibald Haygood
Reuben Ford	976 Lewis Parker
937 William Archy	977 Henry Wood
Mary Ann Divene	Andrew P. McCory
938 Levi Henderson	Lavina Giles
939 William Thomason	Richard Fuller
940 James J. Eastwood	978 John Stephens
941 Elizabeth Horton	979 Alexander Giles
942 Bolin P. Leaptrot	980 John F. Butler
943 Nathan Vealle	981 Lavina Giles
944 George Vealle	982 Hugh Butler
945 Cornelius Cook	Mary Giles
946 Lewis Durden	983 Hillery Ford
Bedy Perkins	984 Henry Hodges
Nicy Durden	985 Barbara Hust
Emaline Crumby	986 Rebecca Griffin
James Thomas	987 Henry Griffin
947 Milly Bennett	988 William Hall
948 Zachariah Brookins	989 J. P. Leverett
949 John Stone	990 Salathiel Holton
950 Benjamin Brookins	991 Sarah Pittman
George H. Hudson	Vandoodle L. R. White
951 Thomas L. Hutchings	James Raynolds
952 John P. Griffin	992 Sarah Hitchcock
Dolly A. Henderson	993 Mary Swint
953 Matthew Durden	994 Nimrod Pittman
Troy Thomas	995 Middleton Pool
954 Major Croom	996 John R. Odum
955 James G. Parish	997 James Renfroe
Franklin Green	998 Sherod Hood
	James Pittman

999	Mary Holmes	1042	William Godfrey
1000	William Hood	1043	William B. Lewis
	Treasy Cook	1044	Peter Yates
1001	Simon Hood	1045	William F. Yates
1002	James Humphrey	1046	Mary Yates
1003	Joseph Hood	1047	Marshal. D. Walker
1004	James Little	1048	Asa Garrett
1005	John Taylor		Wesley Armstrong
1006	William D. Grimes	1049	Edmond G. Amerson
1007	Alesberry Jordan	1050	Ivey Thigpen
1008	James Ray	1051	John Garner
	John Trawick	1052	Jesse Thigpen
1009	Elwell Newman	1053	Wiley Weeks
1010	James Christian	1054	Dennis Thigpen
1011	Green Andrews	1055	Zachariah Sheppeard
1012	Richard Andrews	1056	Sylvanus W. Prince
1013	Mary Odam	1057	Rebecca Harmon
	Eliza Miller	1058	Emanuel Brown
	Mary Jackson	1059	David Tanner
1014	Moses W. Trawick	1060	Franklin Tanner
1015	Elizabeth Bailey	1061	Henry King
1016	Richmond Bailey	1062	John Salter
1017	Moses Garner	1063	Thomas Salter
1018	John Pounds	1064	Ephriam Salter
1019	Solomon H. Barron	1065	David Bailey
1020	George W. Baron	1066	Nathan Barwick
	Martha Womble	1067	Robert W. Fort
1021	Allen Cook	1068	Windfred Fort
1022	Jesse Mills	1069	Peter P. Smith
1023	Elizabeth Walker	1070	J. E. Lewis
	Sarah A. Butcher	1071	Samuel Smith
1024	John Garrett	1072	Allen B. Smith
1025	William F. Womble	1073	Joseph H. Page
	Shelton Perkins	1074	Nancy Brown
1026	Solomon Gladden		Milly Fortner
1027	Treasy Harris		Thomas Sumley
	Dolphin Mills		— Deedom
1028	William Clay	1075	John C. Corbit
	Lyda F. Watkins	1076	James Jourdan
1029	Joseph Harris	1077	William D. Jourden
1030	William R. Lock	1078	Silas Floyd
1031	Francis Durden		Elizabeth McBride
1032	Wiley Durden	1079	S. A. H. Jones
1033	John Vealle		Cherry Malone
1034	Moses Roberson		Elizabeth Dorsey
	Nancy Brailey	1080	Mary Jordan
1035	James Mills	1081	Solomon Newsom
1036	Charles Mills		John W. Shepperd
1037	Drury Taylor	1082	William Taylor
1038	John Mills		Hilery Hooks
	Curtis Hooks		
	Mary Bailey		
1039	Asalph Mills		
1040	Nancy Salter		
1041	John N. Salter		

EXTANT SURVEYOR'S RECORDS

Warrants were secured by petitioning the land courts which were composed of Justices of the County. These records from Books D-L, 1788-1793, show the name of petitioner, date warrant was issued and name of person whose land adjoined. These records may be found in the Georgia Department of Archives and History.

Name	Date issued	Adjoining
Abercrombie, Charles	Aug. 11, 1789	
Anderson, John	Aug. 3, 1789	
	Apr. 1, 1791	
Anderson & Stokes	Oct. 6, 1789	Blackshear
Arline, John	Aug. 3, 1789	Walker
Armstrong, John	May 7, 1792	Tennille, G.
Atwood, Isaac		Spann, Geo.
Baker, Joseph	Feb. 8, 1791	Handley
Ballard, Xpher	Nov. 1, 1790	Tennille
Banks, Elisha Fowler	Nov. 7, 1791	Coleman, Chas.
Banks, Gerrard	Dec. 19, 1785	Lumpkin, C.
	Dec. 19, 1785	Cookers & Dees
Bankstone, Lawrence	Apr. 3, 1793	Brasley, J.
Barren, Joseph	Jan. 4, 1790	Crawford
Barren, William	Apr. 3, 1787	Harris
Bass, Esaw	Jul. 5, 1790	Hillard
Beacher, David	Jul. 5, 1790	Williams
Beckom, Allen	Jul. 5, 1789	Beckom
Beckcom, Samuel	Apr. 6, 1789	Beckom
	June 7, 1790	Brown, Sneed
	Nov. 1, 1790	Beckom
	Dec. 1790	Jackson, R.
	1792	Beckom
	Aug. 1792	Lott
	Aug. 8, 1792	Cobb
	Aug. 6, 1792	Beckcom
	Aug. 6, 1792	McMillon
	Aug. 6, 1792	Beckom
Beckcom, Sherwood	Aug. 6, 1789	Jones
	Oct. 6, 1789	Vacant
	Aug. 6, 1792	Middleton, R.
Beckcom, Simon	Sept. 6, 1789	Thompson, B.
Beckcom, Solomon	Aug. 6, 1792	S. Beckcom
	Aug. 6, 1792	Coventon, J.
Beddingfield, Joseph	May 3, 1790	Vickers & Long
Bennett, Arthur	Sept. 7,	Howard & Hail
Bennit, Capt. Jno.	May 17, 1785	Reynolds, A.
Bentley, William	May 17, 1784	Fort, A.
Bentley, Balaam	May 17, 1785	
Berryhill, Andrew	May 17, 1784	Kilgore, R.
Benion, John	June 4, 1790	Few & Paul

Name	Date Issued	Adjoining
Benion, William	Apr. 6, 1789	English
		Surgis
		Green
Bird, Michel	Feb. 22, 1788	Phillips, J.
Black, John	Aug. 6, 1792	Bowie, J.
	Aug. 6, 1792	Bowie & Jackson
	Aug. 6, 1792	Black, J.
	Aug. 6, 1792	Black, J.
Blackshear, David	July 4, 179-	Lawson & Blackshear
	Dec. 2, 1793	Parrott & Long
Blanchard, Benj.	Sept. 6, 1790	Smith, Thos.
	Sept. 6, 1790	Roe, James
Blount, James	Sept. 7, 1789	Irwin, Alex'r.
	Oct. 6, 1789	Beckcom, Saml.
Bobb, Thomas	Oct. 6, 1789	
Borland, Andrew	Jan. 4, 1791	Greene Co. Line
Bonds, Charles	July 4, 1791	Burton & McGehee
Bowin, James	Aug. 6, 1792	Jackson, Robt.
Bowie, ?	Aug. 6, 1792	Black, John
	Aug. 6, 1792	Camons
	Aug. 6, 1792	Bowin, J.
	Aug. 6, 1792	Camons, Eleazer
	Aug. 6, 1792	Ross,Moses & Brinton
	Aug. 6, 1792	Fagan, Geo
	Aug. 6, 1792	Fagan & Camon, E.
	Aug. 6, 1792	Ross
Bowin, Joel	Mar. 2, 1789	Widow Haskins
Boyd, David	July 7, 1788	Fort
Bozman, Luke	May 7, 1792	Wood & Kelly
Brack, Benj.	May 17, 1784	McGehee Creek
Brack, Eleazar	Jan. 4, 1795	McGehee Creek
Bracken, Isaac	Jan. 7, 1790	Burns & Giddons
Bracken, William	Jan. 4, 1791	Clerk & Powell
	Jan. 4, 1791	vacant
	July 14, 1791	Rees, Joel
Brantley, Thos.	Nov. 7, 1791	Bardale,Kirk,Hill
Braswell, Kendred	May 3, 1790	Powell, Stepto ?
Braswell, Robert	May 3, 1790	vacant
	July 5, 1790	vacant
	July 5, 1790	Stephens & Snell
	Sept. 7, 1787	Braswell
	July 5, 1790	Whitehead, Amos
	July 5, 1790	Snell, Christopher
	Sept. 7, 1789	Brinton, J.
Braswell, Samuel	Aug. 6, 1789	Anderson, Jno.
Briggs, John	May 3, 1790	Pendleton & Spreight
Brinton, Jno.	July 7, 1788	Griffin & Jones
Brinton, William	May 7, 1792	vacant
	Aug. 6, 1787	Goods land
Brooks, James	May 17, 1784	Lawson & Jno.Hill
Brown, Henry	May 7, 1792	vacant
Brown, Joseph	Aug. 6, 1792	Sessions

Name	Date Issued	Adjoining
Burton, John	Dec. 8, 1790	Burton
	Dec. 8, 1790	Eubanks, Dan.
Brunor, John	Nov. 1791	Brinton
Bryan, David	Mar. 6, 1786	Culpepper
Bryant, John	Sept. 6, 1790	unknown
	Sept. 6, 1790	Clerk & Williams
	May 3, 1790	Dees, Duett
Bullard, Willy	May 7, 1792	vacant
Burge, John	Aug. 2, 1790	Peak & Lamar
Burk, Nimrod	Apr. 6, 1789	
Burnat, Solomon	May 2, 1791	Call
Burnet, Daniel	July 17, 1789	
	Sept. 7, 1789	Andrews & McCormic
Burney, David	Dec. 4, 1786	vacant
	Apr. 3, 1786	vacant
Burney, James	Aug. 3, 1789	Gainer & vacant
Burney, John	Aug. 3, 1790	Clerk & Tennille
Burney, Randal	Aug. 1, 1793	Burney
	Aug. 1, 1793	
	Aug. 5, 1793	
	Apr. 1, 1793	Burney
	Aug. 5, 1793	Burney
Burney, Richard	July 5, 1790	Burney
	May 7, 1792	Burney & vacant
		Doctor Dees
Buttery, Zachary	Aug. 2, 1790	Stroud, Jacob
Camp, Samuel	Apr. 6, 1789	Daniell, Benj.
	July 4, 1791	Rutherford
Campbell, William	Sept. 7, 1789	Williams & McGonders
Carnes, Thos. P.	May 7, 1792	vacant
	May 7, 1792	Carnes, Thos. P.
	May 7, 1792	Williams, James
	May 7, 1792	Criswell, David
	May 7, 1792	Criswell, David
	Nov. 7, 1791	Bickcum & Jackson
Carter, John	Dec. 19, 1785	vacant
Caswell, John	Feb. 7, 1792	vacant & Coleman
Cates, Richd. Wyatt	Oct. 6, 1789	Barclay & Oates
Cates, Thos.	Feb. 6, 1792	Boswell
Catchings, Joseph	Dec. 5, 1785	Catchings & vacant
Cave, Wm. (Cane?)	June 4, 1787	Cain & unknown
Cawthon, Wm.	Jan. 4, 1790	Sanford & Weeks
Chance, Henry	Nov. 1, 1790	vacant & unknown
Chance, Sampson	1788	Mackmillian, Robt.
Chance, Vincent	July 3, 1790	vacant
Chandler, Mordecia	May 17, 1784	Catching & Grey
Chandler, Obednya	May 17, 1784	Harshall, M.
Chivers, Joel	Nov. 7, 1791	Survey of Williams
Christmas, Nathl.	Dec. 19, 1785	Walker & Carter
	Dec. 19, 1785	Walker & Reddick
Clerk, Lewis	July 5, 1790	Christmas & Jackson
Clough, Geo.	Dec. 27, 1785	Carr, Henry &
		White, Robt.

Name	Date Issued	Adjoining
Clough, Geo	Dec. 19, 1785	Furlow, Jas. & Sam Huff
	Dec. 19, 1785	vacant
	Dec. 19, 1785	Joseph Phillips
Cobb, John	Dec. 1, 1788	Camons & Miller
Cock, Zebulon	May 7, 1792	vacant
Cole, William	Jan. 4, 1790	Pollard & Smith
Coleman, Jonathan	May 3, 1790	vacant
Collins, John	Sept. 6, 1790	Branton
Collins, William	May 3, 1790	Coleman
Colson, Sanders	July 5, 1790	James Johnson
Conner, Daniel	Dec. 3, 1787	Loyd Kelly
Cooper, John	Aug. 6, 1787	Massey & Shepward
Cooxy, William	May 2, 1791	
Cox, Henry	Sept. 7, 1789	John Coleman
Cox, Josiah	Apr. 6,	
Cox, William	Feb. 8, 1791	Hunts
Criswell, David	Surveyed 1790	Criswell
	Surveyed 1790	Criswell & vacant
Croome, Elijah	?	Sturgis & Hills
	Apr. 3, 1791	Hills & Dillard
Crosby, George	Oct. 6, 1789	vacant
Culpepper, John	Apr. 3, 1786	Jno.Culpepper & vacant
Comons, (Cummings?), Eleazar	Aug. 6, 1789	Commins & Murph
	Oct. 6, 1789	Cook & Hunt
	Oct. 4, 1790	Kelly, Jacob
	Aug. 6, 1792	James Bowie
	Aug. 6, 1792	Fagan & James Bowie
Curry, David	Oct. 6, 1789	Beckcom & Spaldin
Dameson, John	Jan. 4, 1791	Donnelly & Mitchell
Daniell, Benj.	Mar. 7, 1789	Samuel Camp
Daniel, John	May 3, 1790	Burney & vacant
Dannelly, Francis	Dec. 1, 1798	Dickson
Dardins, John	Aug. 6, 1792	vacant
Davis, Thomas	July 5, 1790	Braswell, Robt.
Dawson, James	Aug. 6, 1792	Thos.Carnes & Jackson
	Aug. 6, 1792	Hutchinson, James
	Aug. 6, 1793	Hutchinson, James
	Aug. 6, 1792	Hutchinson, James
Dawson, James & Lancaster	Oct. 6, 1790	Dawson
Dawson, Jas. & Richd. Moore	Oct. 6, 1789	Dawson
	Oct. 6, 1789	Dawson & Lancaster
	Oct. 6, 1789	Dawson
Dawson, Jas. & Morgan	Oct. 6, 1789	Dawson & Lancaster
Deason, John	July 5, 1790	vacant
Debosk, Capt.Peter	July 21, 1785	Davis, Willie

Name.	Date Issued	Adjoining
Delk, Joseph	Aug. 1, 1791	Christmas
Dees, Duett,	July 7, 1789	Jm.Barron & Padgett
	Jan. 4, 1790	Bryant,Jno. & Dees
	Feb. 7, 1791	Johnston
	Feb. 7, 1791	Johnston
Dennis, John	Apr. 4, 1791	Jiddow Solbury
Dixon, Michel	May 3, 1790	Lawrence, John
(Dickson)	June 7, 1785	Grantham
	May 3, 1790	vacant
	May 3, 1790	Marshall
	May 8, 1790	
	May 3, 1790	Joshua Taylor
	May 3, 1790	John Anderson
Dickson, Reuben	surveyed July 12, 1791	Jood, Black
Dixon, Thomas	Apr. 2, 1787	Dixon, vacant
Domini, Frederick	Apr. 3, 1791	Domini & Ray
	Aug. 6, 1790	Allen
Donnaly, John	May 17, 1784	
Douglass, Edw.	Oct. 6, 1789	Crawford & McCormac
Dowder, Richd.	Dec. 8, 1790	Kelly & Jells
Drew, Josiah	Apr. 3, 1787	James Hines
Dukes, Henry(heirs of)	Oct. 25, 1784	Commons
Derdains, John	May 2, 1791	Henry Jone
Cammis, Jonathan	Apr. 1, 1793	Outlaw & Handley
	Apr. 1, 1793	Outlaw & Handley
	Apr. 1, 1793	Goff & vacant
English, Cornelius	Apr. 4, 1791	vacant
	Feb. 7, 1791	Lawson & vacant
Eskridges, Hetor R.	Jan. 4, 1795	Beckcom & vacant
Evans, Robt.	Apr. 6, 1789	S. Beckcom & Littleton
Fagan, George	Aug. 6, 1792	James Bowie
Fauche, Jonas	Feb. 6, 1792	Fenn & Irwin
Favers, Jm.	Dec. 19, 1785	John Linsey & vacant
Few, Ignatius	Apr. 6, 1785	Isaac Perry
	Nov. 5, 1791	Hutchinson & vacant
	Nov. 5, 1791	Fras. Tennille & Few
	Nov. 5, 1791	Hutchinson & Few
Fields, James	Apr. 6, 1789	vacant
Flannakin, Saml.	Dec. 19, 1785	Jm.Hill & Jno.Jhite
Flournoy, Robt.	July 5, 1790	Flournoy & unknown
Flournoy, Thos.	Aug. 6, 1792	Jos. Ryan
Fort, Owne	Aug. 5, 1793	
Forsyth, Robt.	May 2, 1791	Horn & Thompson
	May 2, 1791	unknown
	May 2, 1791	John Anderson
	May 2, 1791	surveyed land
	May 2, 1791	Horn & Fountain
Franklin, Geo.	Apr. 4, 1792	Chas. Culpepper
Flournoy, Thos.	Aug. 6, 1792	Thos. Flournoy & Ryan

Name	Date Issued	Adjoining
Gardener, John	July 7, 1788	Gardner
	July 7, 1788	Gardener
	July 7, 1788	Gardener
	July 7, 1788	Gardener
	July 7, 1788	Gardener
	July 7, 1788	Gardener
	July 7, 1788	Gardener
	July 7, 1788	Gardener
	July 7, 1788	Gardener
	Mar. 2, 1789	Gardener
	Mar. 2, 1789	Gardener
	Mar. 2, 1789	Gardener
	Mar. 2, 1789	Gardener
	Mar. 2, 1789	Gardener & vacant
	Mar. 2, 1789	Gardener & vacant
	Mar. 2, 1789	vacant
Gainor, William	Dec. 1, 1788	Jas. Burney & Wm's.
Gilman, Harmon	(scratched out)	
Glascock, Thomas	Aug. 6, 1792	Robt. Jackson & Renfro
	Aug. 6, 1792	Jno. Wallace & Jackson
Glenn, David & Sessions	Aug. 6, 1792	Jno. Crawford & Black
Goode, Edward	Apr. 2, 1789	Surveyed & vacant
Grantham, Jno.		Dixon & Ellis
	May 3, 1790	Read & Griffin
	May 4, 1790	Griffin
Grantham, Wm.	Aug. 6, 1792	vacant & surveyed
Green, Benj.	July 5, 1790	vacant
Greene, James	Aug. 3, 1789	Saffold & Glenn
	July 7, 1788	Salter, Simon & Walker
Green, Peleg	Oct. 4, 1790	Comens & Jackson
	Oct. 4, 1790	Jamison & Longstreet
	Aug. 6, 1792	Walter Jackson
	Aug. 6, 1792	Walter Jackson
	Aug. 6, 1792	Walter Jackson
Greer, Josiah	Apr. 3, 1786	Major Call
Greyham, James	June 6, 1785	Flenneker & Armour
Griffen, Leonard	Feb. 8, 1791	Tennille & Smith, Lew
	Feb. 8, 1791	Glenn
Griffen, Majer	Oct. 6, 1789	Irwin & vacant
Hadon, Wm.	Nov. 1, 1790	Hardon & Tabar
Hargrove, Josiah	May 3, 1790	vacant
Harris, Jesse	Apr. 4, 1793	Hillar & Helton
Harrison, Benj.	Nov. 1, 1790	vacant & surveyed
	Nov. 1, 1790	vacant & surveyed
	Nov. 1, 1790	vacant & surveyed
	Nov. 1, 1790	vacant & surveyed
	Apr. 6, 1789	vacant & surveyed
Hart, Robt.	Jan. 7, 1793	vacant & surveyed
Hart, Saml.	Feb. 6, 1792	Hannah & Kelly
Hartsfield, Geo.	Nov. 6, 1787	Oconee River
Heaton, Robt.	July 4, 1791	Evans & vacant

85

Name	Date Issued	Adjoining
Hemphill, Wm.	July 4, 1791	Lawson & Hemphill
Herring, James	May 3, 1790	Bracken & Powell
Higdon, Charles	May 3, 1790	vacant
	May 3, 1790	Edw. Irby & vacant
	May 3, 1790	vacant
Highland, Nicholas	Dec. 19, 1785	Christmas
	Dec. 19, 1785	Christmas & Carson
	Dec. 19, 1785	vacant
Hickman, Wm.	Nov. 1, 1790	Germanies & Pauls
Hill, Thos.	Aug. 6, 1787	Jno. Kirk & Brantley
Hillard, Majer	July 5, 1790	David Johnston
Hogg, Jacob	May 17, 1784	Whatly & Heard
Holderness, James	Oct 6, —	Henderson
	Oct. 6, 1789	Coulter, John
Hollenworth, Stephen	Apr. 4, 1791	vacant
Holly, Jonathan	May 3, 1790	Simion Lowry
Holley, Thomas	Apr. 6, —	
Holton, Samuel	May 3, 1790	vacant
Hood, Nathaniel	May 2, 1791	Hardwick & Lott
Hooks, William	July 7, 1788	Hooks & Holland
	July 7, 1788	Tennille & Lingo
Hooper, Absalom	May 17, 1784	R. Whiten & Rutherford
Hopson, Briggs	Aug. 1, 1791	Welch & Ratcliff
	Nov. 5, 1793	Tobias Riams
	Nov. 5, 1793	vacant
Horn, Joab	Dec. 1, 1788	Solm. Wood & Jas. May
Horton, Thomas	Aug. 2, 1790	Horton & unknown
House, Joseph	July 1, 1791	Joseph Hargrove
Howell, Joseph	Apr. 1, 1793	Miles Rachels
Hubert, Mathew	Aug. 6, 1787	Rutherford
Huckeby, John	Aug. 27, 1792	Barfield & unknown
Hudson, Wm.	June 4, 1787	Alexander Irwin
Huff, Samuel	Dec. 19, 1785	Geo. Clough
Hughs, James	Nov. 1, 1791	vacant
	Nov. 1, 1790	Arthur Moore
Hutchinson, James	Oct. 5, 1789	vacant
	Aug. 6, 1792	Thomas Carnes
	Aug. 6, 1792	James Hutchinson
	Aug. 6, 1792	unknown
	Aug. 6, 1792	Thomas Carnes
	Apr. 1791	Few & Bostick
Irwin, Jared	Aug. 3, 1789	Wm. Irwin &
		W. Flemmons
	Aug. 3, 1789	Alexander Irwin
Jackson, Absalom	Nov. 5, 1791	Jackson
	Nov. 5, 1791	Jackson
	Nov. 5, 1791	Jackson
	Nov. 5, 1791	Jackson
	Nov. 5, 1791	
	Nov. 5, 1791	Jackson & unknown
	Nov. 5, 1791	Jackson & Peleg Green
	Nov. 5, 1791	Jackson & unknown
	Nov. 15, 1791	Jackson
	Nov. 15, 1791	Jackson

Name	Date Issued	Adjoining
Jackson, Charles	Apr. 3, 1786	Jas.Ashley & Howard
	June 4, 1787	Jackson & vacant
Jackson, David		
& Kindrick	Feb. 6, 1792	James Kindrick
Jackson, Joseph	Apr. 1, 1793	Howel (?)
Jackson, Robt.	Nov. 1, 1790	Daniel Longstreet
	Nov. 7, 1791	Absolm Jackson
Jackson, Walter	Dec. 8, 1790	Beckcom & Jackson
	June 7, 1790	Longstreet & Jackson
	Aug. 6, 1792	Jackson
	Aug. 6, 1792	Walter Jackson
	Aug. 6, 1792	Walter Jackson
	Aug. 6, 1792	Walter Jackson
	Aug. 6, 1792	Walter Jackson
Jamison, Wm.	Oct. 4, 1796	Longstreet & Beckcom
Jenkins, Francis	July 7, 1788	E.Nails & vacant
Jenkins, Zachariah	Nov. 7, 1791	John Rickardson
Johnson, Benj.	Aug. 1, 1792	B. Johnson & vacant
	Aug. 1, 1792	B.Johnson & vacant
	Aug. 1, 1792	B. Johnson & vacant
	Aug. 1, 1792	B. Johnson & vacant
	Aug. 1, 1792	B. Johnson & vacant
	Aug. 1, 1792	Middleton
	Aug. 1, 1792	Middleton & unknown
	Aug. 1, 1792	Middleton & vacant
	Aug. 1, 1792	Middleton & surveyed
Johnson, Danl.	June 4, 1787	
Johnson, David	July 5, 1790	vacant
Johnson, John	July 5, 1790	Wm. Sanders
Johnson, James Jr.	July 5, 1790	Sanders Colson
	May 3, 1790	Lewis
	July 5, 1790	James Johnson
Johnson, Wm.	Mar. 1, 1789	Glen & Phillips
	July 7, 1788	vacant
	Sept. 6, 1790	Commens
Joins, Edmond	June 15, 1790	Joseph Smith
Jones, Jesse (heirs)	June 7, 1785	Robt. Whiton
Jones, John	Oct. 6, 1789	Jones & McClendon
Jones, Phillip	May 7, 1784	vacant
Kelly, John	Apr. 3, 1787	vacant
	Apr. 3, 1787	vacant
	Aug. 6, 1792	Wm.Thompson & Camp
Kelly, Lloyd	July 5, 1790	Bearfield & Pruett
Kelly, Wm.	Aug. 3, 1789	Glen & White
Kemp, Wm.	Feb. 6, 1792	vacant
	Feb. 6, 1792	Herrins & Marshall
Kendall, David	Apr. 1, 1793	Lamar & Clark
Kendall, Jeremiah	Aug. 3, 1789	David Burney
	Apr. 6, 1789	E.Bugg & Jno.Curry
	July 7, 1788	John Jones

Name	Date Issued	Adjoining
Kendall, Wm.	Apr. 3, 1787	vacant & Sturgis
	May 2, 1791	Wm. Kendall
	May 2, 1791	Curry & Cook
Kettle, Mary	Apr. 4, 1791	Blunt & surveyed
Kimbrough	Apr. 6, 1789	Few & Upton
Kindrick, Barrie	May 7, 1792	Sheppard.Jno. & Wm.
Kindrick, Jonas	Aug. 6, 1792	Irwin & Graybill
Kirk, John	Aug. 6, 1787	Thos. Hill & Brantley
Kitchens, Benj.	Aug. 6, 1792	Kitchen & Jackson
	Aug. 6, 1792	Kitchen & vacant
	Aug. 6, 1792	Kitchen & Jackson
	Aug. 6, 1792	Kitchen & Jackson
	Aug. 6, 1792	Kitchen & Jackson
	Aug. 6, 1792	Kitchen & vacant
	Aug. 6, 1792	Kitchen & vacant
	Aug. 6, 1792	Kitchen & vacant
	Aug. 6, 1792	Kitchen & vacant
	Aug. 6, 1792	Kitchen & vacant
	Aug. 6, 1792	James Bewie
	Aug. 6, 1792	James Bewie
	Jan. 7, 1793	surveys
	Jan. 7, 1793	Benj. Kitchen
	Jan. 7, 1793	surveys
	Jan. 7, 1793	surveys
	Jan. 7, 1793	Benj. Kitchens
	Apr. 1, 1793	Commons
	Apr. 1, 1793	Kitchens & vacant
	Apr. 1, 1793	Jos. Ryan & Kitchen
	Apr. 1, 1793	Jno. Black & Jos, Ryan
	Apr. 1, 1793	vacant
	Apr. 1, 1793	Dawson & Jones
	Apr. 1, 1793	Ryan
	Apr. 1, 1793	Dawson
Lamb, Jesse	May 3, 1790	Duett Dees & Elis Nals
Lancaster, Wm. and Jas. Dawson	Oct. 6, 1789	James Dawson
Jno. Lawson	Sept. 7, 1789	Broadstreet
Leapham, Aaron	Dec. 8, 1790	Harris
Ledbetter, Isaac	Feb. 7, 1792	Sneed & vacant
	Feb. 7, 1792	Lasseter & vacant
Levin, Richard	May 7, 1784	Tennille & Hill
Lightfoot, John	July 5, 1790	vacant
Lingo, Moses	Apr. 6, 1789	vacant & surveyed
Linsey, John	May 17,1784	John Stroud
Long, Nicholas	June 7, 1786	Lamar & Long
Long, Nicholas Jr.	Oct. 6, 1789	Shoals, Dennis, Jacob
	Oct. 6, 1789	Coleman & Adams
	Apr. 6, 1789	N. Long & Mitchell
Longstreet, Saml.	Oct. 4, 1790	Robt. Jackson
	Oct. 15, 1790	Jackson & Longstreet
Lord, Laudwick	Feb. 6, 1790	Armstrong

Name	Date Issued	Adjoining
Lott, —	Apr. 4, 1791	vacant
Lott, Jno.	Aug. 3, 1789	vacant & Lott
Lott, Mark	May 3, 1790	vacant
Lowry, Simeon	June 4, 1787	
Lucas, Moses	Apr. 6, 1789	Grantham & vacant
Lucas, William	May 17, 1784	Wm. Candlar & Ben Catch
Lumpkin, Charles	Dec. 19, 1785	Gerard Banks & vacant
	Dec. 19, 1785	Charles Lumpkin
Madox, William	Aug. 6, 1792	Heard & Rob Day
Marshall, Danl.	May 17, 1784	vacant
	Apr. 2, 1787	Jno. Fenn & Gambol
Marshall, John	May 17, 1784	Jackson & Houston
Marshall, Solomon	Apr. 2, 1787	Irwin & Celmants
	Apr. 2, 1787	vacant & unknown
	Oct. 5, 1789	vacant
Martin, William	May 17, 1784	Gideon Patterson
Mason, Thomas	Aug. 6, 1787	Retherford & unknown
May, Jonas	Dec. 1, 1788	Solomon Wood & Hab. Horn
Mayo, Mark	May 3, 1790	Colemans & vacant
	Apr. 1	Coleman
McCeymore, Emily	July 4, 1791	Renfroe & vacant
McCall, Thos. and Shelman	Feb. 7, 1791	vacant
McClendon, Joel	Jan. 7, 1788	Burney & vacant
	July 7, 1788	McCormack & Baker
McClendon, Lewis	July 5, 1790	Dickson & Jnoes
McCorcle, James	Aug. 2, 1790	Hutson & McCorcle
McCullars, Bryant	Oct. 6, 1789	Richard Call & vacant
	Oct. 6, 1789	vacant & unknown
	Jan. 4, 1791	Duhart & Asa Emanuel
	Nov. 1, 1790	vacant
McDowell, Thos.	May 3, 1790	Solomon Beckum
McGee, Shadrack	July 5, 1790	Jonas Chambers
	July 5, 1790	Isaac Perry & unknown
McLane, Daniel	Apr. 6, 1789	McLane
	Apr. 6, 1789	McLane
	Apr. 6, 1789	McLane
	Apr. 6, 1789	McLane
	Apr. 6, 1789	McLane
	Apr. 6, 1789	McLane
	Apr. 6, 1789	McLane
	Apr. 6, 1789	McLane
	Apr. 6, 1789	McLane
	Apr. 6, 1789	McLane
McMillion, Matthew	Aug. 6, 1792	Samuel Beckcom
McMurry, William	Jan. 4, 1791	Burney,Harris,&Denis
Mercer, Peter	Jan. 4, 1791	vacant
	May 7, 1792	vacant
Middleton, Robt.	June 7, 1790	vacant & Middleton
	June 7, 1790	vacant

Name	Date Issued	Adjoining
	June 7, 1790	vacant & Middleton
	June 7, 1790	vacant & Middleton
	June 7, 1790	vacant & Middleton
	June 7, 1790	vacant & Middleton
	June 7, 1790	vacant & Middleton
	June 7, 1790	vacant & Middleton
	June 7, 1790	vacant & Middleton
	June 7, 1790	vacant & Middleton
	June 7, 1790	vacant & Middleton
	Aug. 6, 1792	Beckom & McMillon
McMillon, Matthew	Aug. 6, 1792	Kitchen & Middleton, Robt.
Middleton, Robt.	Aug. 5, 1793	vacant & unknown
	Aug. 5, 1793	Middleton & vacant
	Aug. 5, 1793	Middleton & vacant
	Aug. 5, 1793	Middleton & vacant
	Aug. 5, 1793	Middleton & vacant
	Aug. 5, 1793	Middleton & vacant
	Aug. 5, 1793	Middleton & vacant
Millar, Jonathan	Nov. 1, 1790	McClendon
Miles, John	Aug. 3, 1789	vacant
Moon, Jacob	May 2, 1795	Jos. Hemp & vacant
Moore, Arthur	July 5, 1790	vacant
	July 5, 1790	vacant
Moore, Thomas	Mar. 2, 1789	Rutherford line
Moore, Richard & Dawson	Oct. 6, 1789	vacant
	Oct. 6, 1789	vacant
Morgan, Wm. & Dawson, Jas.	Oct. 6, 1789	Dawson & Lancaster
Motts, Wm.	Dec. 6, 1790	Daniel & Worthen
Mounger, Sampson	Aug. 6, 1789	Matlock & Kelly
	Aug. 6, 1787	Matlock, Day, Kelly
Murchant, Isaac	Dec. 8, 1790	Rutherford, Radclif
Murchants, John	Dec. 3, 1790	Marshall & vacant
Murphy, Bartholomew	Aug. 2, 1790	Johnston, Martin
Nail, Elisha	Apr. 6, 1789	vacant
	June 7, 1790	vacant
Nall, Martin	June 7, 1790	vacant
	June 7, 1790	Hill & unknown
Neal, Thomas	Aug. 22, 1792	Stephen Mitchell
Neely, John	Oct. 6, 1789	Jackson & Jno. Stuart
Nelson, William	Aug. 6, 1789	vacant
	Apr. 6, 1789	
Newton, Moses	May 2, 1790	Jno. & Abraham Dennis
Nutt, John		Kemp, Harris-Floyd
Odom, Isual	July 5, 1790	Burns, Starret, McGee
Outlaw, Edward	May 17, 1784	vacant
	Apr. 1, 1793	Dr. Eammais & McGeehe
	Apr. 1, 1793	Vivion & Gardner
Paeeb, James	Dec. 1, 1789	Creswell
Parker, Aaron	Nov. 7, 1791	Day, Robt., & Bankston

Name	Date Issued	Adjoining
Parker, Daniel	May 7, 1791	surveyed
Parker, William	Jan. 7, 1793	Cates, Richd. & vacant
Purkins, Adam	May 17, 1784	vacant
Perry, Isaac	Sept. 6, 1790	Robison
	Sept. 6, 1790	Thos. Smith & S. Burns
	Sept. 6, 1790	Perry
	Sept. 6, 1790	Perry
	Sept. 6, 1790	Perry
	July 5, 1790	Oconee River
	July 4, 1790	Shadrack
Phillips, John	Dec. 19, 1785	Mark Lott
Phillips, Joseph	Dec. 19, 1785	Zach Phillips
	Dec. 19, 1785	Jos. Phillips
	Dec. 19, 1785	Jos. Phillips
	Dec. 19, 1785	Jos. Phillips
	Dec. 19, 1785	Jos. Phillips
	Dec. 19, 1785	Oconee
	Dec. 19, 1785	Chas. Dean
	Dec. 19, 1785	Jas. Furlow & Phillips
	Dec. 19, 1785	heirs of Bennis
	Sept. 7, 1785	Michel Bird
	Sept. 7, 1785	Isaac Stokes
	Dec. 19, 1785	Geo. Clough
	June 7, 1785	James Grayham
	June 7, 1785	Winfrey & Walker
Phillips, William	Dec. 19, 1785	Wm. Fitzpatrick
	Dec. 19, 1788	Henry White & Phillips
Phillips, Zachariah	Dec. 20, 1785	Zach Phillips
	Dec. 20, 1785	Zach Phillips
	Dec. 20, 1785	Zach Phillips
	Dec. 20, 1785	Zach Phillips
	Dec. 20, 1785	Zach Phillips
	Dec. 20, 1785	Zach Phillips
	Dec. 20, 1785	Zach Phillips
	Dec. 20, 1785	Zach Phillips & Oconee
	Dec. 20, 1785	Wm. Germany
	Dec. 20, 1785	Wm. Swanson
	Dec. 20, 1785	Jno. Stroud & Phillips
	Dec. 20, 1785	Phillips, Z. & vacant
	Dec. 20, 1785	Phillips, Z. & vacant
	Dec. 20, 1785	Phillips, Z. & vacant
	Dec. 20, 1785	Oconee & Flour
	Dec. 20, 1785	Oconee & Flour
	Dec. 20, 1785	Phillips, Z.
	Dec. 20, 1785	Phillips, Z.
Phillips, Zach	Dec. 20, 1785	Z. Phillips & vacant
	Dec. 20, 1785	Z. Phillips & vacant
	Dec. 20, 1785	Z. Phillips & vacant
	Dec. 20, 1785	Z. Phillips & surveyed
	Dec. 20, 1785	Fras. Tennille

Name	Date Issued	Adjoining
Pollard, William	Feb. 6, 1792	Glascock, Thos. & Jackson
	Feb. 6, 1792	.m. Phillips, A. Jackson
	Feb. 8, 1791	Wm.Pollard & Dawson
	Feb. 8, 1791	.m.Pollard & Dawson
	Feb. 8, 1791	Wm.Pollard & Dawson
	Aug. 6, 1792	Pollard & vacant
	Feb. 8, 1791	Pollard & vacant
	Aug. 6, 1792	Pollard & vacant
Powell, George	Nov. 1, 1790	vacant
Powell, Moses	Apr. 5, 1795	Binion, Jm.& Cain
Powell, Stephen	Feb. 8, 1791	Powell & Clark
Powell, Wm.	Jan. 1, 1787	Armstrong, Jno.&Heard
	Oct. 6, 1789	E. Clerk & Fort
Price, Cader	May 3, 1790	Cader Price & vacant
Pugh, Theophilus	Aug. 6, 1792	vacant
Pullen, Thos.	Oct. 6, 1789	Tennille & Brinton
Rachel, James	Apr. 3, 1786	Kemp & Thos.Howard
Rachel, Miles	Oct. 5, 178?	Upton & Miles Rachel
Raney, John	Sept. 2, 1790	Raney, Benj.& Rogers
Raley, Smith	Aug. 2, 1790	
Randolph, Isaac	Feb. 3, 1794	Randolph & vacant
	Feb. 3, 1794	Sartain & Thomas, G.
	Apr. 3, 1794	Ohoopie-Randolph
	Feb. 3, 1794	Randolph & unknown
	Feb. 3, 1794	Randolph & unknown
	Feb. 3, 1794	Randolph & unknown
	Feb. 3, 1794	Randolph & vacant
	Feb. 3, 1794	Randolph & vacant
Randolph, Isaac	Feb. 3, 1794	
	Feb. 3, 1794	Randolph & Sartain
	Feb. 3, 1794	Randolph & Sartain
	Feb. 3, 1794	Randolph & Sartain
	Feb. 3, 1794	Comens
Ray, James	Sept. 7, 1789	Millar & Irwin
Ray, Zachariah	May 17, 1784	Ramsey
Rayford, Mauris	Apr. 6, 1789	vacant
Reaves, Joseph	July 5, 1790	Arthur Moore & vacant
Renfro, Wm.	May 3, 1790	Howell Hergrove
	?	Carnes, Thos. P.
Reynolds, Absolom	Dec. 24, 1784	
Roan, Tunstel	Mar. 17, 1784	vacant
Roberts, Amos	Dec. 24, 1784	Kelly & Vickers
Robertson, David	Aug. 3, 1792	vacant
Robertson, Edward	Aug. 1, 1791	John Robertson
Roberson, John	Aug. 1792	Ohoopie
Robertson, Joseph	Aug. 1, 1791	Isaac Perry
	Aug. 1, 1791	John Robertson
Robinson, Edward	Sept. 7, 1789	Ohoopie
	Aug. 1791	Leonard Griffin

Name	Date Issued	Adjoining
Robinson, Israel	May 7, 1792	Robinson
	May 7, 1792	vacant
	Aug. 6, 1792	Robinson
	Aug. 6,1792	Robinson
	Aug. 6, 1792	Robinson
	Aug. 6, 1792	Robinson
	Aug. 6, 1792	Robinson
	Aug. 6, 1792	Robinson
	Aug. 6, 1792	Robinson
	Aug. 6, 1792	Robinson
	Aug. 6, 1792	Robinson
	Aug. 6, 1792	Robinson
	Aug. 6, 1792	Robinson
Robinson, Israel	Aug. 6, 1792	Robinson & vacant
Robinson, John	Sept. 7, 1789	Griffin
	July 4, 1791	Jas. Robinson
Robinson, Robt.	Apr. 1, 1793	Miller & McDowel
Roe, Hezekiah	July 4, 1791	vacant
Rogers, Dred	May 17, 1784	vacant
Rollin, Thos.	Oct. 6, 1789	vacant
Ross, Moses	May 7, 1792	Ross Creswell
	May 7, 1792	Ross Creswell
	May 7, 1792	Williams
	Oct. 6, 1789	vacant
	Oct. 6, 1789	vacant & Ross
Roundtree, Wm.	Aug. 6, 1787	Vickers & vacant
	Oct. 6, 1789	vacant
Runnels, Hermon	Aug. 6, 1792	Kelly & Hubert
Rutherford, John	Aug. 6, 1787	Cochran & Fain
	Aug. 6, 1787	Miller
Runnels, Hermon	Oct. 4, 1790	Mason, Jno. & Smith
Rutherford, Saml.	Jan. 15, 1785	Hooper
Ryan, Joseph	Aug. 6, 1792	Ryan & vacant
	Aug. 6, 1792	Jos. Ryan & vacant
	Aug. 6, 1792	Hergrove, Renfro, Holy
	Aug. 6, 1792	Ryan, Jos. & vacant
	Aug. 6, 1792	Ryan, Jos. & vacant
	Aug. 6, 1792	Ryan, Jos. & vacant
	Aug. 6, 1792	Ryan, Jos. & vacant
	Aug. 6, 1792	Ryan, Jos. & vacant
	Aug. 6, 1792	Ryan, Jos. & vacant
	Aug. 6, 1792	Ryan, Jos. & vacant
	Aug. 6, 1792	Ryan, Jos. & vacant
	Aug. 6, 1792	Ryan, Jos. & vacant
	Aug. 6, 1792	Ryan, Jos. & vacant
	Aug. 6, 1792	Ryan, Jos. & vacant
	Aug. 6, 1792	Ryan, Jos. & vacant
	Aug. 6, 1792	Ryan, Jos. & vacant
	Aug. 6, 1792	Ryan, Jos. & vacant

Name	Date Issued	Adjoining
	Aug. 6, 1792	Ryan, Jos. & vacant
	Aug. 6, 1792	Ryan, Jos. & vacant
	Aug. 6, 1792	Ryan, Jos. & vacant
	Aug. 6, 1792	Ryan, Jos. & vacant
Ryan, Joseph	Aug. 6, 1792	Jos. Ryan & vacant
	Aug. 6, 1792	Jos. Ryan & vacant
	Aug. 6, 1792	Jos. Ryan & vacant
	Aug. 6, 1792	Jos. Ryan & Comon
	Aug. 6, 1792	Flournoy, Thos. & Ryan
Salter, James	May 7, 1792	vacant
Samford, Saml.	Dec. 1, 1788	Elijah Padgett
Sanderlin, Robt.	Apr. 6, 1789	Richard W. Cates
Sartain, James	Jan. 4, 1791	Stephen Powell
Scarborough, Aaron	Aug. 2, 1790	vacant
Scarborough, Miles	Oct. 6, 1789	vacant
Scarborough, Moses	Jan. 4, 1791	vacant
Seale, Wm.	May 7, 1792	Murphy & Kelly
Sessions, Joseph	Apr. 6, 1789	Glenn & Col. Sess
	Apr. 6 —	Bazer, Caleb & Phillip
Sharks, Josiah	July 7, 1788	Griffin & Hartsfield
Shelman, Jno. & Thos. McCall	Feb. 7, 1791	vacant
Shaw, Wm.	May 7, 1792	Hall & Forsyth
Shelman, John	Oct. 6, 1789	Jno. Anderson
Shelman, Michael & F. Tennille	Apr. 6, 1789	Kay & vacant
Shelvey, John	June 4, 1787	Long & Shelvey
Smith, George	Dec. 4, 1786	Harrison & Eubanks
Smith, John	Nov. 7, 1791	Thos. Smith & McGehee
Smith, Robt.	Feb. 8, —	Fitz Hunt & Tennille
Smith, Wm.	Apr. 6, 1789	Ragland & Tennille
Sneed, Chs.	Apr. 6, 1789	Thomas Jones
Snell, Christopher	Mar. 2, 1789	vacant
	July 5, 1790	Jas. Johnson
Spann, Geo.	— —	Hill, Wm.& Isaac Atwood
	Feb. 6, 1792	Spann & Few
Spike, Thomas	Apr. 3, 1787	Lides ?
Stanley, Sams	Oct. 6, 1789	vacant
	Apr. 1, 1793	Emmis, Dr. & Stanley
Stephen, Benj.	Nov. 1, 1790	vacant
Stewart, Charles	Apr. 6, 1789	McFarlan & Roberts
Stinson, Nathan	May 2, 1791	Nail, Reubin
Stokes, Jno. & Anderson, Jno.	Oct. 6, 1789	Blackshear & Scarboro
Strawodes, Jacob	Aug. 2, 1790	Zacky Buttery
Stroud, John	Dec. 19, 1785	vacant
	Dec. 19, 1785	Wm. Hill & Andw.Arm
	Dec. 19, 1785	Adam Carson & Lennill
	Dec. 19, 1785	Phillips, Wm.
Sturgis, Andrew	Aug. 6, 1789	Paul
	Sept. 7, 1787	Creswell & Sturgis

Name	Date Issued	Adjoining
Stuart, John	Feb. 21, 1785	
Swanson, Wm.	Dec. 19, 1785	Jas. Phillips
	Dec. 19, 1785	Zach. Phillips
Swella (?), Saml.	Feb. 6, 1792	Wood, Dempsey & Macon
Tanner, Noah	Sept. 6, 1790	vacant
Tapley, Jno.	Jan. 7, 1793	Jno. Barron
Taylor, Joshua	July 7, 1788	Bracken, Wm. & Harrison
Taylor, Wm.	Aug. 5, 1793	Coleman & Creswell
Tennille, Benj.		Middleton
	Mar. 2, 1789	vacant
	Oct. 6, 1789	Burnet
	Mar. 2, 1789	Chandler & Eland
	Apr. 6, 1789	Campbell & Marshall
	Apr. 1, 1791	Beckcom, Sherod
	Aug. 1, 1791	
	Apr. 4, 1791	Jas. Holderness
	Aug. 3, 1789	Few & McClendon
	July 7, 1788	Williford & Brooks
Tennille, & Fitzm. Hunt		Armstrong & Lamar.
Tennille, Frances	Oct. 6, 1789	vacant
	Aug. 1, 1791	Tennille
	Aug. 1, 1791	McMurry, Kirkland
	May 7, 1792	Kendall & Beckcom
Tennille & Michael Shelman	Apr. 6, 1789	Kay
Tharp, Wiley	July 4, 1791	Big survey
Thiner (?), Michael	Oct. 6, 1789	surveyed & vacant
Thomas, Gideon	May 2, 1791	Burney & vacant
Thomas, James	May 7, 1792	Wicker, R. & Tennille, F.
	May 3, 1790	James Thomas
Thompkins, Eliz.	Apr. 6, 1789	
Thompson, Benj.	May 2, 1791	John Robertson
Thompson, John	June 7, 1785	Wm. Fitz & Robt. White
Thornton, Elam	May 3, 1790	Williams & vacant
	May 1793	vacant
	May 3, 1790	Elisha Nail & vacant
Tilman, Littleberry	June 4, 1787	vacant
Tomlinson, Aaron	Apr. 3, 1791	Stuart & Howard
Tomplins, Chas.	Dec. 19, 1785	county line N
	Dec. 19, 1785	vacant
Tompkins, Eliz.	Apr. 6, 1789	Hunt, Fitz.
Troy, Mary	Sept. 7, 1790	Green, Harvey, Forsyth
Underwood, Benj.	Oct. 6, 1789	vacant
Upton, Benj.	Aug. 6, 1792	Burns & Statham
Vickers, Benj.	Dec. 6 —	Hopson & vacant
Vickers, Thos.	Aug. 6, 1792	Thos. Vickers & vacant

95

Name	Date Issued	Adjoining
Vivion, Thacker	Jan. 4, 1790	Bracken & Powell
	Jan. 4, 1790	vacant
Wadsworth, James	Feb. 5, 1789	Daniell
Walker, James	Feb. 8, 1791	David Curry & W.Irwin
Walker, Silvanus	June 6, 1785	vacant
Walker, Thomas	Apr. 6, 1789	vacant
Wamock, John	Oct. 6, 1789	Rougton
Wall, Arthur	June 6, 1785	Phillips,Zach.& Wm.
Wallace, Charmal	Dec. 4, 1786	R. Lawson
Wallace, John	Aug. 6, 1792	Thos. Glascock
	Aug. 6, 1792	Danl. Longstreet
Ward, Moses	Feb. 7, 1791	vacant
Warthen, Richard	Dec. 8, 1790	Warthen,Graves,Lewis
Watson, Benj.	Aug. 6, 1792	Thos. Glascock
Watson, David (ded'd.)	Sept. 7, 1789	Huckagy & W. Dowell
Watts, Jacob	Aug. 1, 1791	Cox & Carr & Burk
	Aug. 6, 1792	Oates
	Aug. 6, 1792	vacant
Watts,Jesse	Feb. 7, 1791	Kelly & Marten, John
Watts, John	Sept. 7, 1789	Chas. Shepherd
		Whitehead & Smith
	Sept. 7, 1789	Young & Havey
	May 2, 1791	Burney, Randal
	Aug. 6, 1792	Boykin
Welsh, Benj.	Aug. 3, 1789	Christmas & Pinker
Wesley, Leumons	June 4, 1787	Kindrick & Chaplin
Whiggins, Wm.	Sept. 10, 1789	
White, James	Sept. 14, 1784	Greer, & Jas. Stuart
White, Joseph	Sept. 13, 1784	John White
Whitehead, June	Apr. 6, 1789	Swain
Whitehead, Thos.	Feb. 6, 1792	Jones & surveyed
Whitman, Jno.	Dec. 19, 1785	Wm. Fitzpatrick
Whitten, Robt.	May 17, 1784	Robt. Day
Wicker, Robt.	May 3, 1790	Brittain
Wiggins, Wm.	Sept. 27, 1784	Crawford,Mart. & Kelly
Wilborn, Curtis	July 5, 1790	Morgan & Sutten
Williams, Chas.	Sept. 6, 1790	Bryant, Jno. & Wm.
Williford, Nathan	Aug. 6, 1787	Burke & vacant
Wilkinson, Reuben	Dec. 8, 1790	Tennille & Marshall
Wood, Abrahm	Sept. 7, 1789	Abraham Wood
Wood, David	May 7, 1792	Miles & Wood
Wood, James	Sept. 7, 1784	Tucker & surveyed
Wood, Solomon	July 7, 1788	Wm. Collins & John May
	Apr. 6, 1789	Evans & vacant
Woodard, Warwick	Aug. 6, 1792	
	Aug. 6, 1792	vacant
	Aug. 6, 1792	

Neal, Thomas, Capt.
Williford, Nathan,Lt
Jorthan,Elijah,Ensign
Rogers, Thomas
Chavis, Gilbert
Medlock, Nehen'l.
Averett, Benjamin
Gilliland, William
Haswell, Richard
Graves, James
Averett, Archibald
Spurlock, John
Clark, Henry
Beckom, William
Worthan, William
Beckom, Solomon
Grantham, John
Bearden, Richard
Bearden, Arthur
Beckom, Saben
Fort, William
Rachels, Valentine
Gayne, James
Jackson, Robert
Beckom, Sherwood
Dickson, John
Mott, William
Dickson, Thomas
Beaty, William
McFarlin —
Hickmon, Theo
Ryan, Morris

Muster Roll,
Capt.Tho.Neal's
Company 1 Bat.
2 Regiment
* * *

**John, Thomas Capt.
Hooker, Stephen,Lt.
Barbree,Isaac,Ensign
Johnson, Charles,Sgt
Miller, George,Sgt.
Ward, Moses, Sgt.
Trowick, Jesse,Sgt.
Thomson, Swan, Cpl.
Vickers, Thomas, Cpl
Mathis, Thomas, Cpl.
Stuart, Charles,Cpl.
Cain, John
Heath, John
Raburn, John
Youngblood, Arther
Butler, Thomas

(**Should be Thomas Johnson)

Rivers, Robert
McClung, Wm. M.
Jackson, William
Ernest, Jacob
Phillips, Fillery
Jackson, Steven
Youngblood,Nathan
Islands, Isiah
Giles, William
Rucker, William
Fitts, James
Barnett, Benj.
Sanderlin,Robert
Reaves, William
Jackson, Jack
Carter, William
Harvey, William
Wodall, David
Barnett, William
Butler, John
Miller, Lewis
Slocom, John
Kilpatrick,James
Hogin, John
Brantley, Benj.
Islands, James
Butler, John
Godwin,Jonathan
Hill, James
Callaway, Jehu
Parker, Jacob
Yarbrough, Wm.
Bonner, James
Johnson, William

Dist. # 5
2nd Btn.
2nd Reg.
* * *

McDowel, Capt.
Townsed, Eli,Lt.
Curton,Boln,Ens.
Kelley, David,Sgt.
Fulsom, John, Sgt.
Motte,Jos., Sgt.
Duckworth,Jacob,Cpl
Wilson, James,Cpl.
Lineacum,Hezek.Cpl.
Robert, Thomas,Cpl.
Chapman, William
White, Damey
Graves, Lewis
Steale, Elr
Ginkins, Allin

Woodard, Work
Casey, James
Wells, Eligah
Ledbetter, James
Stateham, William
Stateham, Charles
Minecre, William
Townsley, Job
Chritte, Thomas
Wolder, Joseph
Motte, Nathan
Fuluham, Mear
Davis, Eligah
Beckcom, Allen
Beckcom, Sherod
Baytry, Samuel
Jackson, John
Recton, Joseph
Rackels, Burrel
Hollomon, Mark
Kelley, Jesse
Wade, James
Fagin, Aron
Grantham, Daniel
Morgin, Assa
Perce, Abner
Brown, Stephen
Iszele, Jesse
Ferris, Moses
Leggett,Jaramiah
Kelley, Thomas
Kelley, William
Kelley, John
Rochels, George
White, Reuben
Dannis, William

Muster Roll
Capt. McDowell's
Company 2 Btt.
2nd Reg.
* * *

Carson, Jos.,Capt.
Whatley,Dan'l.,Lt.
Glass,Zachariah,Lt.
Morgan,James,Cornet
Carson, Adam,Sgt.
Wood, Rich., Sgt.
Herndon, Joseph,Sgt.
Obare, Robt., Sgt.
Gay, Gilbred, Cpl.
Hunt, Wm., Cpl.
Fulsom, John. Cpl.

ilson,, James,Cpl.
Whatley, Elisha
Brown, John
Culver, Nathan
Wood, Etheldred
Roberts, Thomas
Whatley, Jesse
Wilson, Robert
Pickard, Thomas
Lewcos, Moses
Carter, William
Hall, Benjamin
Morgan, Jery
Bankston, William
Jackson, Isaac
Jackson, Stephen
Cobb, Benjamin
Cobb, James
Wicker, Julius
Jones, Henry
Pounds, Merryman
Pool, James
Murphey, Daniel
Tant, William
Bishop, James
Dennis, John
David, Jonathan
Morgan, William
Gay, Joshua
Brasel, Alin
Sexton, Hugh
Miles, Moses
Barkdale, Abner
Lyles, John
Kelley, Thomas
Wood, James
Dawson, James
Asque, Uriah
Page, James
Ilands, Isiah
Ilands, James
Dillard, Thomas
Wood, Aron
Thompson, Elijah
Stanley, Stephen
Beason, Samuel
Jarrell, James
Runnels, Richard
Bankston, Isaac
Going, William
Bankston, Thomas
Langford, James
Akins, James
Scurlock, Presley
McKinzey, William
McKinzey, Randolph

Brewer, Ozburn
Beacham, John
Whatley, Alan
Wooton, Hardy
Woodward, James
Kelly, John
Danielly, Arthur

* * *

McKensey, Capt.
Smith, Wm., Capt.
Ward, John, Lt.
Brinton, Isaiah, Ens.
Smith, Nace, Sgt.
Rushing, James, Sgt.
Burnett, John, Sgt.
Slocomb, John A.
Smith, Nicholas
Avant, Ransom
Pate, William
Lingo, John
Pate, Thomas
Purkins, Elisha
Campbell, John
Pollard, Wm. Jr.
Harris, Henry
Ethridge, Robert
Kelley, Edward
Welborn, David
Ikner, Michael
Hall, James
Clay, David
Simpson, Thomas
Clay, Charles
Renfro, Stephen
Gilmore, John
Wood, Benjamin
Boon, John
Melone, William
Jackson, Jeremiah
Jackson, Thomas
Jackson, William
Taylor, Henry
Reddin, Anderson
Frazier, John
Pollard, Robert
Robinson, George
Hall, John
Ray, Ambris
Holland, John
Holland, Henry
May, John
Blakney, Robert

98

Barnes, Samuel
Renfro, William

2nd Company
1st Batt.
2nd Reg.
* * *

McKenzie, John, Capt.
Cathell, James, Lt.
Miles, Jeremiah, Ens.
McKenzie, Randal, Sgt.
Price, Marady, Sgt.
Biven, Jonathan, Sgt.
Lee, Temple, Sgt.
Walker, Abraham, Cpl.
Williams, John, Cpl.
Parash, Hezekiah, Cpl.
McGinty, Jos., Cpl.
Mobly, Rubin
McGomary, John
Miles, John
Lee, Ransom
Permenter, John
Munk, Mial
Parish, Josiah
Rogers, Joseph
Yarborough, Wm.
Miles, William
Wilson, Samuel

Montgomery, James
Lewas, Daniel
Pearc, John

Cates, Thomas
Downs, Silas
Rogers, Henry
Biven, William
Briggs, Zebiah
Bishup, James

McClenden, Joel
Walker, James
Miles, Abraham
Lee, George
Downs, Isaac
Brown, John
Biven, William, Jr.
McKenzie, Aaron
McKenzie, Wm.
Hogg, James
Marcus, John
Dannelly, Arthur

Parker, Benjamin
Lithgo, Robt.
Blackmore, Abner
Thomson, Jesse
Clay, Charles

Fuller, Isaac
Lishman, Edward
Whitney, John
Hutcheson, Joseph
Barksdale, Abner
Hoye, William
Anderson, Jonathan
Saxon, Hugh
Fields, John
Daughaty, John
Daughaty, Dempsey
Kelly, Jesse
Pinkston, Daniel
Works, James
Wooten, Henry
Liles, John
McCormack, James

Muster Roll
2nd. Co.
2nd. Batt. 2nd. Reg.
* * *

Irwin, Hugh, Capt.
Robison, James Lt.
Whitehead, Rezin,Lt.
Tolar, Lewis,Cornet
Watson, David, Sgt.
Robison, Samuel,Sgt.
Raney, Joseph, Sgt.
Walter, Thomas, Sgt.
Fluker, David
Lyon, Richard
Hagans, James
Fluker, Baldin
Wilson, Robert
Pittman, Jesse
Nusom, Frederick
Curry, John
Hart, Samuel
Barron, Absalom
Wall, William
Wall, Joseph
Niland, John
Morgain, Garlant
Fail, Jeplbey
Prince, Silvenes
Nunn, James
Bassett, Richard
Milton, Teagle
Cahoon, Joseph
Farmer, Thomas
Raskee, James
Lynum, William
Benningfield, Jos.
Graham, Samuel
Purkins, John

Adear, Jacob
Wall, Henry
Watson, Elisha
Rogers, Burrell
Burney, James
Dongar, Philip
Raney, William
Morton, James
Boars, Joal

Cavalry of
1st Regiment

* * *

Spann, George,Capt.
Murphy, Chisnel, Lt.
Cox, James, Ens.
Dillard, Phillip Sgt.
Wilson, James Sgt.
Williams, Joseph
Folk, Joseph
Martin, Thomas
Martin, Levi
Cannon, Calip
Porter, Frederick
Robinson, Edward
Gilmore, Charles
Johnston, Benj.
Martin, James
Highnote, Phillip
Reatherford, Robt.
Johnston, Wm.
Webb, Josiah
Smith, Benjamin
White, John
Dunn, Nehemiah
Winn, Peter
Robinson, Wm.
Robinson, Wm. Jr.
Wilson, Robert
Durdan, Stephen
Wilborn, Curtis
Newman, William
Motley, Robert
Williams, Charles
Cockuham, James
Tomkins, Samuel

Dist. # 2
1st Btn.
2nd Reg.
* * *

Hooker, Nathan Capt.

Robinson, John Lt.
Shelvey,John Ens.
Smith, Jesse Sgt.
Rigbey, Allen Sgt.
Acard, John
Baley, Lewis
Patten, James
Eaken, James
Eaken, Moses
Scurlock, Presley
Robinson, Samuel
Jones, James
Jordan, Baxter
Jordan, Richard
Sinquefield,Samuel
Kinney, John
Greer, James
Smith, Thomas
Jones, John
Jones, James Jr.
Davis, Joseph
McClendon, Wilson
McClendon, Job
Lithgo, Robert

Dist. # 3
1st Btn.
2nd Reg.
* * *

McCavy— Capt.
Cobb — Lt.
Lilly — Ens.
Jiner, John Sgt.
Hearn, Wm. Sgt.
Garner, Urias Sgt.
Hathorn, Tho.Sgt.
Athorn, Anthony
Pray, William
Clay, Peave
Niall, Harris
Hall, David
Jinkins, Wm.
Jackson, Isaac
Jackson, Stephen
Jackson, Tobe
Purkins, John
Sarsit, William
Obannon, Elijah
Dun, Thomas
Hollon, Suel
Cobb, Benjamin
Wicker, Julus
Briant, Benj.
English, John
Cumble, Antony

Jones, Jonathan
Chavis, William
Tomson, John
Acney, William
Pall, James
Jiner, Nathaniel
Morssie, Cashford
Lucke, Moses
Coldman, Curtis
Standly, Shade
Taylor, Right
Burgamy, Wm. L.
Neal, Antony
Ledbetter, Isaac
Garner, Richard
Clunt, James
Howel, Gabriel
Armstrong, Edward
Burd, Shadrick
Powel, Stephen
Ellis, Ephriam
Garmeny, William
Linch, John
Culver, Nathaniel
Daniel, Benjamin
Parker, Abel

    5th Co. 1st Btn.
      2nd. Reg.

      * * *

Parrott, Benj. Capt.
Burk, Nimrod, Lt.
Childers, Richard, Ens.
Farr, Peter, 3gt.
Wilford, Lewis, Sgt.
Hampton, William, Sgt.
Ford, William, Sgt.
Otoe, Jeremiah
Kemp, William
Armstrong, John
Hickman, Joseph
Kemp, Joseph
Kemp, Benjamin
Kemp, Stephen
Higgs, John
Hanner, Thomas
Dennard, Shardach
Dickson, Reuben
Hart, Samuel
Saffold, John
Delk, Joseph

Higgs, Abraham
Roberts, Richard
Spivey, Joshua
Thomas, William
Trapnell, Archibald

Note: This muster
carried no date
nor designation.

Names are written
as they were spelled
on the muster rolls.

100

A list of Captain Edmond Hopson's Company of first class

Militia from the 13 Regiment Washington County, 1814

Hopson, Edmond, Capt.
Hopson, Wm., Lt.
Jimberly, David, Lt.
Price, Joseph, Lt.
Cone, John, Ensign
Bailey, William, Sgt.
Hainey, Ezl., Sgt.
Daniel, John, Sgt.
Curry, David, Sgt.
Thompson, Robert, Cpl.
Moore, George, Cpl.
Harrison, John, Cpl.
Garner, Stephen, Cpl.
Worthy, John, Cpl.
Carter, David, Cpl.
Avant, Ransome
Andrews, Gray
Amison, Benjamin
Brock, William
Butler, Samuel
Burge, Mathew
Brooks, William
Brooks, John
Bulloch, James
Barney, Randall
Brown, Jesse
Cook, John
Cook, James
Cook, Benjamin
Campbell, Elijah
Cooper, John Smith
Chastien, Peter
Clay, William
Carnich, William
Collins, Creed
Carlisle, Dennard
Dixon, Tilman
Driggire, Wynn
Dennard, Abner
Dixon, Robert
Dupree, William
Elliott, Benjamin
Elton, Charles
Ethridge, John
Eda, Richard
Early, Jesse

Frizzle, Thomas
Fisher, Metcalf
Foose, Moses
Gibbs, Harod
Hall, William
Hodges, Seth
Hill, Enoch
Husky, Clayton
Hainy, Levin
Hardiman, Thomas
Hood, Lion
Howard, Harman
Hall, Daniel
Hataway, Bateman
Johnson, Aron
Joins, Ezekiel
Joines, William
Jones, Samuel
Jordan, James
Johns, James
Kendrick, Harvey
Loyd, John
Lowe, William
Lyon, James
Lowery, Samuel
Lyon, Richard
Lewis, Ire
Langarn, Richard
Mays, William
Messer, Wm. B.
Martin, Noah
Martin, Julius
McDade, Charles
Miller, Warren
McGaha, Andrew
Messick, George
McDaniel, Zaddock
Martin, John
Oliver, Phineas
O'Quinn, Bryant
Peddy, Julius
Pope, Wylly
Pinkston, Basil
Parker, Henry
Pace, Nathaniel
Prosser, Jesse

Roberson, Wm.
Rogers, John
Runnells, David
Renfroe, Nathan Jr.
Ray, Ambrose Sr.
Renfroe, Enoch
Rushing, John
Rogers, Daniel
Richardson, Dan'l.
Robertson, Solomon
Shelvy, John
Salter, John
Sinquefield, Asa
Sneed, Ansel
Smith, Jesse
Smith, John Sr.
Smith, John Jr.
Smith, Robert
Smith, Thomas
Stewart, Henry
Stewart, Nath'l.
Safold, Major
Tanner, William
Tanton, Newsom
Tallcnton, Thomas
Veall, George
Wicker, Nath'l.
Whitten, Dempsey
Williamson,
  Anderson
Wallace, James
Webb, John
Waller, John
William, Shadrack
Waggoner, Nicholas

C. D. Dixon,
  Lt. Colo
  13th Reg.
  2nd Brigade
  2nd Division
  Georgia Militia

Governor and Council - Minutes
May 10, 1790 - Dec. 16, 1790
pp. 145-147

Government House, Augusta
6th September 1790

The rank and arrangement of the Militia of Washington County are
established this day in the following order:

Jared Irwin, Esqr. Colo Com. 16th Jan. 1787
John Watts, Esqr. Lt Colo   "
James Evans, Esqr. Major   "

1st Company
Owen Fort, Esqr. Capt. Com 13th April 1786
James Burney, Gent. 1st Lt   "

2nd Company
Thomas McDowell, Esqr. Capt. Com 16th April 1786
John Dennis, Gent 1st Lt   "   7th Oct. 1786
William Johnson, Gent 2nd Lt

3rd Company
Robert Tate, Esqr. Capt. Com 5th Oct. 1786
Samuel Wilson, Gent   1st Lt   "
William Worsham, Gent 2nd Lt   "

4th Company
John Robertson, Esqr., Capt.
Daniel Watley, Gent   1st Lt

5th Company
William Smith, Esqr. Com 2nd May 1787
John Ward, Gent 1st Lt   "
William Campbell Gent 2nd Lt "

6th Company
James Hogan, Esqr   Capt.

7th Company
Charles Stewart, Esqr. Capt. Com 19th May 1787
John Barbre, Gent. 1st Lt   "
William Jackson, Gent 2nd Lt   "

8th Company
William Kemp, Esqr. Capt. Com 23rd June 1787
John Stokes, Gent. 1st Lt   "

9th Company
Edward Hagans, Esqr. Capt. Com 4th July 1787
John Shepherd, Gent. 1st Lt   "
James Howard, Gent. 2nd Lt   "

10th Company
William Irwin, Esqr. Capt. Com 16th October 1787
Jacob Dennard, Gent. 1st Lt   "
Nimrod Burke, Gent. 2nd Lt   "

102

Government House, Augusta
Tuesday, 14 February 1792

General Order:

The following appointments are made in the Washington
County Regiment of Militia by Colo. Jared Irwin:

1st Company
William Cawthorn, 1st Lieut. in the room of Lieut.
James Barney, resigned; Job Horn 2nd Lieut.

4th Company
David Whatley, Capt. in the room of Capt. Robertson, resigned;
James Morgan, 1st Lieut. in the room of Lieut. Whatley, promoted
Allen Whatley, 2nd Lieut.

6th Company
Curtis Wilburn, Capt. in the room of Capt. Hagan, resigned
William Johnston, 1st Lieut; Benjamin Johnston, 2nd Lieut.

8th Company
John Stokes, Capt. in the room of Capt. Kemp, resigned;
Jacob Kelley, 1st Lieut. in the room of Lieut. Stokes, promoted
Moses May, 2nd Lieut.

11th (Additional) Company
Lloyd Kelley, Capt; John Kelley, 1st Lieut; Enoch Storey,
2nd Lieut.

12th (Additional) Company
Nicholas Currey, Capt.; James Burney, 1st Lieut; Benjamin
Kendrick, 2nd Lieut.

By Order of the Commander in Chief
J. Meriwether, Secretary

103

A true List of the voters in Captain Higdon's Company at the
Common Muster ground on the 22nd day of December 1798 for
the purpose of Nominating a first Lieutenant in said company
occasioned by Removal of the former lieutenant it appears that
Needham Cock was fairly elected.

Candidate: Needham Cock

Voters:

William Hart	1	John Overstreet	1
William Chance	1	Josiah Hargrove	1
John Martain	1	Hardy Hargrove	1
Charles Higdon	1	Aaron Niblet	1
Josiah Drew	1	Randal Hargrove	1
Burel Higdon	1	William MacCall	1
Mikagah Bradly	1	James Saulter	1
John Dirdino	1		
William Eles	1		
Edward Irby	1	To his Excelency	
Robert Dickson	1	James Jackson	
Bengman Saulter	1	Governor	
Reubin Martain	1	John Briggs, J.P.	
Joseph Cimbrel	1		
Robert Braswell	1	(Note — names spelled	
Geneper Hall	1	as they appear on re-	
James Lues	1	cord)	

Return of a nomination from
Washington County

Name of Pensioner	Age	Name of heads of families with whom soldier lived 1840
William Williams	86	William Williams
Lustatia Thompson	74	Green H. Warthin
George F. Howard		James Collins
Uriah Peacock	88	Uriah Peacock
Thomas Love	90	Lovey Love
Moses Cox	86	Moses Cox Jr.
Isaac Jones	79	Isaac Jones

* * * * * * * *

NAMES OF THOSE WHO REGISTERED AS REVOLUTIONARY SOLDIERS AND
DREW LAND IN VARIOUS LOTTERIES WHILE RESIDING WASHINGTON CO.

Name	Year of Lottery	Lot No. Dist. No. County	Year draw taken up
Amison, Jesse	1827	113-30D Lee 2-7 D Troup	9-27-1828 8-30-1828
Bedgood, John	1827	30-2D Coweta 137-21D Lee	7-9-1827 7-9-1828
Blanford, Clark	1827	98-5D Muscogee	11-21-1837
Brinkley, Ely	1827	60-12D Lee	Reverted
Burgamy, William	1827	157-5D Lee 165-11D Troup	4-7-1837 12-16-1834
Childers, Richard	1827	27-24D Lee	6-18-1829
Cone, Archibald	1827	57-10D Troup	1-18-1833
Dickerson, Henry	1832	35-9D-2 Sec Cherokee	2-11-1833
Eastwood, John Sr.	1827	135-12D Lee	2-22-1836
Elton, Abram	1827	201-9D Carroll	Reverted
Garrett, Samuel	1827	108-3D Muscogee	10-4-1835
Gilmore, James	1832	292-11D-3rd Sec. Cherokee	11-10-1837

Hay, Isaac	1827	240-21D Muscogee	11-17-1827
Holley, William	1827	106-8D Muscogee	9-29-1829
Holt, Thomas	1827	151-10D Lee	2-9-1837
Howard, Solomon	1827	209-19D Muscogee	12-14-1830
Jenkins, Lewis	1832	60-7D-4 Sec Cherokee	11-26-1839
Joiner, Abraham	1827	178-10D Carroll	Reverted
Jordan, John	1827	11-22D Lee 139-10D Troup	9-18-1829 9-18-1829
Laurence, John	1827	312-dD Coweta 284-17D Muscogee	2-16-1830 12-4-1829
Lee, John	1827	95-28D Lee	Reverted
Lee, Sampson	1827	5-11D Lee	Reverted
Mathis, John	1827	122-3D Carroll 123-27D Lee	12-11-1829 12-11-1829
Middleton, John	1827	144-19D Muscogee	2-4-1833
Mott, Nathan	1827	266-7D Carroll 140-28D Lee	Reverted 1-5-1833
Offcutt, Nathaniel	1832	220-13D-3rd Sec Cherokee	7-1-1843
Peacock, Archibald	1827	210-7D Lee 30-1D Muscogee	9-5-1834 1-4-1833
Peacock, Uriah	1827	237-17D Muscogee	3-21-1831
Prosser, Oty	1827	81-8D Carroll	Reverted
Smith, Colsby	1832	199-25D-2 Sec Cherokee	12-12-1837
Smith, Job	1827	8-7D Lee	4-24-1832
Taunton, Henry	1827	138-14D Lee	Reverted
Thomas, Benjamin	1827	215-30D Lee	5-15-1830
Tindal, Joshua	1820	110-9D Early	10-17-1831
Tomlinson, Aaron	1827	251-2D Coweta	3-4-1828
Tomlinson, William	1832	164-15D-3 Sec Cherokee	t-17-1834

Worthen, William	1827	137-1D Muscogee	12-21-1833
Watkins, Mitchell Sr	1832	129-22D-3 Sec Cherokee	11-7-1836
Watkins, William	1827	120-13D Lee 192-3D Muscogee	11-9-1839 3-3-1836
Watson, Ezekiel	1827	196-3D Troup	12-10-1828
Wiley, Absalom	1827	40-24D Lee	4-20-1827
Williams, William	1827	116-12D Carroll	7-19-1827

The following registered as widows of
Revolutionary soldiers

L. M. Hall	1827	88-13-D Muscogee
Elizabeth Burney	1827	60-3D Troup
Mary Page	1827	122-2D Carroll
Temperance Mayo	1827	76-7D Lee
Reb. Warthen	1827	180-10D Lee
Edy Martin	1827	184-3D Carroll
Mary Thomas	1827	89-1D Muscogee
Fere Hartley	1827	27-18D Muscogee
Penelope Thompson	1827	141-4D Coweta

Austin, John	Catherine Bray	12/21/1828
Allen, David	Carolina Duty	4/8/1829
Adams, Arnold	Nancy Gilmore	7/30/1829
Arnold, Arnet	Mary Mimms	9/24/1829
Ayers, Goodwin	Avy. Mirany Leaptrot	8/31/1830
Arnold, Harrell	Sarah Mimms	1/19/1831
Amerson, Uriah	Elizabeth Taylor	9/26/1833
Andrews, John	Rachel Champion	9/10/1834
Arnold, John	Ann Crafton	12/23/1834
Adkins, Randol	Nancy Harden	11/22/1838
Adams, Benjamin	Ardenna Tanner	3/7/1839
Askew, Frederick W.	Mary Underwood	10/14/1839
Armstron, William H.	Caroline Cox	6/16/1841
Amison, Cullen	Charity Nichols	4/9/1843
Achord, John R.	Elizabeth Posey	2/7/1843
Adams, Hopewell	Amandy Mathis	3/9/1843
Achord, James K.	Mary Massey	2/16/1843
Andrews, Green	Mary Hitchcock	8/26/1847
Ashley, John F..	Winefred H. Howard	1/10/1847
Anderson, John	Elizabeth Gilbert	9/16/1847
Adams, Jordan	Mary S. Mathis	4/27/1848
Armstrong, Ed. F.	Lucretia Womble	7/30/1848
Avant, James	Cressy Cox	12/27/1848
Archer, William M.	Martha Durden	3/4/1849
Achord, Henry A.	Elizabeth A. Johnson	11/7/1850
Alford, William A.	Emily Bowan	8/15/1850
Andrews, Green Lee	Martha A. Pool	5/2/1850
Alford, John W.	Jack Ann Priscilla Wall	12/14/1851
Burgamy, Tobias	Sarah Decanter	4/8/1828
Barwick, Redding	Nancy Wiggins	12/23/1828
Bartlett, Thomas	Nancy Cook	1/1/1829
Bray, Joseph	Sarah Arnold	2/1/1829
Brown, Turner T.	Winnie Avery	10/15/1829
Beddingfield, John H.	Martha Lyon	12/17/1829
Boyd, John	Elizabeth Malplus	5/6/1830
Blount, Daniel	Margaret Irwin	6/11/1830
Barnes, Jacob	Polly Miller	5/21/1829
Brown, Uriah	Mary May	9/5/1830
Bland, John	Emiline Daniel	3/30/1830
Bedgood, Richard	Elizabeth D. Whitfield	12/5/1833
Blair, Robert K.	Zina Jordan	12/5/1833
Brooks, Aaron	Mary McDearman	1/15/1837
Brooks, Johnson	Margaret Swain	12/29/1836
Brookins, Solomon B.	Mary P. Watkins	4/29/1837
Bryan, William P.	Temperance Knight	9/14/1837
Buck, Seaborn W.	Dorothy W. Armstrong	2/24/1839
Brantly, William	Lliza Brantly	1/28/1836
Brantly, Jeptha	Zelphia Boatright	9/13/1838
Bothwell, David J.	Elizabeth Neely	10/4/1838
Brewer, John	Parmelia Thigpen	12/30/1837
Boatright, Edward D..	Patience Bullard	9/1/1839
Blakely, George W.	Priscilla Horton	1/9/1838

Brown, William L.	Matilda Price	2/17/1839
Bell, John	Clarisa Little	12/4/1838
Bailey, David	Winefred Barwick	2/4/1840
Butler, Hughy	Martha Giles	1/7/1840
Barnes, David H.	Martha Ann May	8/9/1839
Bedgood, Serus	Charlotte M. Vickers	12/19/1839
Batts, Jesse	Olive Newsom	4/28/1840
Blackborn, William	Mary Evans	12/8/1840
Brookins, Zachariah	Rebecca Stanly	12/8/1840
Brantly, James M.	Mahala Young	3/4/1841
Boatright, Rolly	Elizabeth Harden	12/11/1838
Barksdale, Alfred	Alicia Patterson	10/13/1840
Brantly, Harris	Permelia Bridges	4/4/1841
Boatright, George E.	Elizabeth Sessions	7/18/1841
Britt, Martin W.	Nancy Tarver	12/13/1837
Bullard Lewis	Elmira Boatright	4/19/1842
Bright, Morgan	Lucinda Osborn	2/22/1842
Barwick, Nathan	Sarah A.S. Sheperd	4/14/1842
Butts, Jesse	Mary Ann Jordan	6/6/1843
Brantly, Thomas M.	Permelia A. Arnold	8/3/1843
Barefield, John	Elizabeth Thigpen	8/17/1843
Bridges, William	Sarah Giles	9/17/1843
Brady, Andrew J.	Elizabeth Raines	2/26/1843
Brantley, James	Siney Hartley	12/21/1843
Bailey, Bird	Louise Messex	2/11/1844
Boatright, James	Rachel Joiner	1/12/1850
Brantley, Thomas	Sarah Hartley	2/29/1844
Bedgood, Lewis	Eliza Crawford	8/18/1844
Bridgers, Alexander	Nancy Bridgers	1/2/1844
Barge, John	Sarah H. Cumming	12/1/1844
Brantley, John	Nancy Young	12/29/1844
Burris, Frederick	Delpha Love	11/9/1849
Boatright, George D.	Artamass Massy	12/26/1848
Brantley, John J.	Nancy Brantley	7/1/1850
Blount, Henry	Carolina Hawkins	12/18/1849
Barber, John W.	Nancy W. Roberts	8/27/1850
Brantley, William G.	Elizabeth R. Kibriel	9/4/1851
Bartman, Bartley M.	Catherine H. Pool	11/5/1851
Bryan, Jason J.	Martha A. Miller	7/23/1851
Barksdale, William	Martha Dugan	2/6/1851
Brown, Thomas	Elizabeth Davis	11/16/1845
Burch, Littleberry	Margaret Wade	5/15/1845
Barwick, William	Sarah Ann Smith	9/28/1845
Brookins, Thomas	Narcissus Vinson	10/20/1839
Bell, James J.	Catherine Powell	11/25/1846
Barrow, Solomon	Martha E. Norris	12/11/1845
Barwick, Jackson	Nancy King	4/12/1846
Bedgood, Henry J.	Elizabeth A. Crawford	10/15/1846
Barwick, Abel J.	Martha Brooks	2/8/1846
Barwick, Stansell	Rebecca Fowler	10/12/1845
Blackburn, Stephen	Nancy A. Williams	12/25/1845
Brown, Henry	Tabitha Guyton	2/11/1845
Bland, Henry	Elizabeth Ann Adams	12/11/1845
Bailey, Richmond	Martha A. Smith	12/2/1845
Brown, Emanuel	Nancy Ann Shepperd	8/19/1847

109

Bryan, James	Cintha L. Barber	10/27/1847
Brantley, Gideon	Eliza Shire	12/21/1847
Brantley, George F.	Emeline Brantley	11/9/1848
Bland, Henry	Martha A.M.Lawrence	9 — 1848
Barron, James	Georgiann Mills	12/17/1848
Brantley, James L.	Rebecca Young	— /11/1849
Barksdale, William	Martha Duggan	2/6/1851
Bangs, Joseph	Martha Brown	7/3/1851
Brown, Richard F.	Martha A. Jackson	8/26/1851
Bryant, John G.	Cherry W. Williams	5/22/1851
Barwick, John	Elizabeth Odum	4/17/1851
Brooks, William J.	Sarah E. Tompkins	7/6/1851
Baker, Joseph	Martha J. Mills	6/5/1851
Butcher, Henry	Mary J. Prescott	12/4/1850
Britt, George W.	Elizabeth Byne	12/4/1851
Brantley, Benjamin	Martha Williams	1/1/1832
Burns, James	Mary Parker	1/6/1832
Barber, John H.	Nancy A. Roberts	8/27/1850
Cason, Dennis	Sarah Massey	1/1/1829
Crafton, William	Minerva Calhoon	1/17/1830
Cox, James	Mary Barwick	3/14/1830
Coston, Thomas	Zelphia Hill	5/5/1830
Collins, Thomas J.	Mary Newsom	6/17/1830
Cole, Wesley T.	Sarah A.C. McAllister	6/17/1830
Chester, Absalom	Nellie Barber	8/10/1830
Cumming, Eli	Mary Brown	8/3/1830
Chivers, Jacob	Judah Barns	2/6/1834
Cane, Benjamin H.	Penena Whittle	6/13/1833
Cullens, Francis B.	Lavenia Smith	12/30/1832
Cordrey, James	Jane Webster	10/18/1835
Collins, John A.	Martha N. Roughton	3/23/1837
Coker, John R.	Martha A. Tarver	2/4/1838
Chamber, Ira	Mary Giles	12/18/1837
Cumbry, Ephriam	Martha Denman	3/20/1836
Cobb, Amos	Eliza Lyons	4/3/1836
Canter, William R.L.	Mary Dickens	11/7/1837
Cook, Cornelius	Sarah Salter	1/19/1839
Coffield, Charles	Lourany Hawkins	1/10/1839
Cawley, Robert W.	Elizabeth Price	12/25/1838
Clance (Chance),Martin	Mary Powell	3/27/1838
Cook, Benjamin R.	Leutresia Hood	1/21/1838
Curry, George W.	Jane Walker	1/1/1840
Cherry, Riley	Charity Wicker	10/29/1839
Curry, David B.	Elizabeth A.Walker	2/27/1840
Calhoun, James M.	Elefair Metts	12/20/1840
Crabb, Wiley	Elizabeth Bedgood	4/25/1841
Clay, Pierce	Mary Ray	11/11/1841
Chipley, J. S.	Ann Hunt	2/6/1842
Calhoun, John F.	Martha Calhoun	1/10/1842
Coffield, John R.	Martha Taylor	7/20/1842
Coston, John	Mrs.Elephair Newsome	11/14/1843
Curry, John A.	Mary Hataway	4/14/1844
Chivers, Larkin	Kissiah Vann	4/27/1845
Curry, Albert G.	Margaret M. Reason	9/4/1845

Cox, John W.	Alaphaire E. Rodgers	10/15/1846
Cumming, Green E.	Ann Pridgen	--- --- ---
Coffield, John D.	Lavania Hall	12/17/1846
Crawford, John W.	Lydia Cutlaw(Outlaw?)	11/12/1846
Crafton, William	Martha Forbes	6/16/1847
Cone, Jonathan B.	Catherine Rushing	4/22/1847
Cone, James B.	Ann L. Walker	9/19/1847
Cox, Young A.	Jane Bland	9/16/1847
Chester, William B.	Mary Jackson	12/5/1847
Crawford, Jesse	Eliza A. Mason	1/19/1848
Coffield, Joseph J.	Bethany Kitchens	1/23/1848
Camp, Clark	Lucinda Giles	3/9/1848
Clark, David E.	Mary A. Corvart	6/15/1848
Cheeley, Thomas J.	Jane R. Wicker	1/4/1849
⎯⎯ Robert J.	Temperance A. Salter	12/19/1848
⎯⎯ John	Almira Bland	1/1/1849
Cook, Calvin	Elizabeth Hodges	1/18/1849
Cobb, Clemmons	Susan Hawkins	12/21/1848
Cook, Samuel	Martha Young	12/15/1848
Chester, Absalom	Elizabeth Lynam	5/17/1849
Cox, James R.	Mary Brookins	12/27/1849
Cox, Wiley	Frances Walker	3/6/1850
Coston, Wiley	Mary A.E. Kneeland	11/25/1850
Cone, William	Martha G. Walker	1/8/1851
Cone, Jesse J.	Frances A. Baker	12/23/1849
Cone, William	Sarah Veal	1/25/1851
Cook, Ailsbury	Mary Ann Bailey	2/27/1851
Carr, Robert J.	Vinia Fort	10/9/1851
Cone, Henry	Faith Ann Taylor	3/20/1851
Cone, William B.	Sarah Ann Warthen	7/6/1851
Croom, Asa D.	Matilda Durden	1/23/1851
Collins, Major L.	Sarah Ann Collins	6/10/1851
Chasteen, William J.	Mary Cox	12/21/1851
Dixon, Shad	Elizabeth Cason	11/20/1828
Duggan, Archelous C.	Elizabeth A. Walker	3/17/1829
Durden, Matthew	Eliza Eastwood	4/30/1830
Dickens, James	Susannah Burgamy	12/20/1829
Dorch, Russell	Ann Holt	5/30/1829
Danavant, Thomas	Isabella Brown	1/18/1835
Dorch, Russell	Coline Hartley	3/6/1838
Dorch, David	Mary Barron	6/2/1836
Dillard, A.	Tabitha Smith	4/3/1838
Dortch, Walter	Elizabeth Bailey	11/4/1838
Dickens, James	Margaret Crawford	12/28/1838
Davis, Deocleatun	Elizabeth Buck	10/7/1838
Dorch, John	Catherine Holt	12/15/1838
Davis, William	Martha Howard	12/27/1841
Donalson, Henry	Brittania Myers	9/29/1841
Dortch, David J.	Nancy Salter	12/16/1841
Donaldson, James M.	Sidney C. Fort	8/24/1843
Dolan, Owen	Martha Hodges	1/4/1844
Daniel, Sampson	Mary Smith	2/7/1844
Daniel, Joseph	Elizabeth Wood	7/9/1844
Davis, Thomas J.	Minerva H. Warthen	6/29/1845

Davis, John	Elizabeth Fenn	11/6/1845
Davis, Enas A.	Mary Fleming	11/5/1846
Durden, Lewis	Sarah A. Holton	1/12/1847
Daniel, William H.	Nancy A.F. Jordan	2/18/1847
Discks(Dicks?),Green B.	Sarah Tyson	4/25/1847
Davis, David	Peney Thomas	1/11/1847
Daniel, Silas	Rebecca M. Irwin	1/12/1842
Davis, Thomas	Seany A. Brown	11/2/1846
Duggan, William	Ann E. Walker	1/11/1849
Durden, Wiley	Elizabeth Simmerson	3/18/1849
Duggan, John M.	Elizabeth W. Jordan	1/8/1849
Durden, Francis	Nancy Wicker	1/9/1850
Davis, Thomas L.	Temperance Bryan	11/21/1849
Dudley, Elum R.	George Ann Brantley	4/23/1850
Davis, William	Martha Mills	11/13/1851
English, John	Levina Coleman	2/3/1830
Edwards, Leroy	Martha Myers	3/17/1839
Emewiler, George W.	Lucy Ann Hitchcock	4/10/1838
Elton, John B.	Susan C. Sherling	12/18/1844
Ennis, James H.	Alphair Rains	7/28/1844
Everett, James D.	Elizabeth Corbet	5/12/1847
———, Alexander	Adeline Duggen	12/31/1848
Ennis, Elias N.	Eliza Davis	9/22/1849
Elton, William	Mariah B. Lindsey	11/30/1848
Elton, Robert	Susan C. Perkins	12/10/1848
Elkins, Timothy	Winnefred H.Tarbutton	3/8/1849
Edge, Zachariah	Nancy Williams	2/15/1849
Elkins, Timothy	Elizabeth A. Massey	1/14/1845
Frances, James	Mary Smith	1/8/1829
Forshee, Elisha	Lydia Durden	3/12/1833
Fort, Arthur	Martha Smith	4/7/1834
Fulghum, John	Elizabeth Harrison	8/13/1836
Frazier, Henry B.	Mary M. W. Odum	9/7/1836
Fields, Bennett	Priety C. Dorch	12/21/1834
Finney, Ezekiel	Jackaline Curry	9/17/1837
Fisher, John	Mary Brantley	3/5/1839
Fountain, W. B.	Letha Elton	12/20/1838
Fluker, Robert T.	Mary Sessions	1/8/1838
Forbes, Benjamin	Sarah Powell	7/16/1839
Frost, Hillary	Elizabeth Bedgood	11/7/1837
Fowler, James S.	Ellefair Chester	3/18/1841
Fields, Samuel	Ann W. Saffold	1/27/1842
Fox, Charles	Mary Pickers(Pichens?)	4/2/1843
Frost, James	Celia Lindsey	12/7/1843
Fountain, William	Cassa Sellers	11/17/1843
Fulgham, Mathew	Penelope Harrison	2/25/1844
Fountain, Nathaniel	Spicy Fountain	1/27/1845
Forbes, Benjamin	Nancy R. Cox	11/25/1845
Fulgham, Jacob D.	Pheraba D. Cone	12/25/1845
Fountain, William	Telytha Dortch	3/8/1846
Fulgham, James	Jane S. Harrison	2/1/1846
Forbes, Robert	Louise Roughton	11/21/1848
Forbes, Joseph	Alafair Smith	7/8/1849

112

Fort, Robert	Jane E. Moor	9/16/1849
Franklin, George	Nancy McCallister	9/13/1849
Grimes, Thomas	Jane Frederick	11/3/1829
Giles, Nathaniel	Levina Wood	2/21/1830
Giles, John	Smithy Nowell	3/11/1830
Gray, William	Delilah Renfroe	3/19/1833
Gilbert, Nathan	Eliza Scroggins	3/22/1834
Griffin, Lewis	Emeline Hall	10/12/1834
Green, Edmund	Mary Jones	2/2/1836
Garner, Joshua J.	Mary Armstrong	11/30/1837
Griffin, William	Penelope Wood	1/13/1836
Griffin, Asa	Jemima Beckum	10/18/1837
Giles, Calvin	Delphia Croom	12/27/1838
Glover, Jesse	Nancy Webster	8/3/1839
Gregory, Allen	Elizabeth Franklin	12/27/1840
Green, Gideon	Mary Ann Perry	11/23/1845
Giles, William W.	Rebecca Wood	1/13/1842
Gilbert, William	Mary Scott	1/9/1842
Goff, William E.	Ruth Orr	4/20/1843
Gilbert, Nathan	Sarah Love	3/23/1843
Gordy, Leonard	Susan Ryland	2/18/1844
Griffin, Hardy	Sarah Boatright	12/26/1844
Garrott, John	Sarah A. Little	12/5/1839
Glover, Benjamin	Matilda King	10/18/1846
Guiner, William W.	Georgiana Newsome	4/26/1846
Giles, Dr. Franklin	Camilly O'Quinn	1/12/1847
Graybill, Tully	Annabella Tucker	3/24/1846
Gray, Zachariah	Mariah Walker	5/23/1847
Gilbert, Nathan	Peggy Powell	1/5/1847
Giles, Nathaniel B.	Ann Hataway	6/15/1848
Gilmore, Alexander	Adaline Duggan	12/3/1848
Giles, John B.	Lucretia Hataway	5/24/1849
Gregory, Samuel H.	Anna Linzey	7/5/1849
Green, Gideon	Emily Covington	6/24/1850
Green, Sherrod	Martha Jones	1/21/1850
Geeslin, Samuel	Elizabeth Duggan	8/19/1851
Hawkins, Dreiory (?)	Artimicy Cook	5/1/1828
Hill, James	Ann C. Townsley	4/9/1829
Hood, James	Sarah Avera	12/10/1829
Hodges, John	Jane D. Bland	12/10/1829
Hilton, Richard	Binka Campbell	1/7/1830
Harrell, David	Dolly Martin	9/1/1830
Harrison, William D.	Margaret Sparks	10/3/1830
Horton, Daniel	Eliza Rials	12/23/1830
Heath, Daniel	Nancy Tison	7/25/1833
Humphries, Matchell B.	Sallie Horton	10/4/1832
Harrard, David	Mary Ann Fish	11/20/1833
Holt, Kitchen	Abigail Britton	9/1/1833
Hamilton, Sherrod	Juda Linnum	1/10/1833
Hall, Reuben	Mary Ann Strange	10/31/1833
Hooks, Hopewell	Sarah Harrison	4/21/1833
Hightower, Warren	Mary Martin	5/22/1834
Hatcher, William	Thany Bray	12/27/1834
Hall, William B.	Alafair Shehee	5/5/1834
		10/2/1834

Hodges, William	Ann S. Floyd	10/18/1836
Harrison, James G.	Rebecca Corsey	4/14/1836
Heath, Henry	Smithey Murphey	8/16/1836
Howell, Raford	Sealy Mathis	8/8/1836
Helton, Washington	Tabitha Bell	11/5/1836
Horton, Harrold	Martha L. Taylor	5/25/1837
Harwick, Robert A.	Eliza A. Alford	3/19/1837
Hall, William H.	Malinda Veal	10/19/1837
Hodges, Henry	Abigail Bateman	2/20/1838
Hattaway, Jackson	Betsy Coffield	9/12/1837
Hicks, William	Caroline Cooper	10/12/1837
Harvard, Stephen	Frances Atkins	1/17/1836
Harrison, James C.	Sarah Taunton	1/11/1836
Hitchcock, Turner R.	Sarah Clay	4/15/1838
Holton, John	Lucresia Daniel	1/15/1839
Hall, William	Liddy Ann New	8/15/1839
Hamilton, Morris R.	Mary Webb	6/2/1839
Hammock, George	Sarah A. Smith	1/21/1841
Hitchcock, Shadrach	Mary W. Williams	7/22/1841
Harris, Daniel	Elizabeth Murphey	1/14/1841
Hataway, Nathan	Arrenia Lingo	11/29/1841
Henderson, Nichols	Mary Durden	12/23/1841
Hartley, Raiford	Permelia Boatright	9/29/1841
Hill, William	Elizabeth Thigpen	6/13/1841
Horton, Josiah	Sarah Page	2/20/1842
Hammock, George	Sarah Ann Smith	1/24/1841
Hood, William	Margaret Renfree	2/20/1842
Hart, Samuel W.	Celia Smith	7/7/1842
Harrison, John	Sarah Frost	5/11/1843
Howard, John	Temperance May	7/2/1843
Hood, Thomas J.	Mary Ann Floyd	12/26/1843
Hodges, Redding	Sarah Renfroe	1/16/1844
Harper, William F.	Rebecca Wood	9/3/1844
Howard, Samuel	Martha Osborn	12/3/1844
Herrington, James	Penelope Amison	7/24/1845
Harris, Joseph	Emily Clay	5/24/1845
Harman, William B.	Mary F. Brown	4/29/1845
Hurst, Henry W.	Martha A. O'Quinn	1/16/1845
Haines, Alvin C.	Elizabeth McCullers	9/16/1845
Harrison, Lewis J.	Elizabeth Page	12/27/1841
Hardin, William R.	Elizabeth Smith	12/3/1846
Harrell, Jackson	Syntha Smith	8/3/1845
Harman, William N.	Rebecca Prince	12/25/1845
Hodges, Augustus G.W.	Ann Avant	12/15/1846
Hartley, Hardy	Jane Brantley	2/24/1846
Hopson, Nathaniel W.	Amanda Wicker	5/28/1846
Hicks, Henry	Ann Pate	3/10/1847
Hataway, John	Martha Lingo	2/11/1848
Hataway, James	Sarah Thigpen	9/19/1847
Heath, William	Asceamy Brady	11/4/1847
Hightower, Joshua	Mary Arline	4/2/1848
Harwick, Thomas W.	Mary Davis	Oct. 1848
Hartley, Burrel	Rebecca Shepperd	4/2/1849
Harris, Wiley	Mary A. Brown	2/18/1850
Hunt, James R.	Laura J. Lucas	9/14/1849

Hanson, Michael	Caroline King	1/2/1850
Hook, James S.	Emily Jane Harris	5/27/1850
Harris, Thomas	Mary Smith	10/1/1851
Hodges, Henry C.	Eliza R. Tucker	9/28/1851
Hooks, Curtis	Clarisa L. Walker	4/31/1851
Hart, Sam W.	Celia Smith	— — ——
Inman, Jeremiah	Mary Ann Gainor	11/11/1838
Irby, Hezekiah	May Culver	4/25/1839
Ivy, John	Martha S. Robinson	12/3/1839
Irwin, Charles A. F.	Martha Floyd	2/9/1847
Irwin, William A.	Sarah A. E. Daniel	12/7/1848
Ingram, Benjamin	Sarah J. Cone	1/19/1849
Johnson, Isaac	Elizabeth Moore	8/5/1828
Jackson, William	Nancy Chambers	2/14/1829
Jordan, Jacob	Harriett Yates	12/27/1829
Jordan, James	Mary Price	1/12/1830
Jones, Seaborn, A.H.	Adriane R. Malone	12/10/1833
Jordan, Baxter	Delania Tarver	10/27/1833
Jordan, Stephen	Elizabeth Newsome	12/21/1837
Jackson, Lewis	Alah Barron	4/27/1836
Joiner, Jared	Sarah Cordery	10/12/1837
Jones, Isaac	Elizabeth Martin	4/27/1837
Joiner, Hewett	Martha Deen	2/7/1839
Joiner, Moses	Rutha Orr	8/9/1838
Johnson, James	Frances Wilson	6/24/1838
Jordan, John	Mary Duggan	11/17/1839
Jordan, William F.	Elizabeth McRea	11/19/1839
Jones, Needham	Margaret A. Waters	106/1839
Jernigan, Jeptha	Alice Speight	12/19/1839
Jordan, Elisha W.	Mary Gilmore	12/30/1838
Joiner, William	Julia Hodges	5/3/1840
Jordan, Thomas	Elcy Adams	10/26/1840
Jackson, James	Nancy Holder	11/1/1841
Jenkins, John	Sarah Ann Hamilton	12/26/1841
Jordan, Cornelius	Harty Haines	12/26/1841
Jones, Silas	Martha W. Sessions	12/13/1843
Jackson, Frederick	Ellen Rockett	2/22/1844
Jordan, Thomas	Mary Mayo	1/7/1844
Joiner, Elias	Martha Smith	1/31/1844
Josey, Samuel	Mary Holt	10/20/1843
Jordan, Benjamin	Rebecca Murphey	10/1/1844
Jordan, Archibald	Ann Watkins	1/4/1844
Jones, William	Louisa Ryland	7/18/1845
Jones, Seaborn J.	Nancy Rains	2/11/1845
Jordan, Middleton	Sarah May	3/6/1845
Jackson, Irwin	Martha Britt	11/29/1845
Jones, Seaborn	Nancy Powell	10/14/1845
Johnson, James J.	Caroline Moye	10/22/1846
Josey, Henry	Ann P. Whitfield	12/24/1845
Jones, Seaborn N.	Rebecca N. Greer	3/16/1847
Jordan, Elsbury F.	Rebecca R. Duggan	12/17/1846
Joiner, Malachi	Ann S. Took	10/21/1847
Johnson, John A.	Eliza Wilson	7/25/1847

115

Jenkins, Martin	Lutetia Hightower	12/23/1847
Jenkins, John	Sephurge(?), Mettz	1/8/1848
Jordan, John	Jane Mayo	2/3/1848
Josey, John W.	Mary E. Adkins	4/20/1848
Jones, Allen	—— Welch	11/1/1848
Jernigan, Augustus	Victoria Warthern	Jan. 1849
——	Carolina Joiner	—/16/—
——	Sarah Braswell	1/18/—
Johnson, William C.	Elizabeth Thigpen	11/21/1837
Josey, Robert J.	Temperance Salter	12/19/1848
Jordan, James	Nancy W. Lord	11/16/1848
Jones, Silas	Mary F. Massey	2/27/1847
Jones, John	Elizabeth Adams	1/20/1850
Jones, Abel	Martha Lee Osborn	6/18/1850
Jones, Josiah	Treacy Knight	12/20/1849
Joiner, Jesse	Emeline Gregory	12/11/1849
Jordan, Laurence	Marian Brookins	7/3/1850
Jackson, Noel	Mary New	9/20/1849
Jordan, Benjamin S.	Sarah G. Smith	9/2/1851
Jackson, James Henry	Susan Roberts	9/4/1851
Jackson, Andrew W.	Mary D. Mills	12/21/1850
Joiner, Elias	Martha Ann Smith	—— —— ——
Knight, Abel	Julian Berryhill	4/26/1829
Kennedy, Leroy	D. Watkins	3/25/1830
Kindred, Kinman	Mary Massey	10/24/1833
Keller, Lewis	Malinda Watkins	1/1/1835
King, Josiah F.	Martha C. Knight	10/15/1835
Key, Sion	Rachael B. Tison	4/21/1836
Kennedy, Archibald	Sarah Robison	3/6/1845
Killebrew, John C.	Sarah A. Collins	1/21/1847
Kenner, Jordan	Mariah Keener	1848 or 183
Kelly, John	Mary Register	11/4/1838
Kennedy, Thomas J.	Winford Williams	12/12/1839
Kingary, Abraham	Lucia Ann Moreman	4/30/1839
Kicklighter, Fred	Mary Ann Hannan	7/25/1840
Kennedy, Samuel W.	Martha Ann Sellers	3/10/1844
Kennedy, Alexander	Martha A. Cox	9/27/1846
Killebrew, Hezekiah	Martha Cumming	1/7/1847
Kitrell, Noah	Isabella Jane Massey	5/27/1847
King, William	Catherine Hanson	2/3/1847
Keen, Willis	Margaret Scott	11/7/1848
Kinman, Alston	Rebecca Williams	9/5/1850
Killingsworth, M. C.	Mary A. Barge	8/21/1849
Kitchen, Boze B.	Nancy D. Harrison	10/19/1849
King, William T.	Rhodah D. Whitfield	2/16/1851
Laton, James	Delphia Boatright	1/3/1838
Lord, Wheatley	Mary Shields	2/7/1830
Little, Gray	Nancy Johnson	12/15/1829
Lancaster, James A.	Emeline Sinquefield	11/14/1830
Law, Samuel	Elizabeth Barwick	12/19/1833
Lambert, Alfred	Martha A. Collins	2/20/1834
Lord, Leandy	Letha Barwick	11/6/1836
Lord, William	Matilda Barwick	9/2/1838

Laton, Hillery	Elizabeth Wise	12/4/1836
Lamb, Quinny	May Whiting	12/12/1838
Lewis, James E.	Harriett Scott	9/13/1838
Lord, John	Mary Green	1/13/1842
Love, Amos	Debby Sellers	10/3/1841
Low, Samuel M.	Elizabeth Sherling	4/13/1843
Lawrence, Newton	Nancy R. Hicklin	11/18/1847
Langmade (?), John S.	Eliza E. Kendrick	8/10/1843
Langmade, Edward	Ann D. Kendrick	6/22/1843
Law, Samuel -	Rebecca Forbs	5/26/1844
Langford, James L.	Mary M. Dales	11/26/1844
Lindey, William	Sarah A. Holder	10/7/1846
Leverett, Daniel M.	Martha S. Achord	9/6/1846
Lang, Henry C.	Nancy Davis	11/25/1846
Lingo, Peter	Margaret Terrell	5/9/1846
Linzy, John	Sarah A. Franklin	1/21/1847
Lloyd, Drury	Housora Tompkins	9/22/1849
Logan, Mathew	Winney Cungame	5/3/1849
Lyons, John	Louisa Franklin	10/15/1850
Lawrence, Sherrod	Mary Brown	6/8/1851
Lord, Ailsbury	Sarah D. Brook	3/23/1851
Lord, Solomon	Mary A. J. Lord	2/10/1852
Laton, James	Zelphia Boatright	1/3/1838
McBeth, James	Mary Ann Beckham	3/11/1829
Mathews, John	Nancy Horton	4/17/1829
Massey, Corde	Sarah Moore	6/7/1829
Miller, Jordan	Delpha Gay	12/3/1829
Mott, Joseph	Penelope Cato	3/2/1830
McVay, Walter	Phoebe Laton	6/15/1830
Mayo, Benjamin	Alaphen Watkins	2/9/1830
Miller, John	Luezer Nowells	9/2/1830
McElvay, George R.	Catherine Rutherford	12/22/1830
Mayo, William	Rachel Smith	12/22/1830
Miller, Jordan	Julian Arnold	1/20/1831
McVey, David	Mary McMullen	12/11/1832
Hoy, Isaac	Letticia Frobs	12/12/1833
Meek, Howell	Elizabeth Fulgham	10/22/1833
May, Reuben	Susannah Cato	12/20/1832
Massey, Kinchell W.	Nancy Irwin	1/21/1834
McGehee, Nathan	Harriett Brantley	10/4/1836
May, Joseph H.	Sidney Howard	12/22/1836
Martin, Henry	Martha Arnold	12/11/1834
Moody, Enoch S.	Elizabeth Marchman	12/31/1834
McVey, Yancy	Jane Duke	11/19/1835
Miller, Lee R.	Martha Smith	7/27/1837
Morrell, Enoch C. S.	Mary A. Whiddon	7/2/1837
McCoy, William	Jane Ranes	2/20/1834
McBride, Thomas J.	Elizabeth Floyd	1/23/1838
Mayo, James J.	Caroline Kendrick	4/20/1836
Martin, James	Milla Oliver	5/5/1836
McLendon, Burrell	Chloe Walters	2/25/1839
Murkeson, George M.	Elizabeth Pierce	12/25/1837
Meeks, William	Sarah Sanders	10/11/1838
Matthews, Reuben A.	Mary Coffield	3/22/1839
Miller, William	Elizabeth Logue	10/31/1837

Merrell, Alderman	Sarah McGearman	3/30/1839
Monroe, Dr. Edward W.	Julia Stanton	11/21/1838
Mills, Mathew	Sarah Griffin	2/25/1841
Miller, Thomas J.	Patience Smith	12/10/1840
Myers, William	Ellen Pate	11/1/1840
McNair, John A.	Arabella Johns	2/21/1841
McIntyre, Thomas	Sarah C. Floyd	1/7/1841
McEwen, William P.	Rutha Sheppard	11/17/1830
Moody, David	Martha Corbet	2/2/1842
McGowan, Jinsy	Jane Dancy	12/13/1841
McBride, William G.	Lutitia A. Greenwood	1/3/1844
Head, James	Frances Johnson	6/2/1844
Moody, Jefferson	Mary Askew	10/5/1843
Malpass, Kennon	Sarah J. Cheely	2/13/1844
Morris, John	Ann Brantley	4/7/1845
Mills, William	Mary Kindman	9/25/1845
Moye, George W.	Susan Barwick	11/2/1845
McMillen, Adolphus	Gelina Bateman	1/11/1846
McWilliams, Thomas N.	Lydia Orr	4/5/1842
Mimms, William	Tibitha W. Woods	2/9/1843
Mill, Jesse	Tempe May	11/5/1839
Massey, James J.	Cealy Elkins	5/22/1845
Mayo, Dempsey W.	Martha Britt	5/10/1846
Miller, Charles	Mary Grove	9/7/1845
Miller, Bright	Grace C. Williams	1/20/1846
Mims, Abner	Pennina Tull	3/23/1847
Meyers, William A.	Sarah Moye	2/24/1847
Mayo, William W.	Sarah A. Adams	5/23/1847
McAfee, Jordan	Elizabeth A. Arnold	12/29/1847
Moye, John R.	Mary A. Donalson	1/30/1848
McConnel, Clark	Hannah A. Warthen	11/15/1847
Meak, Washington	Dardina Brown	12/23/1847
Moore, Lemuel W. H.	Sarah S. Johnson	9/14/1848
May, Lumber (?) J.	Emily Cato	10/24/1848
Morrison, Angus A.	Penelope F. Cato	12/19/1848
Murphy, Henry	Frances A. Trussill	2/6/1849
Morgan, Jesse F.	Amarintha L. Hines	8/28/1849
McVay, Wiley C.	Lucy E. Robison	1/6/1850
Moody, Enoch	Sarry Ann Underwood	12/18/1848
Morris, William	Mahaley Williams	4/26/1849
Nowells, Henry	Elizabeth Long	12/20/1829
Newsome, David R.	Datha Raines (Dartha?)	2/2/1837
New, Ezra	Lucinda Wester	6/26/1838
New, John	Nancy Harrison	7/29/1841
Newsome, Solomon	Eliza Batts	4/28/1841
Newsome, Joedy	Mary Ann Brown	12/1/1844
Northington, Jesse A.	Permelia Renfroe	4/3/1845
Noble, John J.	Mary Paradise	1/22/1843
Norris, Thomas W.	Elizabeth Donalson	9/22/1846
Newsom, Hezekiah	Juliann Caroline Brown	10/29/1846
Newman, Mark	Ann H. Ainsworth	12/18/1849
Norris, Robert C.	Martha J. Armstrong	3/3/1850
New, Stephen F.	Elizabeth Adkins	3/24/1850

118

O'Quain, John	Rachel Giles	12/17/1846
Orr, William	Margaret A. Warren	11/9/1828
Oliver, Asa	Elizabeth Wilson	10/12/1829
Oliver, John L.	Tecy Rye	1/18/1836
Odam, John R.	Mary Taylor	12/26/1844
Odam, John R.	Martha McVey	7/28/1833
Orr, Thomas A.	Mary Hart	3/24/1842
O'Quain, Daniel	Lucy Giles	12/17/1846
Outlaw, Jordan F.	Mary E. Peacock	12/21/1847
Orr, Freeman	Jane Darby	1/23/1849
Paradise, James	Mary Parker	6/17/1828
Pate, Redding	Elizabeth Miller	6/21/1829
Pope, Wiley	Martha Bryan	12/6/1833
Page, John M. E.	Martha Kelly	6/9/1833
Price, Moore	Polly Maxwell	8/20/1837
Price, Littleberry	Elizabeth Frost	1/28/1834
Pitman, John	Nancy Renfroe	1/19/1837
Peacock, GreenB.	Margaret Maxwell	10/20/1837
Price, Nathan	Nancy Jackson	9/17/1839
Powell, Alfred	Winifred Whitaker	3/9/1836
Price, Cullen	Mary Sheppard	12/4/1838
Pounnelle, John	Mary Davis	12/31/1838
Page, Solomon	Elizabeth Scoggins	7/14/1839
Price, Warren	Martha Ely	7/26/1840
Powell, John Jr.	Mary Young	1/11/1841
Price, Joseph	Mary A. M. Prince	1/13/1842
Perry, Elijah	Appy May	1/14/1843
Purce, Philip B.	Mary Peacock	9/30/1841
Phillips, James	Elizabeth Griffin	7/1/1841
Prince, Sylvanus W.	Ann Newsom	2/10/1842
Powers, Virgil	Ann E. Jenkins	5/26/1842
Pearce, John	Martha Cox	11/9/1843
Pitman, Pheuby	Temperance Wood	10/2/1843
Pope, James	Mary E. Page	5/26/1844
Page, John D.	Nancy Wilson	1/27/1845
Price, Moore	Mary Maxwell	8/20/1837
Pevey, Green B.	Martha A. Vinson	10/30/1839
Peacock, Uriah	Mary M. Norris	6/11/1845
Price, Rice	Mary Whitfield	12/27/1844
Partridge, Payton	Milly Carter	1/24/1847
Peacock, Zachariah	Nancy A. Smith	7/1/1845
Peacock, Lewis	Emeline Benson	12/15/1846
Pate, Patrick Y.	Martha Moye	3/31/1847
Powell, Alfred	Mary Oliver	1/10/1847
Prichard, Thomas	Malinda Sheppard	4/6/1847
Page, John D.	Mary Rawls	4/10/1847
Peace, William	Nancy Anderson	7/27/1847
Perkins, Jackson	Beady Durden	12/16/1847
Pournelle, William F.	Lydia M. Brookins	2/14/1846
Pitman, William B.	Sarah J. Brown	11/30/1847
Pace, John C.	Mary E. O'Quin	7/25/1848
Page, Allen A.	Elizabeth Webb	5/30/1849
Pournelle, George W.	Martha A. Ashley	2/25/1851

Rogers, Wiley	Martha Peterson	11/4/1830
Register, Noel	D. Williamson	2/3/1831
Robinson, Thomas R.	Mrs. Sarah Orr Howard	12/17/1836
Renfroe, Nathaniel	Easter Hust	12/15/1836
Rocket, Richard	Ellen Spears	10/25/1836
Renfroe, William	Lady Renfroe	5/26/1836
Rutherford, John B.	Mrs. Arena Smith	4/15/1836
Robison, Harmon D.	Alley Tootle	12/9/1838
Ray, John	Elizabeth Rushing	9/13/1838
Riddle, William C.	Senia Ann Brown	5/21/1840
Rains, Washington	Nancy Crafton	2/10/1839
Robertson, John N.	Sarah L. Parker	12/27/1840
Rains, William	Christiana Eason	2/4/1841
Rushing, John	Winifred Pool	12/19/1839
Raines, Richard	Emily Strange	8/15/1843
Register, Jesse	Georgeann Stokes	5/9/1843
Register, John	Sarah Smith	5/9/1843
Register, John N.	Harriett Williamson	1/18/1842
Rains, Griffin	Nancy Bland	2/4/1844
Renfroe, Everett	Mary Procter	6/31/1843
Rogers, Theophilus	Ann Eliza Brown	11/28/1844
Rogers, Hezekiah	Matilda Giles	12/19/1844
Ray, James	Jane Rushing	1/2/1840
Renfroe, Jared	Nancy Hood	2/24/1846
Rogers, Robert Y.	Martha L. Greer	2/11/1847
Register, William K.	Lucinda Sanders	3/11/1847
Rillingsworth,F. W.	Nancy Lord	10/17/1847
(the above could be Killingsworth)		
Rudisill, John W.	Martha Pournelle	12/14/1847
Roberson, Green R.	Almeda Bridger	9/2/1848
Roughton, Albert L.	Mary A. Moye	2/21/1849
Rachels, Joseph	Nancy Daniel	2/15/1849
Rawlings, Frederick	Susan Tarbutton	2/19/1850
Roberts, Green	Margaret A. Sellers	3/26/1849
Roughton, John W. M.	Cherry A. E. Moye	12/25/1849
Roberson, Rufus A.	Charlotte M.Hall(or Hale)	11/14/1850
Rodgers, Levi H.	Martha Hust	12/23/1850
Rogers, J. F.	Elizabeth A. Williams	1/22/1851
Reaves, Joseph	Catherine Smith	1/31/1850
Roberts, John W.	Sarah A. Ross	7/1/1850
Roughton, Zachariah	Sarah A. Bynum	1/27/1850
Sparks, Thomas N.	Nancy McCollins	2/19/1829
Smith, Patrick	Sarah Bryan	7/16/1829
Schnell, Barnaby	Catherine McCain	9/24/1829
Stubbs, Gabriell	Gracy Collins	11/19/1829
Stone, William	Elizabeth Powell	4/15/1834
Spurlock, Samuel	Mahaly Bedgood	12/4/1829
Summer, Jethro	Jinsey Phillips	4/4/1830
Sneed, William	Ann Speight	2/11/1830
Spann, John	Matilda Seal	2/26/1830
Sterling, William	Nancy Hay	1/1/1833
Staunton, William	Elizabeth Beckham	6/2/1833
Smith, Phineas	Sarah A. Price	8/28/1834
Sammonds, James B.	Winney McVey	2/15/1836

Sheppard, David	Temperance Lightfoot	2/5/1835
Salter, Ephriam	Elizabeth Langford	2/17/1837
Smith, James	Milla M. Landon	4/27/1837
Smith, Thomas R.	Rebecca Register	6/11/1837
Salter, Toliver	Sarah Brown	11/20/1837
Salter, Thomas S.	Nancy Mayo	11/15/1836
Shirling, Richard	Vicy Barnes	9/6/1838
Skrine, Benjamine	Va. A. Davis	4/19/1839
Sanders, James	Eliza Hanson	3/27/1839
Smith, James R.	Mary A. Hunt	11/10/183-
Smith, William	Mary Hutchinson	9/30/18—
Swint, John	Jane Pool	12/3/1840
Stone, John	Martha A. Glenn	2/27/1842
Salter, William G.	Charlotte M. Tarver	12/2/1841
Strange, John J.	Mary Ann Smith	12/21/1842
Smith, Peter P.	Nancy Price	7/29/1842
Smith, James	Amaline Rains	4/27/1837
Snider, Thomas B.	Irena Horton	4/23/1843
Sheppard, Charles H.	Elizabeth A. McCullers	4/13/1843
Smith, William F.	Malindy I. Williamson	5/17/1843
Sherling, James	Alafair Fowler	4/21/1843
Sanders, Jeremiah	Martha Smith	2/8/1844
Smith, Jonathan	Eliza Brady	1/22/1844
Sellers, Daniel	Catherine Sellers	7/11/1844
Smith, William	Elizabeth Hart	1/10/1844
Salter, John N.	Mary Thigpen	5/13/1844
Smith, William	Asena Brantley	12/5/1844
Smith, Elijah M.	Martha A. Garner	1/27/1845
Smith, William L.	Elizabeth Ann Elkins	10/23/1845
Sheppard, John	Dolly Emeline Tompkins	4/3/1845
Smith, William A.	Sarah Webb	11/27/1845
Sheppard, Daniel	Tilly Mathis	10/13/1844
Smith, J. F.	Pamealann Peacock	10/9/1846
Stephenson, John A.	Sarah Daniel	11/24/1845
Sparks, Morgan	Emily Collins	10/19/1845
Smith, Thomas B.	Mary N. Smith	12/3/1845
Strange, John J.	Penelope A. Davis	4/22/1847
Smith, Thomas S.	Edy Elkins	2/4/1847
Strange, Thomas C.	Elephair Cox	2/4/1847
Sheppard, Charles H.	Sarah J. McCuller	5/4/1847
Sherling, James H.	Martha Fowler	5/23/1847
Sheppard, Zachariah	Julia A. Page	10/7/1847
Sheppard, Robert J.	Mary Bland	12/2/1851
Smith, Cato H.	Mary Morrell	10/17/1847
Scott, Winfield	Lydia McAfee	3/19/1848
Sellers, William James	Mary Pope	9/24/1848
Sherling, James Sr.	Sarah Williamson	10/11/1848
Sheppard, Green L.	Nancy Page	1/5/1848
Smith, William K.	Caroline King	5/20/1849
Snider, Thomas B.	Mary G. Veal	3/18/1849
Stanley, Samuel B.	Celia A. Giles	10/6/1850
Shirey, B—	Elizabeth Brantley	5/14/1850
Saffold, Isham H.	Martha A. L. Prescott	10/24/1849
Smith, James S.	Sarah Calhoun	3/16/1849
Smith, John H.	Elizabeth Tarbutton	6/7/1849

121

Smith, Henry	Marian Logan	9/9/1849
Scott, Thomas	Rebecca Tootle	10/9/1849
Stephens, Charnie	Eliza W. Parker	12/28/1850
Shirling, William F.	Susan Wiggins	7/17/1851
Sheppard, William	Martha Sheppard	12/13/1851
Tompkins, Samuel	Emeline Sanders	2/8/1829
Tanner, Thomas	Mary Ann Williamson	2/5/1829
Tucker, Elijah	Lucy Eckles	12/17/1829
Tanner, Isaac	Mary King	9/14/1834
Tennille, Francis	Ann B. Jordan	8/16/1836
Took, David	Phoebe Womble	5/20/1836
Towsand, Aaron	Feddy Lyons	7/20/1837
Taylor, John	Mary Meeks	9/16/1838
Tanner, William H.	Rebecca Adams	12/6/1838
Thompson, John P.	Sarah Hall	12/26/1838
Thigpen, John	Elizabeth A. Mims	1/2/1840
Tarbutton, Joseph	Rebecca Kennedy	8/4/1840
Taylor, William R.	Gracy Ann Hust	12/19/1840
Taunton, Eli	Marie Sumerlin	1/20/18—
Tompkins, Burrell	Mary Lord	10/22/1840
Tanner, Franklin	Mary Ann Jane Brown	3/11/1841
Tootle, Shadrack	Rebecca Hardin	1/3/1842
Taylor, William	Permilla O. Dupree	8/18/1842
Taunton, Newsom	Elizabeth Amison	8/10/1843
Tompkins, William P.	Mary Ann E. Sheppard	7/18/1843
Tanner, Mitchell	Emily Parker	3/26/1843
Thigpen, Green	Mary Nobles	6/2/1844
Talbot, Brabazor (?)	Caroline Cumming	9/19/1844
Tompkins, Francis	Sarah Sheppard	12/12/1845
Tennille, Francis D.	Catalina Warthen	8/7/1845
Tanner, Solomon	Elizabeth Tompkins	9/24/1846
Taylor, James R.	Olivia Bryant	1/22/1846
Tucker, John R.	Mary A. Cox	4/2/1846
Tompkins, James M.	Elizabeth Donaldson	5/14/1846
Tharp, John	Mary Wilson	5/2/1847
Tanner, David	Sarah Brown	11/11/1847
Tanner, Miles	Catherine Jordan	6/4/1848
Tompkins, Robert	Elizabeth Lord	8/27/1848
Thigpen, James R.	Frances Womble	4/19/1849
Turner, Ladock	Sarah Rawlings	12/13/1848
Thornton, Azariah B.	Druscilla B. Wood	2/6/1849
Thomas, William	Rebecca Strange	8/22/1850
Thigpen, Jesse	Lucretia Meeks	8/21/1849
Tanner, David	Barbara Hodges	11/5/1850
Tanner, Mathew	Martha A. C. Snell	2/7/1851
Umphreys, Mitchell B.	Martha Horton	3/21/1841
Umphy, James	Elizabeth Cone	4/8/1841
Ventress, Francis	Elizabeth H. Low	1/30/1831
Veel, John T.	Sarah J. Hall	2/14/1833
Vaun, James	Kesiah Cunningham	9/5/1836

Veal, Burrell	Julia A. Gladden	2/1/1849
Vinson, David H.	Barbara H. Hill	3/7/1850
Vining, Thomas	Mary E. Posey	1/3/1850
Van, Calvin	Jane Bedgood	4/10/1845
Wood, Jared	Elizabeth Gary	12/20/1828
Walker, David	Theny Barron	1/25/1829
Wood, Henry	Fanny Kingman	2/24/1829
Williams, Daniel	Sarah Tootle	3/1/1829
Wright, Wingfield	Elizabeth Forehand	9/23/1829
Wallace, William	Rachel Holt	9/28/1829
Wiggins, Joshua	Martha Dorch	11/19/1829
Walker, William H.	Clarissa R. Williams	12/31/1829
Wicker, Alfred	Lavina Holton	9/2/1830
Whiddon, Hampton	Elena Sheppard	12/11/1830
Whittle, James	Harriet G. Renfroe	8/1/18—
Williams, Daniel	Rebecca Blackburn	2/27/1837
Webb, Crawford	Martha Miller	12/24/1834
Wilcher, Edmund V.	Elizabeth Jones	10/15/1837
Watkins, Mitchell	Patience McCandless	12/26/1837
Williams, Moses	Nancy Taylor	3/18/1834
Webster, Lewis	Rebecca Chivers	11/4/1834
Watkins, Bryant	Elizabeth Mayo	10/31/1833
Welch, Washington	Temperance Sparks	12/20/1836
Whitaker, John B.	Frances A. Pippin	4/22/1835
Wright, John B.	Mourning Smith	1/12/1837
Wood, Henry H.	Mary Gilbert	12/28/1836
Ware, Arthur G.	Nancy Jordan	12/13/1838
Whiddon, Dempsey	Mary Wise	9/20/1838
Williams, Robert	Phoebe Horne	2/25/1838
Wright, Thomas	Holland Webb	9/29/1837
Wood, Thomas	Martha Chester	12/13/1838
Wilson, John	Miley Martin	1/4/1838
Wilcher, Edmund	Elizabeth Jones	10/15/1837
Welch, Asa	Emily Johnson	1/28/1838
Wells, John R.	Cherry Ann Joiner	12/6/1838
Williams, Samuel	Matilda Hoye	5/27/1838
Wiggins, William	Emily Jordan	3/17/1839
Williamson, Mathew C.	Maria Harwick	2/3/1840
Williams, John	Mary Johnson	6/30/1840
White, Robert	Clarisa Lumlee	4/17/1840
Wood, James H.	Angeline Howard	3/21/1841
Welch, Allen H.	Elizabeth Wiggins	5/11/1841
Wilson, Robert L.	Martha A. C. Cummins	9/9/1841
Walden, Kenon	Nancy Calhoun	5/22/1840
Watkins, William	Mary Ann Bishop	12/16/1841
Walker, Seaborn B.	Susannah Wicker	9/30/1841
Williams, Godfrey	Mary E. Price	9/26/1841
Walker, Marshall	Keziah Vinson	2/15/1842

Wise, John	Elizabeth Boatright	3/20/1842
Williamson, Richmond N.	Nancy A. Mayo	8/31/1843
Whiddon, Eli B.	Winifred C. Bailey	9/24/1843
Watson, William J.	Jane Thorp	3/26/1843
Watkins, William	Elizabeth Clay	3/3/1844
Williams, George	Jane Kersey	2/27/1844
Whitfield, Sheldon	Juliann Bedgood	11/20/1843
Welch, Warren	Almeda Ainsworth	7/14/1844
Webb, William A.	Elizabeth Martin	2/9/1845
Warthen, Lovard	Elvira L. Brown	2/9/1845
Walker, William W.	Penelope B. Cone	12/24/1844
Wood, James N.	Sarah A. Fisher	2/6/1845
Welch, William	Ann E. Register	2/19/1845
Wamble, Kinchin	Sarah W. Tennille	12/3/1840
Walker, John	Elizabeth Butcher	7/15/18—
Williams, John	Joicy Collins	12/14/1845
Williams, Jesse	Eliza Wamble	11/5/1845
Wood, Benjamin	Ann B. Darby	9/3/1846
Wicker, Nathaniel	Emeline Lewis	10/29/1846
Wood, William	Sarah Darby	1/22/1846
Webb, Benjamin	Trecy Mathis	12/6/1846
Webb, John Calvin	Ann Mariah Mathews	1/31/1847
Whitfield, Napoleon B.	Martha Hicks	2/18/1847
Whitfield, Charles	Adeline Hicks	2/18/1847
Walden, Ira	Elefair Sheppard	11/3/1847
Williamson, Mathew C.	Mary E. Smith	4/6/1848
Webb, John C.	Almira Rabutton	5/2/1848
Wicker, Ansel W.	Melvina Mills	11/16/1848
Willingham, Memory P.	Nancy Hardison	9/2/1850
Walker, William D.	Eliza A. Barnes	12/5/1850
Woodburn, John A.	Harriett C. Wood	2/6/1850
Willis, Jeremiah	Nancy A. Dorch	12/7/1850
Young, David	Elizabeth Jones	10/6/1836
Young, Andrew J.	Martha G. Prince	4/25/1844
Young, William Green	Elizabeth Jenkins	2/25/1844
		2/25/1844

The following is a list of the names of children returned
to me by the Justices of Peace as entitled to a participation in the poor school fund of the County of Washington
for the year 1835--their tuition paid for out of said fund:

MALES   Age

Irwin Lumley	10	William H. Howard	12
Daniel Lumley	12	Samuel Howard	10
Jeremiah Womble	14	David L. Howard	8
Egbert Womble	9	William Smith	8
Thial Holton	8	James Smith	10
Stephen Holton	10	Isaac Smith	12
William Williams	11	Benjamin Williams	11
Thomas Wicker	13	Isaac Jonson	11
James Howard	12	Lorenzo D. Stanley	10
Hezekiah Vincent	11	Alexander Duke	11
William R. Mills	9	Isiah Jones	8
Green Young	8	Abel Jones	10
Jared Johnson	13	John Martin	13
William Smith	14	Freeman Jonson	11
James Smith	11	Washington Ridgin	13
———, Smith	9		
George Smith	8	FEMALES	
Thomas Brantley	11		
James Brantley	13	Nancy Wicker	9
I. M. Brantley	8	Martha Howard	10
Benjamin Brantley	9	Missouri Howard	8
Arthur Dupree	10	Mary Jonson	9
James Dupree	12	Elizabeth Jonson	11
John Dupree	8	Mary Young	10
Franklin Elliott	9	Sarah Williams	11
James Elliott	11	Charlotte Dupree	13
Anson Trawick	14	Rhoda Pope	11
Bryant Trawick	12	Mary Trawick	12
Angus Lucas	8	Julia Lucas	10
James Wicker	11	Charity Wicker	11
Ansel Wicker	9	Catherine Morrison	8
David Vincent	11	Martha Morrison	9
Alexander Morrison	13	Edy Bridges	14
Joseph Morrison	11	Nancy Bridges	10
Frederick Burriss	12	Beedy Burriss	14
William Burriss	10	Mary Peacock	15
Uriah Peacock	10	Mary Tison	13
Alfred Young	14	Elizabeth Tyson	11
Rabun Croom	9	Rachel Croom	13
Malachi Young	10	Adaline Croom	13
George Croom	11	Martha Croom	9
Russell Knight	19	Nancy Moore	11

Jane Moore	9	Martha Duke	12
Margaret Renfro	8	Mary Duke	10
Sally Ridgin	10	Martha Jones	9
Nancy Smith	13	Nancy Jones	11
Mary Smith	11	Seaney Fort	13
Amanda Echols	9	Jane Donalson	9
Sarah A. Williams	8	Rebecca J. Cox	10
Mary Young	11	Mary F. Cox	9
Mary Jonson	10	Elizabeth A. Arnold	11
Eliza Jonson	12		
Melvina Barnes	9		
Mary Stanley	8		
Jane Duke	8		

* * * * * * * * * *

The following names are the children schooled by the Poor School Fund Washington County 1832:

Name	Age		
David Chambers	8	Thomas King	11
Willis Chambers	10	William King	9
Henry Johnson	10	Benajah King	13
John Carter	9	William Purser	12
Asam (?) McCandliss	7	John Purser	10
Esair McCandliss	7	Alfred Purser	8
Ezre McCandliss	11	Middle (?) Haygood	11
Hiram Williams	13	Francis Blount	9
Godfrey Williams	10	Benjamin Cox	14
Walter Williams	8	Virgil Hotton	11
Norman Williams	12	Joshua Fuller	9
William T. Scott	9	Stephen Fuller	—
James Chambers	12	Blanay H. King	10
John Chambers	9	Thomas Dickins	9
John Tison	11	Hansill Dickins	8
Gideon Tison	9	William Anderson	9
William Fountain	8	Stephen Swilley	8
John Fountain	10	Daniel Moody	13
Biar Fountain	12	Morgan Kemp	10
Wiley Costan	11	Eli Messie	9
William Ezzell	10	Franklin Murkinson	8
George Boatright	9	George Herndon	9
Jefferson Hood	8	John Edy	14
Reason Hood	10	John Anderson	13
Morgan Tanner	9	Alex Duke	9
Vincent Tanner	11	James Sherlin	8
David Mills	9	John E. Sherlin	10
James Cox	8	Hardy Huse	9
John Cox	10	G.W.B. Sanders	13

H. Morris	13	Raford Hartley	9
Edmund Thompson	13	Burrell Hartley	11
Middleton Jordan	13	Hardy Hartley	13
James Helton	12	J. F. Coffield	10
John Cambell	6	William F. Coffield	8
Horgan Sparks	15	John A. Wicker	7
Freeman Johnson	13	James B. Coffield	7
Richard Hotton	14	Jeremiah Sanders	14
Jordan Womble	10	James Sanders	12
Henry Butcher	12	Jackson Perkins	13
Richard Andrews	8	Jesse Crawford	14
William Wilson	11	William Crawford	8
Ervin Lumly	10	Oliver Braddy	14
Daniel Lumley	12	A. J. Braddy	10
Jackson Craft	8	J. T. Braddy	8
James Smith	11	Thomas Calhoon	14
Robert Perkins	8	William Calhoon	12
Phillip Perkins	10	Raymond	8
Ephriam Salter	9	James Hay	9
Thomas Salter	7	Green Young	17
John Salter	11	A. J. Young	15
George Salter	13	George Young	13
N. B. Giles	10	James Young	11
John Dickens	11	Bentley Stewart	14
Thomas Calhoon	14	Alexander Stewart	12
Horgan Kelly	13	J. B. Stewart	8
Mitchell Tanner	10	John G. Rogers	10
John Jackson	16	Edmund Thompson	10
William F. Adams	16	Horgan Sparks	14
John Holt	10	Nathan Renfro	18
Esau Holt	8	Joseph Renfro	12
John Wise	11	Hardy Hughes	14
James King	9	Green Barnes	14
Henry King	11	Franklin Barnes	12
Morgan Howard	10	David Barnes	16
Samuel Howard	12	Jared Whiddon	10
James Howard	8	Eli Whiddon	12
James Wicker	8	William Barrick	10
Thomas Wicker	13	Dempsey Whiddon	11
David Vinson	9	Samuel Bedgood	17
Isham Nowell	11	John Bedgood	14
Augustus Nowell	9	Francis Shepherd	10
Hardeman Smith	10	Warren Jackson	11
Isaac Smith	12	Henry T. Hudson	13
Peter Bray	9		
Benjamin Bridges	12		
Alfred Young	11	Edy Ivy	10
John Williams	14	Elizabeth Elkins	9
Jacob Tison	13	Edy Elkins	11
Daniel Tison	11	Celia Elkins	13
Noan Tison	10	Nancy King	14
Frederick Burns	10	Rachel Holt	9
William Burns	8	S. Ivy	10
James Coston	10	S. Dudley	9
William Coston	8	M. Barnes	8
Ansel Wicker	10	M. Colwell	14

Name		Name	
M. Whiddon	10	M. Taylor	13
S. Whiddon	12	M. Perry	10
R. A. Whiddon	10	N. Howard	8
S. Whiddon	12	W. Howard	10
A. A. Whiddon	8	S. A. Howard	12
E. Sherlin	9	M. E. Howard	14
S. Sherlin	11	C. Howard	9
J. Duke	9	R. Duke	11
M. Duke	7	T. Womble	10
D. Renfro	11	E. Craft	8
H. Renfro	13	S. Craft	10
H. Renfro	15	C. Lumly	13
N. Rogers	10	H. White	10
M. Price	10	Mar. White	8
L. Helton	16	S. A. Butcher	11
E. Crawford	12	S. Sanders	15
L. Braddy	12	N. Thigpen	10
A. Braddy	9	H. A. Thigpen	6
Z. Calhoon	12	M. Jordan	11
H. Calhoon	10	M. Rogers	13
N. Calhoon	14	E. Saunders	17
J. Calhoon	9	N. Duke	9
S. Stewart	10	A. Smiley	8
B. Giles	7	N. Anderson	11
L. Sanders	8	M. Murkinson	12
M. Samders	6	H. Todd	13
S. Griffin	15	N. King	10
H. Giles	11	H. King	12
L. Giles	6	J. Haygood	10
S. Hartley	9	E. Blount	11
C. Hartley	11	F. Blount	13
S. Hartley	13	N. Blount	9
H. Young	9	N. A. McCoy	14
H. Williams	10	M. A. White	12
H. Tison	11	S. A. Holton	9
M. Forbes	9	P. Renfro	13
B. Burriss	12	N. King	10
N. Bridges	13	H. McDaniel	8
H. Powell	10	Mary McDaniel	10
N. Anderson	11	C. McDaniel	12
C. Wicker	9	J. McDaniel	14
S. A. Little	11	J. Hood	10
S. Nowell	13	M. Carter	8
H. A. Odom	13	J. Carter	10
B. King	9	E. Carter	11
H. King	11	J. Davis	13
H. Jackson	17	V. Davis	9
H. Jackson	10	A. Davis	11
E. Hetts	13	H. Edge	8
E. Hetts	11	V. Edge	10
J. Hetts	9	V. Fountain	11
E. Tanner	10	H. Fountain	11
D. Taylor	11	S. Fountain	13

P. Boatright	9	M. Horton	10
L. Boatright	8	S. Horton	12
L. Jenkins	9	L. Scott	10
D. Jenkins	11	P. McCandliss	12
W. Carlisle	10	M. Williams	10
E. McAfee	9	L. Johnson	13
E. Corbit	10	W. Corbit	10
M. Corbit	9	H. Corbit	12
E. Tison	11	B. Tison	8
M. Tison	13	M. Tison	10
S. Hamilton	11	N. Tison	12

This schedule contains the children returned by the Justices of Peace as entitled to a participation in the Poor School Fund and taught and paid for out of said funds as will fully appear by a reference to a statement of receipts and explanation hereunto attached. Given under my hand this 16th day of November 1832.

Sherrod Sessions
Trustee Poor School Fund

129

WASHINGTON COUNTY TAX DEFAULTERS

The tax digests in which the following lists of tax defaulters were included have been lost or were burned in courthouse fires.

The custom in early Georgia was to publish in the local or nearest newspaper a list of those who were in default of paying their taxes for the current year, and it is these published accounts of defaulters which have survived.

There were, of course, many reasons why people were in default; travel was difficult to the county seats where the courthouses were located; many of the tax payers had moved but were still being carried on the tax rolls, etc.

It is difficult to establish the exact location of a person's land from the early tax digests. The militia districts within the county were also the tax districts, and the captains of the militia districts changed almost every year. Therefore, when a man's name appears in a certain captain's district one year and in another captain's district the next year, it does not mean that the man moved, simply that someone else had been elected or appointed captain of the same district.

TAX DEFAULTERS
1791

Capt. Hagan's Dist.

Joel Chivers

Capt. McDowell's Dist.

Josiah Swearingen
William Wauls
Robert Jackson
James McMullen
John Quails

Capt. Whatley's Dist.

Josiah Gay
Joseph Carson
William Hall
James Sims
Isaac Brown
Albright Averitt
William Tannet

Abel Johnston
John Numon
Edward Carpter
Archibald Averitt

Capt. Faust's Dist.

Philip Pitman
Nicholas Welch
Lemmons Wesley
James Sartain
Bradley Hall
John Swilley
Joseph Chaplin
Edward Hambleton
John Crother
Thomas Mikell
Edward Carrigan
Zachariah Buntery
Gideon Thompson

Capt. Smith's Dist.

William Irwin
Thomas Airs
Benjamin Wood
William Hall

Capt. William's Dist.

Benjamin Johnson
John Tompkins
Enoch Penson
Israel Smith

Capt. Irwin's Dist.

William Dennard
James Harris
John Taber
Edward Young
Jesse Pollet
Alexander Irwin
John Simmons
Voll Harden
Reubin Dickson
James Robertson
Samuel Langdon

Capt; Stokes' Dist.

Robert Hemphill
John Smith
John Swilley
Archibald Aylett
Isaac Lafearse
James Vessells
William Smith
Solomon Spears
John Newsom
William Cocks
Zachariah Pair
George Chalmers
William Hampton
William Leghorn
Thomas Bedford
Joseph Belk
Thomas Die
Frederick Newsom
John Mims
John Ford
Jones Griffin
Mr. Hampton
Jeremiah Oates

Capt. Stewart's Dist.

William Harvey
David Barbery
Thomas Airs
John Peres
Lewis Miller
Andrew Frasher

TAX DEFAULTERS
1793

Capt. Sheppard's Dist.

Edward Hopson
Benjamin Ketcher

Capt. Bonner's Dist.

Charles Herrington

Capt. Curry's Dist.

Moses Ross
Thomas Shealds

Capt. Hampton's Dist.

Ephriam Greene
Reddick Garner
David Irwin
Edward Carlile
Andrew Heartshorn
Seaborn Odum
Alexander Finney
Samuel Boggs
John McFarlin
Robert Jackson
Reason Binum
John Spurlock
William Smith

Capt. McDowell's Dist.

James Maroney

Capt. Spann's Dist.

James Cohorn
Peter Winn

Capt. William's Dist.

John Wade
Reese Harris
David Castleberry
William Harris
A. C. Irwin

Capt. Harrison's Dist.

John Smith

Capt. Kelly's Dist.

Martin Johnson

Capt. Hooker's Dist.

John Kinney
Thomas Crocker
John Colton
Allen Rigbey
James Patten

Capt. Bryant's Dist.

John Padgett

Southern Centinel &
Universal Gazette
Augusta, Georgia

TAX DEFAULTERS
1794

Capt. Hooker's Dist.

Caleb Hinton
John Perkins
Thomas McLendon
Mark McLendon
Sewel Holland
John Dunn
Lewis Bailey
John Hims Jr.
John Broughton
Mathew Spikes
Hugh Bell
James Harris
William Braswell

Lewis Herndon
Edward Hampton
James Vessells

Capt. Parrot's Dist.

Allen Haden
Thomas Harvey
William Cox
Joseph Herndon
William Harris
Benjamin Parrott Sr.
Abraham Higgs
Solomon Hamill

Capt. Curry's Dist.

George Taft
—— Ward
Thomas Smith
John Blake
James Taylor
Shachack Taylor
Matthew Yolden
Samuel Wars
Joseph Raney

Capt. Kendrick's Dist.

Jeremiah Russell 3r.
Benjamin Kitchens
Samuel Smith

Capt. Sheppard's Dist.

Hugh Gallman
Malachi Britt
Jonathan Britt

Capt. Hampton's Dist.

Robert Cummings
John Nelms Sr.
Josiah Underwood
Thomas Safebury
Jesse Levily
William Riley
John Nelms Jr.
James Welton
William Hunter
Amos Wheelon
Thomas Underwood
Widow Wiggins

Capt. Williamson's Dist.

William Dennard
William Carlisle

List signed and by
John Watts, Receiver
Tax Returns.

* * *

TAX DEFAULTERS
1798

Certified by John
Howard, Receiver
of Tax Returns.

Capt. Nicholas Curry's Dist.

James English
Lemuel Evans
Robert Carpenter
Thomas Prestwood
Allen McClayne
James Neeland
Richard Horn
Elias Acock
Menan Coleman
Mycajah Bateman
Ebeneezer Fife
John Duprey
Dennis Williams
David Witherspoon
Samuel Swilley
George Taff
Benjamin Robertson
Elias Wester
Thomas Duncan
John May
Evan Andrews
Drewry Patterson
Reubin Tucker
Jeremiah Conney
Thomas McLendon
David Fourman
Levi Horton
Isaac Wade
James Pool
Gabriel Lennon
Freeman Williams
William Bargainer

Nicholas Swilley
William Spivey
Jane Smith

Capt. Edward Bryan's Dist.

Joel Lewis
Jesse Harris
Simon Johnston
Isaac Watson
Isham Carr
G. Elvington
Nathaniel Burnett
James Roland
Drewry Gulbert
Elijah Walton
Jacob Smith
Richard Braswell
John Arline
Elisha Watson
Silas Watson
John Smith

Capt. J. Wicker's Dist.

Thomas Crittenton
John Howell
Stephen Jackson
Isham Jackson
William Ray
Thomas Glass
William Beaty
Samuel Larkin
Richard Warthen
William Perritt
Gabriel Howell
John Winters
Jonathan Deason
James Smith
James Parneel
John Coleman
John Smith

Capt. Burrel
    Kendrick's Dist.

Joshua Howard
James Howard
William Joiner
William Thompson
James Brantley
Levi Bennett

Capt. John Sheppard's Dist.

James Howard
William Mallory
William Greer
Richard Ball
John Raney
John Howell
Stephen Hood
William Nelson
Frederick Regan
Moses Harris
Wheeler Reubin
John Hatcher
William Spivey
Samuel Howard
John Brottan
Edward Hopson
Hudson Lord
John Tomlinson
Bashaba Walker
Jesse Bateman
Job Cobb
Thomas Brown
John Cooper
Amos Wheeler
John Robertson
John Spivey

Capt. B. Parrott's Dist.

David Scarborough
William Dennard
Nathaniel Daniel
Robert Glenn
L. Scarborough
Richard Roberts
Nathan Spikes
David Glenn
William Glenn
Harrison Harris
John Fisher
Shadrack Dennard
Benjamin Kemp
John Graham
Samuel Hart Jr.
Samuel Harris
Wyatt Bettis
William Wallace
William Braswell
James Sheppard
Samuel Hart Sr.
James Frederick

Capt. James Dixon's Dist.

Eb Haden
John Haden
Jacob Dennard
Nobles Porter
William Coulter
Lewis Fowler
Clement Davis
Davis Robertson
Reubin Lawson
John Wooten
John Burk
Samuel Haden
Joseph Parker
Isaac Dennard
Thomas Lenton
Joseph Herndon
Jesse Brown
William Fenney
William Ross
Reubin Neel
Isham Collums
John Herndon

Capt. Geo. Spann's Dist.

Blann Bleckley
Parting Lamkins
George Robertson
Benjamin Kitchens

Capt. Daniel McDowell's Dist.

John Robertson
Joseph Williams
Henry Stewart
Elijah Blann
William Denton
William Robertson
William Kimney
Charles Stewart
John Crumby
William Perkins
David Evans
Spencer Crosby
Jesse Cooksey
Isham Aldridge
Randall McKenzie
Charles Johnston
Richard Lee
Spencer Mattocks
Charles Smith

John Lithcow
John Clark
James Jones
William Smith
John Crosley
Elibrad Pipe
Joseph Ryley
John Smith
James Montgomery
Benjamin Langston

Richard Jordon
Elijah O'Bannon
William Wood
Nimrod Nunn
Kite Motherhead
Isham Hall
Leonard Mattocks
George Dillard
Edward Ryley

White's Historical Collections of Georgia lists the following as early settlers of Washington County:

Alexander Irwin
William Johnson
Jared Litwin
John Robertson
Philemon Franklin
Joseph Avant
James Thomas
William Irwin
Samuel Sinquefield
John Martin
Hugh Lawson
William Sapp
John Jones
Jonh Stokes
John Irwin
George Galphin
John Nutt
George Fluker
Jacob Kelly
John Rutherford
Elisha Williams
Jacob Dennard
Joseph Beddingfield
Aaron Sinquefield
John Sheppard
John Daniel
Joshua Williams
Benjamin Tennille

John Burney
John Shellman
Niles Murphy
John H. Montgomery
Mr. Saunders
James Thomas
John Dennis
D. Wood
William Warthen
William May

Grand Jurors:
July Term, 1791

Solomon Wood, Foreman

William Cain
John Martin
John Sheppard
Alexander Johnson
John Harvey
Ezekiel Daniel
John Ward
Daniel Conner
Thomas McDonald
David Jackson
Edward Hagans
Charles Statham
Reubin Wilkinson
Morris Raiford
John Armstrong
John Dennis
William Johnston

Grand Jurors:
September Term, 1796

H. Brazeal, Foreman

William Bracken
Benjamin Griffin
Cabel Cannon
James Thomas
George Spann
John Burney
John O'Neal

John Jones
William McMurry
John Nutt
C. Murphy
William Bealty
Nicholas Curry
Thomas Holly
Thomas English
William Hooks
Stephen Hooker
Solomon Howars

Grand Jurors:
March Term, 1799

David Blackshear, Foreman

Amos Daniel
Laban Beckham
Reubin Williams
John Smith
Henry Slappy
Holiday Hatley
William Norman
Charles Moorman
Philip Dillard
James Blount
William Elliott
Richard Deens
Andrew Kennedy
Nimrod Burke
Othneil Weaver
Joseph Blackshear
William McGee

SOME DEPOSITIONS

Elijah Blackshear and Isom Carter before David Blackshear
swore they went to house of Reuben Wilkinson and found house
burnt and part of carcases of three people supposed to be
Wilkinson, wife and a negro. 30 Nov. 1795

Capt. Benjamin Harrison 1794 swore that Indians stole horse
Samuel Shurlock attested. 2 Aug. 1802
Jesse Powell also attested

136

Samuel Sparks swore that 13 April 1796 Indians stole 4
horses from Josiah Sparks.
James Smith attested 2 Aug. 1802.

Edward Blackshear made oath that Indians stole from William
Buck Jr. a horse in March 1793 - sworn to 4 Aug. 1802.

Mrs. Jane Pugh made deposition that in Spring 1793 Indians
killed William Pugh (son of Francis and Jane Pugh) and stole
negro, horse, hogs.
Benjamin Harrison attested 7 Aug. 1802.

Jesse Powell swore Indians stole horse from him 1792.
James Wood attested 7 Aug. 1802.

Nimrod Burk Esq. swore Indians stole 2 horses from him 1787
William Denard and Jacob Denard attested 11 Nov. 1802.

William Allen of County of Warren in State of Kentucky
appoints Adam Harden, attorney, to recover slave Betty and
her 3 children. 28 Aug. 1800.
Rec. in Clerks Office - Superior Court in Book P folio 115
Thomas B. Rutherford, Clerk.

Before Samuel Robison, J. P. and Charles Ray, J. P. came
John Frasher and swore that he was at the house of Amos
Wheeler where the day before said Wheeler had bought a horse
from an Indian.

We do certify that Sampson Culpepper, being
an officer done service under our direction
in the above case to the amount of $6.
Samuel Robison, J. P.
Charles, J. P.
* * * * * * * * * * *

First Court Held Washington Co. 22 May, 1787. Henry Osborne,
presided.

Grand Jurors:

Alexander Irwin, foreman	Samuel Sinquefield
Elisha Williams	Joseph Avant
William Johnson	William Irwin
Philemon Franklin	William Shields
John Robertson, Sr.	John Shafford
John Burney	John Rutherford
John Martin	Jacob Dennard
James Thomas	Joseph Beddingfield
Benjamin Tennille	Aaron Sinquefield
Joshua Williams	John Daniel Sr.

137

A return of depredations committed by the Indians since
Jan. 1787

	No. Killed	No. Wounded	Age
Johnston children			
his son	1		10
his daughter	1		8
Oliver Martin	1		50
William Drake	1		30
John Vann	1		25
James Harris	1		25
Reuben Cook	1		33
David Shepherd	1		17
Edmon Burk	1		14
John Pinkerton	1		37
Capt. James Wood	1		—
Robert Hudspeth Warlick	1		40
Scantling A. Soulder	1		—
Lt. Griffin Hogan	1		25
Lt. Daniel Sikes	1		45
Allen Spurlock	1		—
Usley Carthon	1		—
James Ellis	1		60
Jackson family			
his wife	1		31
his son	1		11
4 daughters	4		7-6-5-3
James Jackson	1		35
Nancy Avon	1		14
William Franklin Portess		1	—
Charles Culpepper		1	20
William Powers		1	—
David Scarbrough		1	12
Elizabeth Sikes		1	—
Jackson's daughter		1	12

I do hereby certify that the within is a just and true return of the depredations committed by the Indians agreeable
to an order from the Honorable the Executive Council of the
14th of June last. Signed: Sept. 18, 1788
Jared Irwin, Colonel

138

Archy, William 78
Ard, James 26
  Margaret 42
  Neil 26
  Reuben 26
Arington, James Cato (?) 73
  John H. 73
Arline, James 57
  John 3, 26, 80, 133
  Mary 114
Arm, Andw. 94
Armour, (?) 85
Armstron, William H. 108
Armstrong, (?) 88, 95
  Alex 58
  Alex (Jr.) 58
  Alex. 45
  Alex. (Jr.) 45
  Alexander 3, 26
  Alexdr. 60
  Ancarl (?) 62
  Burton 66
  Dorothy W. 108
  Ed. F. 108
  Edw. 60
  Edward 45, 55, 74, 100
  Edward F. 74
  James 3, 52
  James G. 73
  Jesse 26, 52, 54
  Jno. 92
  John 3, 80, 100, 136
  Martha J. 118
  Mary 113
  Wesley 79
  William H. 68
Arnold, Ambrose 51
  Arnet 54, 108
  Arnette 64
  Elizabeth 42, 64
  Elizabeth A. 118, 126
  Harrel 64
  Harrell 54, 108
  James 52
  John 108
  Julian 117
  Martha 117
  Permelia A. 109
  Sarah 108
  Thomas 50, 56
  William 48, 52
Arrenton, Isaac 47
Arrington, Hardy 66
Asbury, Jonathan 3
Ashley, Jas. 87
  John F. 108
  Martha A. 119
Ashly, John F. 70
Ashmore, John 3
Askew, Frederick W. 108
  Mary 118
Aslomes, Huel 64
Asque, Uriah 98
Athorn, Anthony 99
Atkins, David 75
  Frances 114
  John 56
  Joseph 58
  Randal 57
Attiway, Susan 59
Atwood, Isaac 80, 94
Aubry, Alexander 3
  Jacob 3
Austin, John 108
Autrey, Alexander 3
Autry, Absalom 3
  Alexander 3

Autry (cont.)
  John 3
Avant, Ann 114
  Barbary 71
  Isiah B. 68
  James 108
  John F. 77
  Joseph 135, 137
  Ransom 98
  Ransome 101
Avent, Isaiah 52
  J. B. 54, 62
  James R. 71
  John F. 62
  Joseph 3, 64
  L. S. 57
  R. D. 54
  Ransom 26, 52, 62
Avera, John 45
  Lander 51
  Patience 51
  Sally 48
  Samuel 45, 57
  Sarah 113
  Thomas 26
Averett, Archibald 97
  Benjamin 26, 97
  Henry 26
  John 3
Averitt, Albright 130
  Archibald 130
Avery, Alexander 3
  Jonathan 26
  Samuel 3
  Sanders 26
  Sarah 3
  Sarah (Mrs.) 53
  William 26
  Winnie 26
Avon, Nancy 138
Aycock, Benjamin 3
  Elius 3
  Richard 3
Ayers, Abraham 3
  Daniel 3
  Goodwin 108
  James 3
  Thomas 3, 26
  William 3
Aylett, Archibald 131
BAker, Thomas H. 56
Baber, Nellie 110
Babre, John (Lt.) 102
Bacon, John 3
  Nicholas 3
  Reuben 3
Bafield, (?) 86
Bagby, George 3
Bage, Benj. F. 64
  Mary A. 116
Baggs, Ezekiel 26
  John 3
  Joseph 3
Bagley, Benjamin 42
Bailey, Azariah 3
  Bird 109
  Burrell 42
  Burwell 65
  David 3, 47, 62, 79, 109
  Elizabeth 61, 79, 111
  James 47
  John 46, 51, 65
  Keziah 42
  Lewis 132
  Mary 79
  Mary Ann 62, 111
  Richard 79

Bailey (cont.)
  Richmond 109
  William 3, 47, 55, 62, 68, 101
  Winifred C. 124
  Wm. 66
Baily, Bird 71
  John 56, 71
Baker, (?) 89
  Blake 45
  Frances A. 111
  Francis 3, 26
  John 26, 46
  John (Jr.) 55
  Jonath. (Sr.) 55
  Jonathan 26, 69
  Jonathan (Jr.) 60
  Jonathan (Sr.) 60
  Jonathan G. 67
  Joseph 3, 26, 80, 110
  Joshua 3
  Mary 74
  T. H. 62
  Thomas 26
  Thomas H. 3, 42, 56
  Thomas W. H. 67
  William 26
Baldwin, David 3
  John 3
  Mordecai 3
  Robert 3
  William 3
Baley, David 27
  Harrison 27
  James (Sr.) 27
  John 27
  Lewis 99
  William 27
Ball, Anson 27
  John 27
  Richard 27, 134
Ballard, Christopher 3
  Joshua 3
  Winnifred 47
  Xpher 80
Bangs, Joseph 110
Banks, Elisha Fowler 3, 80
  Gerard 3, 89
  Gerrard 80
  Joseph 63
  Reuben 3
Bankston, (?) 90
  Isaac 98
  James 3
  Laurence 3
  Thomas 98
  William 98
Bankstone, Lawrence 80
Barber, Asa 50
  Cintha L. 110
  Frederick 47
  Jacob 27
  John H. 110
  John W. 75, 109
  Joseph 3
  Mary 77
  Rebeca 71
  Richard 3, 27
  Thomas 3, 69
  William 27, 42, 50
Barbery, David 131
Barbre, Isaac 3
  Jesse 4
Barbree, Isaac 97
Barclay, (?) 82
Barcley, John 4
Bardale, Kirk 81

Barefield, James 65
  Jesse 27
  John 4, 74, 109
  Richard 4, 27
  Solomon 4
Barfield, James 75
Bargainer, John 27
  William 27, 133
Barge, Abel 50
  Abraham 42
  Hannah 65, 71
  John 109
  Lewis H. C. 73
  Richmond 51
  Sarah H. 73
Barkdale, Abner 98
Barksdale, Abner 99
  Alfred 109
  William 109, 110
Barkshare, Richard 4
Barlow, Henry 4, 27, 53
  John 27
  William 4, 27
Barlowe, Edith 49
  Henry 49
Barnadore, Nancy 46
Barnap, (?) 4
Barnes, Colman 42
  D. H. 66
  David 127
  David H. 53, 61, 68,
    72, 109
  Dempsey 42
  Eliza A. 124
  Franklin 127
  Green 127
  Jacob 53, 64, 108
  John 4, 27, 46, 57
  John (Sr.) 42, 60
  Joshua 27
  M. 127
  Melvina 126
  Samuel 98
  Vicy 121
  William 46
Barnett, Abraham 4
  Anabella 42
  Benj. 97
  Claiborne 4
  Joel 4
  John 42, 51, 57
  Joshua 4
  Nancy 61
  Robert (Jr.) 27
  Robert (Sr.) 27
  Samuel 4
  Sarah 51
  Tillman 42
  William 97
Barney, James (Lt.) 103
  Randall 101
Barns, John 72
  Judah 110
Baron, George W. 79
  James 68
Barow, Solomon 109
Barren, Joseph 80
  William 80
Barrentine, Wm. 53
Barret, Jane 71
Barrett, Thomas 54
Barrick, William 127
Barrington, William 42
Barron, Absalom 99
  Alah 115
  Barnabas 57
  Barney 27
  Frances 60

Barron (cont.)
  James 27, 58, 63, 110
  Jno. 95
  Mary 111
  Solomon H. 79
  Theny 123
  Thomas 27
  William 57
  Wm. 84
Barronton, William 4
Barrow, Barma 63
  Barnabus 74
  Barney 45, 47
  James 47
  Milly 27
  William 4, 27, 46
Bartemore, Benjamin 4
Bartlett, Lainda 56
  Lucinda 50
  Thomas 42, 108
  William 4
Bartman, Bartley M. 109
Barton, Willoughby 4
Barwick, Abel J. 69, 109
  Benj. 66
  Benjamin 45, 54
  Elizabeth 116
  Jackson 109
  James 69
  James E. 68
  Jesse 66
  John 4, 47, 54, 61,
    69, 110
  Letha 116
  Mary 110
  Matilda 116
  Nathan 79, 109
  Redding 108
  Samuel 53
  Stansell 109
  Susan 118
  William 47, 54, 60,
    69, 109
  Winefred 109
Basdale, Jeffrey 4
Bass, Esan 4
  Esaw 80
Basset, Richard 27
Bassett, George 4
  Richard 99
Batchelor, Cornelius 4
Bateman, Abigail 114
  Bryant 50
  Claibourne 51
  David 27, 48, 55, 66
  Gelina 118
  Jason 4, 57, 64
  Jesse 134
  Jesse (Sr.) 27
  John 51
  Mycajah 133
  Theophilus 4, 27, 51
  William 27, 51
  William (Sr.) 27
Bates, John 4
  William 54
  Wm. 63
Batts, Eliza 118
  George 75
  Jesse 63, 109
  Nathan 56
Baytry, Samuel 97
Bazel, Arthur 63
Bazer, Caleb 94
Beach, Asabel 67
Beacham, John 98
Beacher, David 80
Beal, Archibald 4

Beal (cont.)
  Hezekiah 4
  William 67
Bealty, William 136
Beard, Edmond 4
Bearden, Arthur 97
  Richard 97
Bearfield, (?) 87
Beasley, Burwell 4
  John 4, 48
  Richard 4
  William 27
Beason, Samuel 98
Beaty, James (Sr.) 27
  Samuel 27
  William 27, 97, 133
Beaver, Anthony 4
Beavin, William 4
Beckcom, (?) 83, 84, 87,
    95
  Allen 4, 97
  Laban 27
  Russell 27
  S. 80, 84
  Saml. 81
  Samuel 4, 89
  Sherod 4, 95, 97
  Simon 4
  Solomon 4, 27
  William 27
  Zachariah 27
Beckham, Abel 59
  Allen 4
  Elizabeth 120
  John 4
  John Y. 4
  Laban 136
  Mary 60
  Mary Ann 117
  Moody 72
  Osborn 59
  Samuel 4
  Simon 4
  Solomon 4
Beckom, (?) 80, 90
  Abel 46
  Allen 80
  Daniel 46
  John 46
  Saben 97
  Samuel 80
  Sherwood 80, 97
  Simon 80
  Solomon 80, 97
  William 97
Beckum, Jemima 113
  Lawson 72
  Solomon 89
Beddingfield, Alan 27
  John H. 42, 108
  Joseph 27, 80, 135,
    137
  Lewis 27
Bedford, Thomas 131
Bedgood, Elizabeth 110,
    112
  G. 75
  Henry W. 109
  James M. 42
  Jane 123
  John 27, 48, 55, 75,
    105, 127
  John (Jr.) 27
  John (Sr.) 48
  John R. 4
  Juliann 124
  Lewis 109
  Mahaly 120

Borland, Andrew 4, 5
  Nathan 5
Bostick, (?) 86
Boswell, (?) 82
  James 4, 5
Bothwell, David J. 108
Bowen, Charles 27
  Emily 108
  Harrod 27
  Herod 50
  Herrod 53, 65
  Joel 5
  John 27
  Malachi 46
  Mary 72
  Nathan M. 71
  Oliver 5
  Windal 5
Bower, Ephraim 5
Bowie, (?) 81
  J. 81
  James 5, 83, 84
  Reason 5
Bowin, J. 81
  James 81
  Joel 81
Boyd, David 81
  Edward 5
  John 27, 53, 108
  Martha A. 69
  Thomas 5
Boykin, (?) 96
  Francis 5, 27
  Jesse 5
  Sarah 27
  William 5, 27
Boys, Thomas 27
Bozeman, Joseph 5
Bozman, Luke 81
Brack, Benj. 81
  Benjamin 5
  Eleazar 81
Bracken, (?) 86, 96
  Isaac 81
  James 27
  William 81, 136
  William (Jr.) 27
  William (Sr.) 27
  Wm. 95
Brackens, Benj. 62
Bracker, William 5
Bracks, Eleazer 5
Braddy, A. 128
  A. J. 75, 127
  Charles 54
  J. T. 127
  John 59, 64
  L. 128
  Oliver 127
  Oliver B. 75
Bradley, Abraham 5
  Charles 42
  Jesse 27
Bradly, Mikagah 104
Brady, Andrew J. 109
  Asceamy 114
  Druscilla 47
  Eliza 121
  John 50, 75
Braedy, William 5
Brailey, Nancy 79
Braken, Isaac 5
  William 5
Brandon, Jacob 5
Branham, Spencer 5
  Susan 52
Brannan, Samuel 5
Brannon, Thomas 5

Brantley, (?) 86, 88
  Aaron 5, 53, 76
  Abbie 49
  Aggy 63
  Ann 118
  Aron 47
  Asena 121
  Benj. 97
  Benjamin 27, 76, 77,
    110, 125
  Benjamin H. 5
  Celia 63, 76
  Edw. 53, 63
  Edward 5, 48, 55, 61,
    69, 76
  Edwin 63, 76
  Elizabeth 121
  Emeline 110
  George Ann 112
  George F. 76, 110
  Gideon 71, 110
  Green 42, 48, 54, 73
  Greene 62
  Harriett 117
  Harris 27, 42, 49, 53,
    56, 60, 73, 77
  I. M. 125
  Jack 63
  James 5, 27, 49, 53,
    69, 76, 109, 125,
    133
  James (Jr.) 63
  James (Sr.) 63
  James L. 76, 110
  Jane 114
  Jephtha 66
  Jeptha 5, 68
  John 49, 53, 109
  John F. 5, 42, 53, 63,
    69
  John J. 109
  Joseph 27, 42
  Mary 112
  Nancy 109
  Patsey 49
  Solomon 27
  Spencer 5, 27, 48, 49,
    53, 63, 69
  Thomas 5, 27, 49, 58,
    76, 109, 125
  Thos. 81
  William 42, 55, 69, 77
  William (Jr.) 42
  William (Sr.) 42
  William G. 109
  William M. 73
  Wm. 42, 65
  Z. 54
  Zachariah 47
Brantly, Aaron 63
  Benj. 63
  Eliza 108
  Harns 63
  Harris 109
  James M. 109
  Jeptha 108
  Spencer 63
  Thomas M. 109
  William 108
  Wm. 63
  Zachariah 67
Branton, (?) 83
Brantram, John 52
Brasel, Alin 98
Brasiel, Matthew 72
Brasill, John 5
Brasington, O. P. 68
Brasley, J. 80

Brassel, Arthur 53
  Elias 77
Brassil, William 72
Braswell, (?) 81
  Benjamin 5
  Ferdinand 5
  George 5
  John 5
  Kendred 81
  Kindred 5
  Mathew 27
  Reddick 27
  Richard 27, 133
  Robert 5, 81, 104
  Robt. 83
  Sampson 27
  Sampson (Sr.) 27
  Samuel 5, 81
  Sarah 116
  Swanson 5
  Wilie 27
  William 132, 134
Bray, Benjamin 49
  C. D. 70
  Catherine 108
  Jarrod 57
  John 56
  Joseph 52, 59, 108
  Peter 27, 49, 127
  Sarah 42
  Thany 113
  Thomas 5
Brazeal, H. 136
  Henry 27
Brazel, Elias 60
Brazwell, Benjamin 5
Bready, William 5
Breck, William 5
Bremer, John 5
Brett, George 76
  Henry 42, 65, 76
Brewer, John 108
  Osburn 98
  William 5
Brewster, Hugh 5
Brewston, John 5
Briant, Benj. 99
Bridger, Almeda 120
Bridgers, Alexander 109
  Nancy 109
Bridges, Abigail 73
  Benjamin 127
  Blake 50
  Edwin 67
  Edy 125
  John 74
  Joseph 27, 51, 54
  N. 128
  Nancy 125
  Permelia 109
  Permila 63
  Rebecca 27
  Sialas 53
  William 5, 49, 109
  William F. 49
Briges, Samuel 27
Briggs, John 5, 81, 104
  Zabiah 98
Bright, Levi 5, 27, 45
  Meley 58
  Morgan 109
  Morgan W. 73
  Neely 73
  Nelly 60
Brinkley, Eli 27, 45
  Ely 105
  John 5, 27
Brinton, (?) 81, 82, 92

Brinton (cont.)
Isaiah 98
J. 81
Jno. 81
John 5
William 5, 81
Britain, James 5
Britt, David 5
George W. 110
Henry 57
James 48, 55
Jesse 5, 27, 48
John 5, 27, 48
Jonathan 132
Malachi 132
Martha 115, 118
Martin W. 109
Obed 57
Brittain, (?) 96
Britton, Abigail 113
Broadstreet, (?) 88
Brock, Eleazer 5
Jackson 69
Jesse 63
John 48
Unity 69
William 101
Brook, Sarah E. 117
Brookin, Nancy 46
Brookins, Benj. 55
Benjamin 47, 78
Charles V. 51
H. 66
Haywood 54, 67
Lydia M. 119
Marian 116
Mary 111
Solomon B. 108
Thomas 28, 109
Zachaariah 109
Zachariah 78
Brooks, (?) 95
Aaron 66, 108
Dolly 69
Edmund 28
Jacob 5
James 28, 48, 56, 69,
81
Jesse 5
John 28, 101
Johnson 61, 108
Martha 109
Robert 54, 69
Robert G. 66
Rogers 5
Sarah 52
William 28, 101
William J. 110
Brosiel, Timoth (?) 69
Brottan, John 134
Brotton, John 28
Broughton, John 132
Brown, Alan (Sr.) 28
Allen 5
Andrew 5
Ann Eliza 120
Asa 28
Clark 70
Dardina 118
Dempsey 5, 28
Ebenezer 69
Edmond D. 74
Elvira L. 124
Emanuel 5, 54, 61, 79,
109
Frederick 5
George 58
Handley 53, 61

Brown (cont.)
Henry 5, 81, 109
Hezekiah 5, 46, 54, 61
Isaac 130
Isabella 111
James 28
Jean 5
Jesse 5, 28, 101, 134
Jesse D. 52
John 5, 42, 48, 55, 98
John (Jr.) 28
John D. 42, 60, 74
John R. 67
Joseph 5, 81
Juliann Caroline 118
Leah 73
Lewis 71
M. 42
Martha 110
Mary 5, 76, 110, 117
Mary A. 114
Mary Ann 118
Mary Ann Jane 122
Mary D. 58
Mary F. 114
Morgan 45, 53, 62, 66
Nancy 66, 79
R. S. 65
Richard 70
Richard F. 110
Richard S. 5
Samuel 50, 53, 64
Sarah 42, 60, 61, 72,
121, 122
Sarah (Widow) 42
Sarah J. 119
Sarah W. 73
Seany A. 112
Senia Ann 120
Sneed 80
Solomon 53
Sophia 60
Stephen 97
Tabitha G. 67
Thomas 5, 28, 109, 134
Turner 45, 58
Turner F. 55
Turner T. 74, 108
Uriah 60, 108
William 5, 28, 45, 46,
55, 59, 61
William C. 5
William G. 67
William L. 73, 109
William O. 74
Wm. L. 60
Brownen, Isaac 5
Browner, Charles 5
John 5
Brumley, Micajah 28
William 28
Brunor, John 82
Brunson, Daniel 28
David 5
Ebeneezer 5
John 5
Brunston, William 5
Bryan, Augustus 28
David 82
Edward 28
Edward (Cpt.) 133
James 110
James S. 75
Jason W. 109
Joseph 5
Martha 119
Penelope 75
Sarah 120

Bryan (cont.)
Temperance 112
William G. 75
William P. 108
Bryant, (?) (Cpt.) 132
David 5, 28, 49
Duncan 5
Jason 48, 55, 65
Jno. 84, 96
John 5, 82
John G. 110
Lewis 28
Olivia 122
Buck, Elizabeth 111
J. J. 62
James A. 42
S. W. 62
Seaborn W. 108
William 5, 28, 52, 54,
62, 78
William (Jr.) 137
William (Sr.) 5
Wright W. 67
Buckhalter, Jacob 5
John 5
Joshua 5
Michael 5
William 5
Buckhanan, E. 73
Buckhanner, Eliz. 61
Buckhannon, Betsy 42
Buckner, Uriah G. 67
Bugg, E. 87
Jacob 5
Jeremiah 5
John 5
Nicholas 5
Buie, Betsy (?) 47
Buk, William (Sr.) 28
Bulger, John 46
Bullard, Lewis 42, 67,
109
Lydia 48
Patience 108
Wiley 5
Wilie 28
Willy 82
Bullin, John 28
Bullington, Reuben 62
Bulloch, James 101
Bullock, Benjamin 28
Carter 28, 46
James 28
Buntery, Zachariah 130
Burch, Charles 5
Edward 5
Littleberry 109
Burd, Shadrick 100
Burford, Daniel 5
Leonard 5
Mitchell 5
William 5
Burgamot, William 6
Burgamy, Drury 46
Susannah 111
Tobias 42, 58, 60, 108
William 6, 28, 46, 58,
105
William (Sr.) 42
William J. 42
Wm. L. 100
Burganny, Tobias 72
Burge, John 6, 28, 82
Mathew 101
Buris, Hanford 42
Burk, (?) 96
Daniel 28
Edmon 138

144

Burk (cont.)
Elnathan 28
John 134
Nimrod 28, 82, 137
Nimrod (Lt.) 100
Burke, (?) 96
Charles 6
David 6
Nimrod 6, 136
Nimrod (Lt.) 102
Burkes, Isham 6
Burnat, Solomon 82
Burnes, James 64
Joseph 28
Burnet, (?) 95
Daniel 6, 82
Burnett, Daniel 6
John 6, 98
Nathaniel 133
Burney, (?) 82, 83, 89,
95
Arthur 28
Brandal 6
David 6, 82, 87
Elizabeth 28, 48
Elizabeth (Widow) 107
Ellis 28, 48
Harris 48, 89
James 6, 82, 99
James (Lt.) 102, 103
Jas. 85
John 6, 82, 135, 136,
137
Randal 6, 82, 96
Richard 6, 82
Silas (?) 48
Willis 6, 28, 48
Burnhart, George 6
Burns, (?) 81, 95
Andrew 6
Ansford 63
Frederick 127
James 53, 110
S. 91
Starret 90
William 127
Burnsides, John 6
Burris, Alfred 53
Frederick 109
Hansford 6
Burriss, B. 128
Beedy 125
Frederick 125
William 125
Burt, Moody 6
Burton, (?) 81, 82
John 82
Richard 6
Bush, John 6
Levi 6, 28, 50
Levi (Jr.) 28
Nathan 6
Bussey, Hezekiah 6
Thomas 6
Busson, Jesse 28
Bustle, Isaac 46
John 46
Nancy 46
Priscilla 46
Solomon 46
Butcher, Elizabeth 124
Henry 67, 110, 127
S. A. 128
Sarah A. 79
Thomas 45
Butler, Bryant 28
Daniel 6
Ford 28

Butler (cont.)
Hugh 78
Hughy 109
John 97
John F. 78
Nancy A. 78
Samuel 101
Thomas 97
William 51
Buttery, Zachariah 6
Zachary 82
Zacky 94
Butts, Jesse 109
Bynam, Garner 55
Henry 58
Tarnar 55
William 46
Byne, Edmund 6
Elizabeth 110
Bynum, Hessy Ann 73
Sarah A. 120
Turner L. 60
William 28
Byrn, Mary 76
Cade, Drury 6
Cader, Francis 6
Cahoon, James 6
Joseph 99
Cain, (?) 82, 92
John 6, 97
Lidda 54
Nathaniel 28, 50
William 6, 136
Wm. T. 42
Calhoon, M. 128
Minerva 110
N. 128
S. 128
Thomas 127
William 127
Z. 128
Calhoun, Abraham 6
Allen 59, 64
Ervin 28
James 28, 58
James M. 42, 110
John F. 110
Martha 110
Nancy 65, 123
Orra 64
Philip 28
Samuel 59
Sarah 121
William 59
William G. 71
Wm. G. 65
Calk, James 6
Call, (?) 82
(?) (Maj.) 85
Major 85
Richard 6, 89
Callaway, Jehu 97
Cambell, Gilbert 6
John 127
William 6
Camby, Leroy 58
Camon, E. 81
Camons, (?) 81, 83
Eleazer 81
Camp, (?) 87
Clark 111
Mary 59
Samuel 6, 82, 83
Thomas 6
William 6
Campbell, (?) 95
Binka 113
Burrel 46

Campbell (cont.)
Elijah 101
George 28
John 6, 98
John (Rev.) 28
William 6, 28, 82
William (Lt.) 102
Canada, David 71
James 42
Canady, John 6
Candlar, Wm. 89
Candler, Henry 6
John 6
William 6
Cane, Benjamin H. 110
Wm. (?) 82
Caniell, Benj. 83
Cannon, Caleb 6, 28, 136
Calip 99
Elisha 51
Elizabeth 68
Richard 52
William 48, 53
Canter, Richard 59
Richard D. 46
Sarah 42, 72
William A. D. 72
William R. L. 110
Cantey, James 6
John 6
Carlile, Edward 131
Mathew 56
Carlisle, Dennard 101
John 6
Mathew 28
Matthew 64
Micajah 28
Susanna 50
W. 129
William 28, 133
Winnifred 28
Carmichael, James 45
Carnes, Thomas 86
Thomas P. 6
Thos. 83
Thos. P. 82, 92
Carney, Matthew 6
Onsbey 6
Carnich, William 101
Carpenter, Peter 6, 28
Robert 133
William 28
Carpter, Edward 130
Carr, (?) 96
Henry 82
Isham 6, 28, 133
Patrick 6
Robert E. 76
Robert J. 111
Thomas 6
Carrell, William 6
Carrigan, Edward 130
Carson, (?) 86
Adam 94, 97
David 6
Jos. (Cpt.) 97
Joseph 130
Samuel 6
Thomas 6
Carswell, Mathew 67
Matthew 6
Carter, (?) 82
David 6, 51, 56, 101
E. 128
Ezekiel 48
George 28
Giles 6, 49
Isabella 71

Carter (cont.)
Isom 136
J. 128
John 82, 126
Kindrell 42
M. 128
Milly 119
Rachel 28
Silas 6, 48, 54
Silas (Sr.) 48
Susan 66
Thomas 28
William 6, 58, 59, 97, 98
Carthon, Usley 138
Cartice, John 6
Cartledge, James 6
Samuel 6
Carvello, Constantine 78
Casey, James 97
Cason, Dennis 42, 56, 64, 71, 110
Elizabeth 111
George 28
Henry 51, 54
Whitehouse 28
William 28, 51, 54
Casson, Rebecca 61
Castavous, Micajah 6
Castellon, Michael 6
Castelow, James 52
William 28, 52
Castin, James 72
Castleberry, David 132
Henry 6
Jacob 6
Jeremiah 6
John 6
Peter 6
Caston, John 77
Thomas 42
William 42
Caswell, John 6, 82
Catch, Ben 89
Catching, (?) 82
Joseph 6
Seymour 6
Catchings, (?) 82
Benjamin 6
Joseph 6, 82
Cates, Hilsey 74
Richard W. 94
Richd. 91
Richd. Wyatt 82
Thomas 6, 98
Thos. 82
Cathell, James (Lt.) 98
Cato, Ailcy 59
Emily 118
Francis 46
James 6, 55, 60, 73
John 78
Penelope 117
Penelope F. 118
Susannah 117
Caudry, Jonathan 6
Cavannah, Edward 28
Cave, Wm. 82
Cavender, Mary 28
Cawill, William 51
Cawley, Robert W. 110
William 28
Cawthon, William 6
Wm. 82
Cawthorn, Josiah 6
William 6
William (Lt.) 103
Celk, Jacob 8

Celk (cont.)
Joseph 8
Celmants, (?) 89
Cernigin, Caty 77
Certam, James 6
Cessna, John 6
Chalmers, George 131
Peter B. 28
Chamber, Ira 110
Chambers, David 126
Hardion K. 78
Ira 62
James 126
John 6, 126
Jonas 89
Joseph 67
Kincey 75
Nancy 115
Peter 49
Simeon P. 57
Willis 126
Chambliss, Samuel 46
Champion, Rachel 108
Champlis, Christopher 6
Chance, Henry 6, 82
Isaac 6
Martin 110
Sampson 6, 82
Simpson 6
Vincent 6, 82
William 104
Chancily, William 50
Chandler, (?) 95
Abednego 6
Edmund 28
Mordecai 6
Mordecia 82
Obednya 82
Chany, Emanuel 6
Chaplin, (?) 96
Joseph 130
Chapman, William 6, 97
Chappel, John 28
Wiley 28
Chappell, John 6
Chastain, Blasingame 28
Peter 28
Sarah 69
William 28
Chasteen, Blas 48
Peter 48
Raney 48
William J. 77, 111
Chastien, Peter 101
Chavis, Gilbert 97
Jeremiah 6
William 100
Cheely, Henry 72
Sarah J. 118
Cheeves, Abner 50
Lucy 69
Chelley, Thomas J. 111
Cherrey, Samuel 28
Cherry, Mary 72
Riley 62, 110
Spencer 42
William 54
Chester, A. 53
Absalom 110, 111
Absolom 49
Asolona 63
Berrill 77
Elizabeth 70, 77
Ellefair 112
Martha 123
Rebecca 77
William 77
William B. 111

Chester (cont.)
William G. 71
Chevalier, Chas. Francis 6
Chevers, Larkin 53
Childers, David 6
John A. 62
Richard 28, 50, 57, 100, 105
Thomas 7
Childress, Richard 6
Childrey, Drury 28
Elizabeth 28
John 7
Martha 28
Childry, Thomas 7
Childs, Isaac 28
Martha 50
Moses 7, 28
Chileney, William 7
Chipley, J. S. 110
Chisolm, John 7
Chivers, Jacob 63, 110
Joel 7, 28, 82, 130
Larkin 7, 75, 110
Mary 75
Nancy 45
Rebecca 123
Thomas 7
Chives, Abner 66
Chrisba, Allen 72
Christian, James 62, 79
Christmas, (?) 82, 84, 86, 96
Nathaniel 7
Nathl. 82
Robert 7
Christy, Allen 60
Chritte, Thomas 97
Cimbrel, Joseph 104
Clance, Martin 110
Martin S. 65
Mary 70
Clark, (?) 87, 92
Daniel 28
David E. 76, 111
Elijah 7
Henry 97
John 135
William 7
Clarke, David 50
Gibson 7
John (Sr.) 7
Clay, Chalender 28
Charles 98
David 7, 28, 98
Elizabeth 124
Emily 114
John 42, 58
Peave 99
Percibal 7
Pierce 28, 51, 110
Pirce 58
Sarah 114
William 42, 50, 54, 61, 79, 101
Clayton, John 7
Clemens, Hosea 7
Clements, Ezekiel 42
Clemonds, Hosea 28
Clerk, (?) 81, 82
E. 92
Lewis 82
Clifton, Nathan 54
Cloud, Jeremiah 28
Clough, Geo. 82, 83, 86, 91
Clunt, James 100

Coalson, William 7
Coats, John 7
  Lasley 7
  Nathaniel 7
Cobb, (?) 80
  (?) (Lt.) 99
  Amos 63, 110
  Benjamin 98, 99
  Clemmons 111
  Ezekiel 7
  James 7, 98
  Job 134
  John 83
  Joseph 7
  Joshua 28
Cobbs, Elizabeth 28
  Jacob 28
  James 7
  John 7
  Joshua 7
Cochran, (?) 93
  John 65
  William 7
Cock, Needham 104
  Zebulon 83
Cocke, Zebulon 7
Cocker, Edward 7
Cockerham, James 7
Cocks, Charles 28
  Daniel 28
  Henry 28
  James 7, 28
  James (Jr.) 28
  John 28
  Richard 28
  Thomas 28
  William 131
Cockuham, James 99
Coe, Joseph 58
Coffield, Betsy 114
  Charles 110
  J. F. 127
  James B. 127
  John 55
  John D. 111
  John R. 110
  Joseph J. 111
  Mary 117
  William F. 127
Cofield, Charles A. 72
  Chas. A. 61
  John 46, 60, 73
Cogburn, Cyprus 46
  George 28
Cohonn, Sarah 49
Cohoon, Adam 49
  Alan 49
  James 51
  Sarah 49
  William 49
Cohorn, James 131
Coker, Daniel 59
  John R. 110
  William 28, 48
Coldman, Curtis 100
Cole, Benjamin 7, 49, 57
  Josiah 7
  Wesley T. 110
  William 7, 83
Coleman, (?) 82, 83, 88,
    89, 95
  Caty 75
  Chas. 80
  Curtis 7
  David 42, 57, 60
  Elizabeth 28, 74
  Harris 7
  Ishum 45

Coleman (cont.)
  James 7
  John 7, 83, 133
  Jonathan 7, 83
  Jones 7
  Lavina 112
  Menan 28, 133
  Moses 7
  Robert 45
  Thomas 7
Colemans, (?) 89
Collier, William 7
Collins, Abhu 28
  Barbara 28
  Creed 49, 101
  Emeline 73
  Emily 121
  Frederick 47
  Gracy 120
  Jackson 61
  James 7, 60, 105
  James M. 69
  John 7, 29, 46, 83
  John A. 110
  John G. 58
  John S. 55
  Joicy 124
  Joshua 46, 55
  L. (Maj.) 111
  Lewis 49
  M. D. 53
  Martha A. 116
  Mary 60
  Sarah A. 116
  Sarah Ann 111
  Thomas 46
  Thomas J. 110
  Thos. J. 42, 60
  Viny 74
  William 7, 29, 49, 83
  Wm. 64, 96
Collums, Isham 134
Colson, Sanders 7, 83,
    87
Colter, John 7
Colton, John 132
Colvin, John 29, 52
Colwell, M. 127
Comens, (?) 85, 92
  David 46
  Eleazer 29
  Eli 46
  Robert 46
  William 46
Comins, David 7
  Eleazer 7
Commens, (?) 87
Commins, (?) 83
Commons, (?) 84
Comons, Eleazar 83
Conaway, Charles 73
Cone, Abel 57
  Archd. 60
  Archelaus 46
  Archibald 58, 72, 105
  Archilas 58
  Archilles 60
  Elizabeth 122
  Henry 111
  Jackson 78
  James 7, 46, 58, 60,
    74
  James B. 111
  Jesse 29
  Jesse B. 60, 74
  Jesse W. 74, 111
  John 7, 52, 101
  John D. 58

Cone (cont.)
  Jonathan B. 74, 111
  Levi 51, 57
  Lewis 47
  Mary 52
  Nancy 62, 78
  Penelope B. 124
  Pheraba D. 112
  Sarah J. 115
  Seaborn 62, 77
  Thomas 57
  William 7, 67, 78, 111
  William B. 111
Coney, Aquilla 29
Congres, Rachel 62
Connell, Jesse 7
Connelly, James 7
  John William 7
  Patrick 7
Conner, Daniel 7, 83,
    136
  John 7
Conney, Jeremiah 133
Connor, Daniel 7
Conyers, Henry 52
  Jacob 42
  Rachel 52, 55
  William 52
Cook, (?) 83, 88
  Abraham 45
  Ailsbury 111
  Alen 45, 59, 60, 79
  Artimicy 113
  Benjamin 29, 45, 58,
    101
  Benjamin R. 110
  Calvin 77, 111
  Cornelius 7, 78, 110
  David 7
  Deborah 29, 44, 47
  Edward 55
  Giles 7
  James 50, 54, 101
  James L. 60
  James S. 55, 72
  John 7, 47, 49, 101
  Julius 29
  Lucy 29
  McKean 7
  McKeen 57
  Mike 45
  Nancy 60, 108
  Nathan 50
  Reuben 7, 29, 138
  Rodiska 71
  Samuel 56, 64, 71, 111
  Savary 48
  Starling 42
  Sterling 53
  Thomas 29
  Treasy 79
  William 74
  William B. 74
Cooke, George 7
Cookers, (?) 80
Cooksey, Jesse 134
  William 7
Cookson, Elizabeth 29
Cooler, Caroline 70
  Rebecca 71
  Richard 71
  Robin 71
Coop, Henry 7
Cooper, Caroline 114
  Isaac 7
  James 7
  John 7, 29, 83, 134
  John Smith 101

Cooper (cont.)
Joseph 7
Obediah 29
William 7
Cooxy, William 83
Copeland, Elisha 29
William 29
Corbet, Elizabeth 112
Martha 118
Sarah 58
Corbett, Groove 51
Corbit, E. 129
John C. 79
M. 129
W. 129
Corday, John 62
Cordery, Sarah 115
Cordrey, James 110
Jonathan 29
Jonathan (Jr.) 29
Jonathan P. 42
Cordry, Daniel 56
John 68
John D. 77
Jonathan 47, 53
Lovinzy 72
Prudence 29
Corsey, Rebecca 114
Corssey, Alfred 58
Corvart, Mary A. 111
Coseys, Alfred 42
Costan, Wiley 126
Costin, John 63
Lott 63
Coston, James 127
John 7, 56, 110
Thomas 7, 42, 53, 110
Wiley 111
Wiley J. 73
William 127
Cotten, John 48
Coulter, John 86
William 134
Coup, Henry 7
Nichale 7
Courney, Alfred 72
Coursey, Alfred 46, 60
William 7
Coventon, J. 80
John 29
Covington, Cloe 57
Emily 113
John 49
Coward, Polly 42
Cowart, Penny D. 63
Cowen, Edward 7
William 7
Cowens, Eleazer 7
Cox, (?) 96
Aaron 51, 58, 64, 70
Benjamin 126
Betsy 49
Bryan 71
Bryant 65
Caroline 108
Cressy 108
Cullen 57
Darius 47
David 56
Denous (?) 53
Elephair 121
Franklin 77
Henry 7, 56, 62, 77, 83
James 42, 50, 52, 54, 99, 110, 126
James R. 111
John 7, 54, 58, 62,

Cox (cont.)
78, 126
John W. 111
Josiah 7, 83
Martha 70, 119
Martha A. 116
Mary 69, 111
Mary A. 122
Mary F. 126
Moses 52, 59, 66, 70, 105
Moses (Jr.) 64, 105
Nancy R. 112
Rebecca J. 126
Richard 77
Robert 64, 78
Robert F. 77
Thomas 7
Tilliam 7
Wiley 111
William 58, 83, 132
William W. 77
Williamson 49
Wm. 62
Young A. 77, 111
Crab, Riland 75
Robert 49
Crabb, Lydia 75
Robert 53
Robt. 64
Wiley 110
Craft, E. 128
Jackson 127
Jno. 42
S. 128
Selia 58
Crafton, Ann 108
Bennet 67
Malton 52
Martha 64, 70
Mathew 55
Nancy 120
William 42, 55, 71, 110, 111
Wm. 65
Craig, Elizabeth 76
Crane, Lewis 7
Crawford, (?) 80, 84
Anderson 7
Charles 7
E. 128
Eliza 109
Elizabeth A. 109
Jesse 111, 127
Jno. 85
John 7
John W. 111
Margaret 111
Mart. 96
Samuel 7
Strother 7
Thomas 7, 49, 59, 64
William 127
William H. 76
Cresswell, David 7
Gilbert 7
Creswell, (?) 90, 94, 95
James 7
Robert 7
Ross 93
Samuel 7
Crew, Elisha 50
Crews, Elizabeth 67
Etheldred 29
Cribbs, Gilbert 7
Thomas 7
Criddle, Thomas 7
Crispus, James 7

Criswell, (?) 83
David 82, 83
Crittenden, John 7
Crittenton, John 7
Thomas 133
Croby, George 29
Crocker, Thomas 132
Croker, William 7
Crook, Robert 45
Crookshanks, Patrick 7
Croom, (?) (Maj.) 7, 57, 78
Adaline 125
Asa D. 111
Emmara 56
Emra 7
George 125
Jennet 59
Major 7, 57, 78
Martha 125
Rabun 125
Rachel 125
Richard 77
Zelphia 113
Croome, Elijah 8, 83
Crooms, (?) (Maj.) 62
Jennett 62
Major 62
Penny A. 62
Crosby, Abraham 29
George 8, 83
Lydia 29
Spencer 29, 134
William 8
Crosley, John 135
Cross, Edward 8, 47
Crother, John 130
Crowell, Henry 45
Crumbley, Anthony 29, 52
Anthony (Sr.) 52
George 52
Crumbly, John 29
Crumby, Emaline 78
John 134
Crumley, Anthony 8
Crumly, Ephraim 66
Crutchfield, John 8
Culbreath, John 8
Peter 8
Cullens, F. B. 62
Francis B. 110
Frederick 29, 62
W. W. 54
Cullins, Alice 29
Augustua A. 67
Ferd 59
Franklin B. 77
Culpepper, (?) 82
Benjamin 29
Charles 29, 138
Chas. 84
David 29
Henry 29
Jno. 83
Joel 29
John 8, 83
John (Jr.) 29
John (Sr.) 29
Malica 29
Sampson 8, 137
Sampson (Jr.) 29
Sampson (Sr.) 29
Culver, May 115
Nathan 98
Nathaniel 100
Cumble, Antony 99
Cumbry, Ephriam 110
Cummin, Eli 60

Cumming, Caroline 122
  Eli 110
  Green E. 111
  I. 42
  Martha 116
  Sarah H. 109
Cummings, David 57, 73
  David E. 73
  Eleazar (?) 83
  Eli 55, 72
  Green E. 72
  Robert 72, 132
Cummins, David 8, 60
  Eli 8
  John Cunningham 8
  Martha A. C. 123
  Richard Cureton 8
  Robert 8, 55, 60
  W. 8
  William 8
Cungame, Winney 117
Cunningham, Kesiah 122
  Thomas 59, 65, 75
Cunyers, Jacob 77
Curl, John 8
  Wilson 49
Currey, Lolsley 42
  Nicholas 29
  Nicholas (Cpt.) 103
  Samuel 29
Currie, John 8
Curry, (?) 88
  (?) (Cpt.) 131, 132
  Albert G. 73, 110
  Alexander 8
  Benjamin 29, 45
  David 8, 56, 60, 83,
    96, 101
  David B. 110
  Elizabeth 73
  George 55
  George W. 110
  Jackaline 112
  Jno. 87
  John 8, 29, 46, 48,
    55, 58, 60, 73, 99
  John (Jr.) 46
  John A. 110
  Margaret 29, 46
  Nicholas 47, 136
  Nicholas (Cpt.) 133
  Robert 8
  Solzy (?) 47
  Thompson 29
  William 8
  William W. 73
  Wm. W. 60
Curton, Boln. 97
Cutchings, Meredith 8
Cuthbert, Alex Daniel 8
Cutlaw, Lydia 111
Cutts, Crecy 49
  Elijah 57
  Elisha 49
  Joseph 8, 29, 49
Dailey, J. D. 77
  Vines 64
Daily, Vines 42
Dales, Mary M. 117
Dameron, John 8
Dameson, John 83
Dampier, Daniel 8
Danavant, Thomas 111
Dancy, Jane 118
Daniel, (?) 90
  Aaron 29
  Abraham 8, 29
  Alexander 54

Daniel (cont.)
  Amos 8, 29, 42, 46,
    136
  Asa 29
  Benjamin 8, 100
  Charles 8, 29
  Edmund 8
  Elizabeth N. 71
  Emiline 108
  Eustis 8
  Ezekiel 29, 56, 64,
    75, 136
  Ezekiel (Jr.) 29, 49
  Ezekiel (Sr.) 49
  Francis 51
  James 8
  Janus 48
  Jesse 62
  John 8, 48, 53, 63,
    69, 83, 101, 135
  John (Sr.) 137
  Jonas 8, 29
  Jos. 29
  Joseph 48, 54, 65, 68,
    111
  Keneth 51, 53
  Kenneth 42
  Lewis 29
  Littleton 45
  Lucresia 114
  Mary 42, 59, 64
  Mathew 29
  Mores 64
  Moses 29, 42, 77
  Nancy 120
  Nathaniel 134
  Peter 51
  Priscilla 29
  Rufus 46
  Sampson 76, 111
  Sarah 121
  Sarah A. E. 115
  Silas 71, 112
  Stephen 8, 29, 47
  Thomas 8, 51
  William 8
  William H. 72, 112
  Wright 29
  Zachariah 42, 57
Daniell, (?) 96
  Benj. 82
  Benjamin 8
Danielly, Arthur 98
  James 8
  John 8
Daniely, Daniel 8
  James 8
Danil, William 73
Dannard, Jacob 8
Dannelly, Arthur 98
  Francis 83
Dannis, William 97
Darbe, Jacob 8
Darby, Ann B. 124
  Armistead 47
  Courtney 71
  James 54, 62
  Jane 119
  John 8
  John Calvin 124
  Richard 8
  Sarah 124
Darcey, James 8
Darcy, Benjamin 8
Darden, Francis 29, 72
  George 8
  Jacob 8
  Stephen 8, 73

Dardien, John 8
Dardin, John 8
  Stephen 57
Darding, John 8
Dardins, John 83
Darek, John 65
Daughaty, Dempsey 99
  John 99
Davenport, LQC 8
  Thomas 8
David, Jonathan 98
  Richard W. 46
  William 8
Davidson, Asa 59
  James 8
  Joseph 8
Davis, A. 128
  Absalom 8
  Amanda 68
  Baldwin 47
  Benjamin 8
  Blanford 8
  Chesley 8
  Clement 29, 134
  Clementus 8
  David 112
  Deocleatun 111
  Deoclesion 47
  Diocletion 8
  Diocliton 29
  E. A. 58
  Edmund 45
  Eligah 97
  Elijah 29, 46
  Eliza 112
  Elizabeth 109
  Enas A. 112
  Enos A. 8, 63
  Goodrum 47, 53, 72
  Goodrun (Sr.) 48
  Goodwin 66
  Irwin 64
  J. 128
  Jacob 8, 75
  James 8
  Jane 72
  Jesse 29
  Joel 8, 52
  Joel A. 54, 63, 75
  John 8, 29, 47, 58,
    73, 112
  Jonathan 29
  Joseph 8, 29, 99
  Joseph G. 77
  Lewis 8, 42, 47
  Lewis (Sr.) 47
  Mary 114, 119
  Mathew 29
  Meredith 8
  Moses 8
  Nancy 56, 61, 117
  Penelope A. 121
  Robert (Jr.) 8
  Sally 47
  Samuel 8
  Solomon 8
  Thomas 8, 72, 83, 112
  Thomas G. 72
  Thomas J. 111
  Thomas L. 75, 112
  V. 128
  Va. A. 121
  Vincen 45
  William 8, 54, 78,
    111, 112
  Willie 83
  Wm. 62
Davison, Caleb 29

Davison (cont.)
J. H. 66
Smithwick 29
Dawkins, Frances 48
Dawson, (?) 83, 88, 90, 92
E. John 29
James 8, 29, 83, 88, 98
Jas. 83, 88, 90
Richmond 8
Day, Ambrose 8
Henry 8
Rob 89
Robert 8
Robt. 90, 96
DeYumpert, Alsey 46
Deampher, Aylesey 8
Dean, Chas. 91
Elizabeth 64, 71
Frederick 29
Joel 42, 48
John 8
Micajah 29
Moses 29
Rachel 51
Thomas 8, 52
Dear, Richard 29
Dearizeaux, Stephen 8
Deas, DeWitt 8
James 8
Deason, Absalom 29
Absolom 51
Jonathan 29, 133
Rachel 8
Sheppard 51
Debosk, Peter 8
Decanter, Richard 29
Sarah 60, 108
W. R. L. 60
Deckins, Lewis 64
Declendemes, Matthew 8
Deedom, (?) 79
Deek, Joseph 8
Deen, James 56
Jesse 57, 64
Joel 56
Martha 115
Deens, Richard 136
Dees, (?) 80, 82, 84
(?) (Dr.) 82
Doctor 82
Duett 84, 88
Delaplaigne, Peter E. 8
Delk, David 29
Jacob 29
Joseph 29, 84, 100
Samuel 29
Thomas 29
Denard, Joseph 137
William 137
Denis, (?) 89
Denkins, Gilbert 8
Denman, Charles 8
Martha 110
Denmark, Shadrack 8
Dennard, Abner 29, 101
Isaac 29, 134
Jacob 29, 134, 135, 137
Jacob (Lt.) 102
James 29
John 29
Rebecca 8
Shadrach 100
Shadrack 8, 29, 134
Thomas 29
William 29, 131, 133,

Dennard (cont.)
134
Dennis, Abraham 8, 90
Isaac 8
Jacob 8
Jno. 90
John 8, 84, 98, 135, 136
John (Lt.) 102
John (Sr.) 29
Dennison, Daniel 9
Densby, Jacob 9
Dent, John 9
Denton, William 134
Depree, Jeremiah 30
Reid 30
Depriest, James 29
Derdains, John 84
Derdan, Frances 58
Mathew 59
Stephen 56
Deveaux, Peter 9
Devenport, Joel 29
Dew, Arthur 29
Diamond, Reuben 29
William 29
Dickens, Gillum 65
Isaac 60
James 111
John 127
Joseph 60
Lewis 9
Mary 110
Sarah 60
Dickenseeds, Edward 9
Dickerson, Henry 42, 105
Dickins, Gillum 55
Hansill 126
Isaac 58, 72
James 58
John 58
Joseph 58
Robert 59
Thomas 126
Dickinson, Charles 48
Dicks, Green B. (?) 112
Dickson, (?) 83, 89
Aaron 29
B. John 29
David 9
James 9, 29
Jeremiah 9
Jeremiah (Sr.) 29
John 97
Michel 9, 84
Reuben 9, 29, 84, 100
Reubin 131
Robert 9, 104
Thomas 9, 97
William 29
Wm. 29
Die, Thomas 131
Dillard, (?) 83
A. 111
Allen 56
B. (Mrs.) 54
Bathsheba 42
Dempsey 56
Edmund 50
George 9, 29, 135
Mary 51
Nathan 29, 50
Nicholas 9, 29
Philip 136
Phillip 9, 29, 99
Sampson 29
Thomas 98
Dinton, Edward 30

Dirdino, John 104
Discks, Green B. 112
Dison, Alvin 69
Divene, Mary Ann 78
Dix, Andrew 9
Dixon, (?) 84, 85
Alla 52
Anna 30
C. D. (Lt.) 101
James (Cpt.) 134
L. John 30
Michael 9
Michel 84
Robert 9, 101
S. Tilman 30
Shad 111
Shadrack 56
Thomas 42, 56, 59, 84
Tilman 52, 101
Dolan, Owen 111
Dolen, Owen 68
Dolittle, Wm. 66
Domin, Frederick 9
Domini, (?) 84
Frederick 9, 84
Dominy, Frederick 30
Donaldson, Elizabeth 122
James M. 75, 111
Robert 64, 68
Wm. 65
Donalson, Elizabeth 118
Henry 111
Jane 126
Mary A. 118
Dongar, Philip 99
Donnaly, John 84
Donnelly, (?) 83
John 9
Dooley, George 9
Doolittle, William 68
Dorch, David 47, 54, 61, 111
John 55, 61, 111
Martha 123
Nancy A. 124
Priety C. 112
Russel 61
Russell 111
Walter 30, 62, 67
Dorsey, Elizabeth 79
John 30
Leakin 30
Dortch, David J. 76, 111
Mary 76
Telytha 112
Walter 111
Douglas, Alexander 9
Edward 9
John 9
William 9
Douglass, Edw. 84
Dowder, Richd. 84
Dowdey, Richard 9
Dowell, Thomas 9
W. 96
Downs, Isaac 98
Silas 60, 72, 98
William 9
Drake, F. B. 66
Francis 54
Richard 66, 68
William 138
Drew, Jesse B. 54
Josiah 84, 104
Driggire, Wynn 101
Driver, David 50
Dublain, George W. 51
Dubose, Jeptha 30

Dubose (cont.)
Reuben 47
Duckworth, Jacob 9, 97
Randol 78
Dudley, Adison E. 70
Arthur 50
Edam 54
Eden 42, 48
Elam 47, 48, 54, 61
Eliam 9
Elum R. 112
S. 127
Susanna 73
Dudly, John 63
Dudney, Arthur 55
Duett, (?) 82
Duffill, Thomas 30
Dugan, Martha 109
Duggan, A. C. 59
Adaline 113
Archelias C. 74
Archelous C. 111
Asa 58, 60, 74
Elizabeth 113
Jesse J. 74
John 9, 30, 45, 55,
60, 74
John H. 45, 55, 62, 74
John M. 74, 112
Martha 110
Mary 115
Rebecca R. 115
William 46, 77, 112
Duggen, Adeline 112
Duggin, Cloana 30
Edmond 30
Duhart, (?) 89
Jno. W. 9
Duke, Alex 126
Alexander 125
Buckner 9
J. 128
James 9
Jane 117, 126
John Taylor 9
M. 128
Martha 126
Mary 126
R. 128
William 9, 48, 53
Dukes, Henry 9, 84
Dun, Thomas 99
Duncan, David 9
James 9
Jos. 9
Matthew 9
Miles 9
Thomas 9, 30, 133
Dunevent, Nancy 46
Dunn, Jacob 30
John 132
Luke 9
Nehemiah 99
Dunst, Moses (?) 47
Dupree, Arthur 125
Charlotte 125
Jacob 65
James 42, 48, 54, 57,
125
Jesse 51
John 125
Lewis 56
Permilla O. 122
T. R. 56, 62
Tim. 50
William 101
Duprey, John 133
Durbin, Luke 9

Durdan, Stephen 99
Durden, Beady 119
Frances 9, 51, 61
Francis 42, 79, 112
Lewis 30, 62, 78, 112
Lydia 112
Martha 77, 108
Mary 114
Matilda 111
Matthew 78, 111
Nicy 78
Sarah A. 68
Stephen 61
Wiley 79, 112
Durdin, Mathas 62
Durham, Mary 30
Samuel 78
Duty, Caroline 108
Dyer, John 30
Rachel 50
Eads, John 9
Eady, John 9, 44
John (Jr.) 30
John (Sr.) 30
Eaken, James 99
Moses 99
Eakins, Alexander 30
James 30
Eammais, (?) (Dr.) 90
Eammis, Jonathan 84
Early, Jesse 30, 50, 57,
101
Earnest, George 9
Jacob 9
Earp, Cullin 30
Eason, Christiana 120
Isaac 9, 58, 65
Eastwood, Elijah 30, 51,
78
Eliza 111
James 42
James J. 78
John 57, 62
John (Sr.) 105
Marium 57
Mary A. 62
Mirium 42
Echols, Amanda 126
Melviria 77
Patience 42
Zelphia 59
Eckles, Lucy 122
Eckols, Joel 9
Ecoles, Catherine J. 72
Ecols, Joel 30
Eda, Richard 101
Edge, (?) 76
Daniel 62
Jonathan 62
M. 128
V. 128
Zachariah 112
Edmonds, David 30
Edmondson, John 30
Edwards, Andrew 30
Britton 47
Elizabeth 30
Gray 9
John 30, 45, 53
Leroy 42, 64, 68, 112
Peter 9
Thomas 30
William 57
William (Jr.) 30
William (Sr.) 30
Edy, John 126
Edzil, Elbert L. 73
Eikner, Philip 78

Eikner (cont.)
Sampson 78
Eiland, Absalom 9
Eland, (?) 95
Elands, Absalom 9
Elbert, Sam'l. (Gen.) 9
Elder, Robt. B. 42
Eles, William 104
Eli, E. B. 9
Rhoda 65
Elkins, Cealy 118
Celia 127
Edy 121, 127
Elizabeth 127
Elizabeth Ann 121
Green 77
John 64, 69
Owen P. 68
Timothy 112
William 77
Wm. 62
Ellington, John 59
Elliott, Benj. 63
Benjamin 9, 46, 56,
101
Bryant 125
Franklin 125
James 125
William 9, 30, 136
Ellis, (?) 85
(?) (Maj.) 49, 54, 64
Ephraim 30
Ephriam 100
James 69, 138
John 58
Major 49, 54, 64
Mayor 42
Pitman 70
Robert 9
Solomon 9
Stephen 9
Elmore, Stephen 30
Elton, Abraham 30
Abram 52, 105
Charles 48, 53, 101
Eliz. 42
John 48, 56, 77
John (Sr.) 63
John B. 112
Letha 112
Robert 52, 112
William 112
Elvington, G. 133
Ely, John 9, 47, 56
Martha 119
Emanuel, Asa 9, 89
David 9
Emewiler, George W. 112
Emmis, (?) (Dr.) 94
English, (?) 81
Cornelius 9, 84
James 133
James S. 9
John 9, 30, 99, 112
Joseph 30
Robert 30
Sampson 47
Thomas 9, 30, 136
Ennett, Elizabeth 72
Ennis, E. N. 72
Elias N. 112
James 49, 77
James H. 112
Jonathan 9
Ernest, Jacob 97
Erwin, William 77
Eskridges, Hetor R. 84
Esom, Mezzak 30

Espey, James 9
Etheridge, Enoch 58
Ethridge, Abel 30
  Calley 30
  Enoch 48, 61
  John 101
  Merit 30
  Robert 98
Eton, Robert 9
Eubank, Daniel 9
Eubanks, (?) 94
  Dan. 82
Evans, (?) 85, 96
  Benjamin 9
  Burwell 30
  Daniel 9
  David 9, 134
  Gibson 9
  James 9, 30
  James (Maj.) 102
  Jasper W. 71
  Jehu 30
  John 9, 30, 71
  Josiah 9
  Lemuel 133
  Mary 109
  Robt. 84
  Stephen 9
  William 9, 30
  Zacheus 9
Evens, Peter 57
Everett, David 58
  James E. 112
Everitt, James B. 71
Eves, Nathaniel 9
Exum, Benjamin 30
Ezzell, William 126
Fagan, (?) 83
  Aaron 9, 30
  Geo 81
  George 9, 84
  James 74
Fagin, Aron 97
Fail, Jeplbey 99
  Thomas 9
Fain, (?) 93
Fair, Jacob 9
  Peter 9
Fairchilds, Lofton 30
  T. John 30
Fandley, Norris 9
Farmer, John 9, 30, 48
  Thomas 42, 99
  William 48
Farr, Peter 100
Fason, William 51
Fauche, Jonas 84
Faulconer, Jacob 9
Faust, (?) (Cpt.) 130
Favers, Wm. 84
Feagan, Aaron 9
Featherstone, Howell 9
Felps, David 9
Fenn, (?) 84
  Eli 9, 46, 60
  Elizabeth 112
  Fravier 9
  Jno. 89
  John 9
  William 9
  Zachariah 9
Fenney, Euphama 9
  William 134
Fennill, John C. 73
  John T. (?) 73
Fentress, J. C. 55
Ferrell, James 9
  Jane 60

Ferris, Moses 97
Few, (?) 80, 84, 86, 88,
  94, 95
  Benjamin 9
  Igantius 9
  Ignatius 84
  William 9
Field, Samuel 67
  William 62
Fields, Bennett 112
  James 9, 84
  John 99
  Samuel 112
  William 78
Fife, Ebeneezer 133
Finchwell, Joseph 9
Finley, James 10
Finn, Eli 55
Finney, Alexander 131
  Arthur 30
  E. (Mrs.) 53
  Euphemia 74
  Ezekiel 75, 112
Finny, Eupherna (?) 61
  Ezekiel 60
Fish, Joseph 53
  Joseph J. 10
  Joseph John 50
  Mary Ann 113
  William 56, 64
Fisher, Charles 49
  John 30, 70, 112, 134
  M. F. 70
  Metcalf 10, 51, 54,
    65, 101
  Sarah A. 124
  William 58
  Wm. 42
Fitts, James 97
Fitz, Wm. 95
Fitzpatrick, Frederick
  10
  Joseph 10
  William 10
  Wm. 91, 96
Fizzel, Jane 58
Fizzle, Jane 45
Flannakin, Saml. 84
Fleming, John 48
  Mary 112
  Robert 10
  William 10
Flemming, Oliver 56
Flemmons, W. 86
Flenneker, (?) 85
Fletcher, James 30
  John 30
  Joseph 30
  Wiley 30
Fling, John 10
Flour, (?) 91
Flournoy, (?) 84
  R. W. 66
  Robert 10
  Robert W. 67
  Robt. 84
  Thomas 10
  Thos. 84, 94
Floyd, Ann S. 114
  Elizabeth 117
  James N. 10
  Margaret 74
  Martha 115
  Mary Ann 114
  Paleman 10
  Pateman (?) 10
  Sarah C. 118
  Silas 55, 66, 79

Flucker, George 10
Flukaway, R. Randolph 30
Fluker, Baldwin 10, 30,
  50, 99
  David 30, 99
  Gemimah 30
  George 135
  Milton B. 42
  Robert 57, 69
  Robert F. 65
  Robert T. 112
  William 10
Folds, George 10
Foley, Watson 69
Folk, Henry 30
  John 30
  Joseph 30, 99
  Lucretia 30
  Mark 30
  William 30
Folker, Joseph 54
Fonkee, Elisha (?) 60
Fontain, William 58
Foobs, Benjamin 63
Foose, Jesse 51
  Moses 42, 57, 101
Forbes, Benjamin 10, 53,
  76, 112
  Joseph 77, 112
  Louisa 69
  M. 128
  Martha 111
  Robert 112
  Sarah 71
Forbs, Benjamin 49
  Dickson 72
  John 50
  Rebecca 117
Ford, Anna 57
  Hillery 56, 78
  John 131
  Joshua 10
  Reuben 78
  William 100
Forehand, Amos 30
  David 49
  Elizabeth 123
  Jerry 49
  Jordan 10, 49
Forgerson, Robert 30
Forrest, Hillory 10
Forshe, John 42
Forshee, Elisha 112
  John 57
Forsyth, (?) 94, 95
  Robert 10
  Robt. 84
Fort, (?) 81, 92
  A. 80
  Arthur 10, 112
  John 49
  Owen 10, 65
  Owen (Cpt.) 102
  Owen H. 43, 76
  Owne 84
  Robert 113
  Robert W. 79
  Seaney 126
  Sidney C. 111
  Thomas 10, 30
  Vinia 111
  William 97
  Windfred 79
Fortner, Milly 79
Fortune, Jacob 10
Foson, William 10
Foster, John 10, 49
  John H. 54

Foster (cont.)
William 10
Fouche, Jonas 10
Foulds, George 10
Fouler, John 30
Fountain, (?) 84
Biar 126
Ivy 69
John 75, 126
M. 128
Nathaniel 112
S. 128
Spicy 112
V. 128
W. B. 112
William 10, 112, 126
Wm. 43
Fourman, David 133
Fowler, Alafair 121
Elizabeth 71
J. D. 65
James S. 112
Jeremiah 51
John 50, 54, 57, 65
Lewis 134
Martha 71, 121
Nathan 10
Rebecca 109
Thomas S. 71
Fox, Charles 112
Frances, James 112
Nancy 65
Francis, Cordall 10
Cordel 48
Cordial 56
Cordy 75
Emily 76
Nancy 76
Franklin, Elizabeth 63, 113
Geo. 84
Geo. F. 62
George 10, 30, 53, 113
George T. 77
James 46
Jesse M. 77
Josiah 48
Louisa 117
Philemon 135, 137
Philimon 10
Samuel O. 10, 66, 69
Sarah A. 117
Thomas 30
Vashti 46
Vashty 56
William 10
Frarser, Wilkins (?) 60
Fraser, Andrew 10
Malikah 10
Frasher, Andrew 131
John 137
Frasier, Stephen 43
William 43
Frasure, Wilkinson 58
Frazer, Andrew 10
Malikah 10
Wm. 46
Frazier, Henry B. 112
Jemima 45
John 30, 98
William 30
Frazure, Margaret 59
Frederick, Delilah 30
Francis 10
James 134
Jane 113
Thomas 10
Freel, Lewis 10

Freeman, Fanny 47
Holeman 10
John 10, 51
William 10
Freil, John 10
Friday, David 30
Frizzle, (?) 30
Bryant 30
Ellisshaba 30
Gale 30
Thomas 30, 47, 101
Frobs, Letticia 117
Frost, Allen 65
Elizabeth 119
Hillary 112
James 58, 75, 112
Ruben 75
Sarah 114
Fryer, Wm. 46
Frzier, Jemima 45
Wm. 46
Fulford, Bryan B. 75
Sarah 75
Fulgam, Jacob D. 72
James 72
John G. 72
Mathew 72
Fulgham, Elizabeth 117
Jacob D. 112
James 112
Jesse 30
Mathew 112
Micajah 30
Fulghum, John 112
Fuller, Chloe 52
I. 43
Isaac 10, 30, 99
John 10, 30
John (Sr.) 10
Joshua 10, 126
Peggy 59
Richard 78
Stephen 126
Fullford, Bryant 63
Fulsom, John 97
John. 97
Fulton, R. L. 67
Samuel 10
Samuel (Jr.) 10
Fuluham, Mear 97
Fuqua, Prater 10
Thomas 10
Furgurson, Daniel 48
Furguson, Benjamin 52
Furlow, Jas. 83, 91
William 10
Fusils, Thomas 10
Fussell, Ezra 10
Gaffold, William 10
Gainer, (?) 82
James 47, 54, 76
James J. 76
Jesse 10
Martha 48
Michael 51
Samuel 30
William 30, 48, 75
Gainor, James 63
Mary Ann 115
William 85
Gallman, Hugh 132
Galman, Harmon 10
Galphin, George 10, 135
John 10
Thomas 10
Gambol, (?) 89
Gample, John 10
Ganer, William 10

Gardener, (?) 85
John 85
Gardiner, John 10
Gardner, (?) 85, 90
Aaron 30
Ashel 30
B. Jesse 30
Celia 62, 74
Ezekiel 47
G. Jason 30
Ishum 48
Jacob 30
John E. 45, 57
Lewis 10
Licia 46
Mark 30
Thomas 30
William 10
Garess, George 43
John 43
Garmeny, William 100
Garnel, Eli 10
Garner, Henry 45, 56, 60, 74
Jacob 10, 30, 59
James 57
John 60, 79
Joshua 60
Joshua J. 74, 113
M. (Sr.) 43
Martha A. 121
Moses 79
Moses (Sr.) 74
Patience 60
Piercy 62
Reddick 30, 131
Redick 10
Richard 100
Stephen 45, 101
Urias 99
William 74
Garrett, Asa 45, 60, 79
Elizabeth 74
John 10, 79
Samuel 30, 45, 105
Garros, Amos 58
Garrott, Asa 59
John 113
Gary, Elizabeth 123
Gaskins, Corda 76
Gaston, Alexander 10
David 10
Gates, Philip 10
Samuel 30
Gatlen, Feriby 60
Gay, Delpha 117
Gilbred 97
John 63
Joshua 98
Josiah 130
Gayne, James 97
Geeslin, Samuel 113
Gelber, D. E. 65
Gendol, Jacob 54
George, Daniel 30
William 10
Germanies, (?) 86
Germany, John 10
Samuel 10
William 10, 31
Wm. 91
Gernigan, Lewis A. 68
Gibbons, (?) 81
Gibbs, Harod 101
William 10
Gibert, Mary 123
Gibson, Adam 10
James 31

Gibson (cont.)
John P. 74
William 31
Gidden, Richard 10
Gilbert, Drery 10
Drury 31, 65, 70
Elizabeth 108
Hilkiah 31
Japtha 31
Jesse 31
John 31
Nathan 65, 71, 113
Thomas 10
Thomas (Sr.) 31
Washington 70
William 31, 50, 57,
65, 71, 113
Giles, Alexander 57, 62,
78
Alexander H. 77
Calvin 78, 113
Celia 43
Celia A. 121
Franklin (Dr.) 113
John 10, 55, 58, 60,
113
John B. 113
L. 128
Lavina 78
Lucinda 111
Lucy 119
M. 128
Martha 109
Mary 59, 78, 110
Matilda 120
N. B. 127
Nathan 58
Nathaniel 62, 113
Nathaniel B. 72, 113
Rachel 119
S. 128
Sarah 109
William 55, 62, 78, 97
William W. 78, 113
Gilis, William 57
Gillett, Elijah 10
Gilliland, Thomas 10
William 10, 97
Gillum, Miles 47
Gilman, Harmon 85
Gilmore, Alexander 113
Charles 99
Charles H. 10
Francis 68
George 31
Hugh 50, 54
James 10, 31, 43, 47,
50, 58, 105
James (Sr.) 31
James H. 62, 78
John 47, 58, 61, 72,
98
John (Jr.) 31
John (Sr.) 31
John H. 10
Mary 61, 115
Nancy 108
Sarah 31
Thomas 49
William 31
William M. 74
Wm. M. 62
Ginkins, Allin 97
Gladden, James 31
Julia A. 123
Solomon 79
Gladdin, James 51
Solomon 55

Gladen, James 10
Solomon 61
Glamkin, John 10
Glascock, Thomas 10, 85
Thos. 92, 96
William 10
Glaspy, John 10
Glass, Joel 10
John 10
Thomas 133
Zachariah (Lt.) 97
Glen, (?) 87
Otway 52
Glenn, (?) 85, 94
Ann 31
Betty (?) 72
Daniel 10
David 10, 85, 134
John 31, 51, 54, 66
Martha A. 121
Patience 55, 64, 70
Robert 10, 134
Robert (Jr.) 31
Robert (Sr.) 31
Thomas 51
William 10, 134
William B. 43
Glover, A. 57
Absalom 10
Benj. 65
Benjamin 10, 113
Jesse 10, 75, 113
Mary 65
Stephen 10, 31
William 10
Godby, William 10
Godfrey, William 79
Godwin, Alan 48
Elias 48, 57
Jonathan 97
Goff, (?) 84
Amos 76
Sarah 55
William 65
William E. 76, 113
Going, William 98
Golden, Benjamin 31
John 10, 31
Goldsberry, Jonathan 10
Golightly, James 31, 43
S. 43
Susannah 55
Go-d, McKerness 31
Goode, Edward 11, 85
Goodgame, Alexander 47
George 43
Goodrum, Lydia 51
Goods, (?) 81
Goodson, Abram 57
Edwin 43, 56
Thomas 53
Gordan, Benjamin 11
Gorden, Benjamin 55
Richard 56
Gordon, Allen 31
Ambrose 11
Benjamin 11, 48
Kenneth 31
Richard 31, 47
Gordsby, Cary 11
Gordy, Leonard 113
Goza, Elijah 31
John 31
Joshua 31
Grady, Frederick 49
Graham, John 134
Samuel 31, 99
Grant, Daniel 11

Grant (cont.)
Peter 11
Thomas 11
Grantham, (?) 84, 89
Daniel 97
Jno. 85
John 11, 97
William 11
Wm. 85
Granway, Alfred 75
Graves, James 97
Lewis 97
Richard 11
Thomas 11
Gray, Enoch 11, 46, 58,
61
James 11
John 11
Joseph 45
Thomas 11
William 73, 113
Wm. 61
Zachariah 69, 113
Graybill, (?) 88
Henry 11
John W. 68
Tully 69, 113
Grayham, James 91
Grear, Robert 11
Greazell, George 11
Green, (?) 81
Benj. 85
Benjamin 11
E. 73
Edmund 113
Ephraim 31
Franklin 78
Gideon 113
Harvey 95
Isaac 11
James 11
Jesse 31
John 11, 31
Leonard 11
Leonard (Jr.) 31
Mary 117
McKeen 11, 50, 57
Peleg 11, 85, 86
Rebecca 77
Sheppard 69
Sherrod 72, 113
Thomas 11
William 47, 55
William (Sr.) 11
Greene, Benjamin 11
Edmund 65
Ephriam 131
Gideon 43
James 11, 85
Leonard 31
Thomas 43
Tilman 60
William 11, 31
Greenle, Eliza 45
Greenwood, Benj. L. 65
Lutitia A. 118
Greer, (?) 96
Aaron 11
David 52, 62
George 52
Gilbert 11
James 99
Josiah 11, 85
Martha L. 120
Rebecca N. 115
Thomas 11
William 11, 134
Gregory, Allen 113

Gregory (cont.)
  Emeline 116
  Henry 68
  Samuel H. 113
  William 43, 51, 53,
    63, 70
Greiner, Charles A. 43
Grey, (?) 82
Greyer, Elizabeth 31
  George 31
  Richard 31
Greyham, James 85
Grice, Fatha 11
  Jesse 11, 31
  Richard 31
Grier, David 56
  George 58
Griffen, Leonard 85
  Majer 85
Griffin, (?) 81, 85, 93,
    94
  (?) (Maj.) 11, 31
  Allen 31, 50
  Asa 72, 113
  Benjamin 11, 136
  Comfort 31
  David 47
  Elizabeth 119
  Enoch 11, 52
  Evington 31
  Farnafol 11
  Francis 70
  Hardy 113
  Henry 78
  James 45
  John 11
  John P. 78
  Jones 131
  Joseph 31
  Larkin 53
  Len 31
  Lenn 11
  Leonard 92
  Lewis 52, 113
  Major 11, 31
  Mary 52
  Mathew 11
  Miller 31
  Rebecca 61, 78
  S. 128
  Sally 51
  Sarah 57, 118
  Sheppard 63
  Thomas 58, 73
  Thos. 60
  William 11, 31, 45,
    55, 61, 68, 113
  Wm. 66
Griffith, Samuel 11
Grimes, Nathan 11
  Thomas 11, 113
  William D. 79
Grimsbey, John 11
Grindstone, John 31
Griner, Phillip 11
Grinsteed, William 31
Grooks, John 62
Groom, (?) (Maj.) 51
  Catherine 31
  Elijah 11
  Emmry 51
  Jesse 11, 31, 51
  Major 51
  Wiley 31
  Wylly 51
Grooms, Wiley 11
Grove, Mary 118
Groves, John 11

Groves (cont.)
  Sarah 71
Guilder, Jacob 31
  Sinnet 31
Guiner, William W. 113
Guiton, Tabitha Ann 43
Gulbert, Drewry 133
Guthrie, William 46
Guthril, John 11
Guyton, Tabitha 109
Hadden, William 11
Haden, Adam 137
  Allen 132
  Ed 134
  John 134
  Nancy 108
  Samuel 134
  Voll 131
Hadon, Wm. 85
Hagan, (?) (Cpt.) 103,
    130
Hagans, Edward 11, 136
  Edward (Cpt.) 102
  James 99
Hail, (?) 80
  Edward 31
Hailey, Holliday 31
Haines, Albin O. 43
  Alvin C. 114
  Alvin O. 68
  Bethel 43
  Ezekiel 31
  Harty 115
  Leonard 43
  Leven 31
  Nathan 31
  Nathan (Jr.) 43
  Nathan W. 11, 43
  Yeoman 67
Hainey, Ezl. 101
Hains, Jane 72
  Nathan W. 71
Hainy, Levin 101
Hair, Winnefred 61
Hale, Charlotte M. 120
  Mary E. 77
Haley, Holliday 11
Hall, (?) 94
  Benjamin 98
  Bradley 130
  Charlotte M. 120
  Daniel 101
  David 99
  Edward 11
  Eliza 77
  Emeline 113
  Francis M. 77
  Geneper 104
  Isham 135
  James 11, 31, 61, 98
  James H. 68
  John 31, 98
  L. M. (Widow) 107
  Lavania 111
  Lydia 48, 51
  M. M. 66
  Reuben 62, 113
  Samuel 31
  Sarah 66, 68, 122
  Sarah J. 122
  Tho. 31
  William 31, 48, 51,
    56, 78, 101, 114,
    130, 131
  William B. 113
  William H. 11, 78,
    114
  Wm. 62

Hall (cont.)
  Wm. (Sr.) 61
  Wm. C. 66
Hambleton, Duncan 31
  Edward 130
Hamill, Solomon 132
Hamilton, Calvin 43
  Duncan 50, 57
  Erwin 76
  John W. Cox 69
  Mary 77
  Morris R. 64, 114
  S. 129
  Samuel 46, 58
  Sarah Ann 115
  Sherod 77
  Sherrod 64, 69, 113
  Thomas 11
  William 11, 43
Hamlin, Richard 11
Hammett, James 11
  William 11
Hammitt, Sitha 11
Hammock, Amelia 11
  Benedict 11
  Daniel 31
  George 114
  John 11
  John (Sr.) 31
Hammond, George 11
Hamock, George W. 75
Hampton, (?) 131
  (?) (Cpt.) 131, 132
  Edward 31, 132
  Mary 46
  Mr. 131
  Thomas 31
  William 31, 100, 131
Hancock, Elisha 31
  William 31
Hand, Abraham 47
Handley, (?) 80, 84
  George 11
  James 11, 48
  Jesse 31
Hanes, Nathan 63
  Nathan W. 63
Hanford, Betsey 46
Hannah, (?) 85
  Thomas 11
Hannan, Mary Ann 116
Hanner, Thomas 100
Hannl, Michael (?) 63
Hanson, Catherine 116
  Eliza 121
  Michael 11, 56, 67,
    115
Harbuck, Michael 11
  Nicholas 11
Hardaman, Elizabeth 31
Hardee, Collins 11
  Diana 65
  Isaac 11
  Theophilus 45
  Thomas 31, 57
  Whitt 45
Hardeen, James 45
Hardeman, Thomas 51
Harden, Adam 31
  Elizabeth 109
  John 31, 51, 54
  Nicholas 31
Hardeson, Elizabeth 51
Hardie, William 11
Hardiman, Thomas 101
Hardin, James 51
  John 66
  John F. 59

Hardin (cont.)
  Rebecca 122
  William R. 114
Hardison, A. Acman 68
  Frederick 45
  John 52
  Nancy 124
  Thomas 31
  William 47
  William L. 71
  Wm. L. 54, 65
Hardon, (?) 85
Hardwick, (?) 86
  Robert A. 43
  Thomas W. 75
  W. P. 54, 75
  William P. 11
  Wm. P. 63
Hardy, Alan 31
  Alan (Jr.) 31
  Collins 52
  Diannah 70
  James 31
  John 31, 52
  Penny 71
  Thomas (Jr.) 51
  Thomas (Sr.) 51
  William 52
Hargrove, Hardy 104
  Howell 11
  Joseph 86
  Josiah 11, 85, 104
  Randal 104
  Richard 74
  William 50
Harkins, Thomas 11
Harlow, H. 39
  James 39
  John 39
  William 39
Harman, William B. 114
  William N. 114
Harmon, Rebecca 79
  William B. 67
  William M. 61
Harper, George 11
  John 31
  Joseph 11
  Robert 11
  Samuel 11
  William 11
  William F. 114
Harrard, David 113
Harrel, Bailey 31
  James 31
  Jesse 31
  Joseph 31
Harrell, Bailey 11
  David 43, 53, 113
  Edward 11
  Henry 31
  Jackson 114
  Jesse 43, 50, 54
  John 59
  Solomon 31, 43, 50, 54
  William 11, 31
  Zachariah 11
Harrill, George 48
Harrington, John 11, 59
  Thomas 11
Harris, (?) 80, 88
  Alsey 31
  Ann 68
  Archiles 11
  Benjamin 31
  Buckner 11
  Chruchwell 43
  Churchwell 31, 51

Harris (cont.)
  Daniel 11, 31, 54, 63,
    75, 114
  David 11, 31
  Edmund 11
  Emily Jane 115
  George 11
  Harrison 31, 134
  Henry 98
  James 11, 31, 46, 51,
    131, 132, 138
  Jesse 11, 85, 133
  John 61, 70
  Joseph 79, 114
  Mary 31
  Mathew 11
  Mathew (Rev.) 31
  Moses 11
  N. F. 53, 66
  Nathan 11
  Reese 132
  Samuel 47, 134
  Sarah 31
  Thomas 115
  Tracy 61
  Treasy 79
  Trecy 56
  Tyre G. 11
  Walton 11
  Wiley 67, 114
  William 31, 43, 132
Harrison, (?) 94, 95
  (?) (Cpt.) 132
  Benj. 85
  Benjamin 11, 137
  Benjamin (Cpt.) 136
  Edward 11
  Elizabeth 112
  Gabirel 12
  Gabriel 43, 55
  James 60
  James C. 74, 114
  James G. 61, 114
  James U. 12
  Jane S. 112
  John 75, 101, 114
  John L. 60, 72
  Joseph 12, 46, 48, 54,
    58, 61, 65, 72
  Lewis J. 75, 114
  Nancy 118
  Nancy D. 116
  Penelope 112
  Sarah 113
  Thomas B. 71
  William 12
  William D. 74, 113
  Wm. 60
  Wm. D. 43
Hart, Barnabas 43
  Barney 49
  Elizabeth 121
  George 12
  Henry 32
  Joel 12
  Jonathan 43, 49
  Joseph 12
  Mary 119
  Nancy 43, 53, 63, 76
  Reuben 12, 32
  Robert 12
  Robt. 85
  Sam W. 115
  Saml. 85
  Samuel 12, 32, 99, 100
  Samuel (Jr.) 134
  Samuel (Sr.) 32, 134
  Samuel W. 114

Hart (cont.)
  William 104
  William S. 76
Harthhorn, John 32
  Thomas 32
Harthorn, Thomas 12
Hartley, Barwell 54
  Burrel 47, 114
  Burrell 127
  Burrill 76
  Burwell 12, 63
  C. 128
  Coline 111
  Fere (Widow) 107
  George 12
  Hardy 53, 63, 69, 76,
    77, 114, 127
  Henry 12
  Hillery 47, 56
  James 12
  James (Jr.) 48
  James (Sr.) 47
  Pherraby 59
  Raford 68, 127
  Raiford 114
  Riley M. 67
  S. 128
  Sarah 109
  Siney 109
Hartly, Raiford 12
Hartsfield, (?) 94
  Andrew 32
  Geo. 85
  George 12
Harvard, Stephen 114
Harvel, Samuel 12
Harvey, Benjamin 32
  Blassingame 12
  Charles 12
  Evans 12
  James 12, 32
  Joel 12
  John 12, 32, 136
  Michael 12
  Thomas 12, 32, 132
  William 97, 131
Harville, John 32
Harwick, Maria 123
  Robert A. 114
  Thomas W. 114
Haskins, (?) (Widow) 81
Hassard, David 43
Hasteen, William 52
Haswell, Richard 97
Hataway, Ann 113
  Bateman 101
  James 114
  John 114
  Lucretia 113
  Mary 110
Hatcher, Archibald 12
  Eldridge 76
  Henry 12
  Jeremiah 12
  John 12, 32, 134
  William 113
Hateway, David 46
Hathaway, Nathan 114
Hathorn, Tho. 99
Hatley, Holiday 136
  John 32
Hattaway, Baten 72
  Baton 60
  Davis 60
  Jackson 114
  John 72
  Nathan 73
  Penelope L. 72

Hattiway, Daniel 55
Haughton, Joshua 12
   Thomas 12
Haul, George 12
Havard, John 49
Havetey, Robert 45
Havey, (?) 96
Hawkins, Benjamin 50
   Carolina 109
   Dreiory (?) 113
   Drewry 55
   Drury 60
   Francis 12
   Henry 60, 72
   Lourany 110
   Samuel 12
   Sarah J. 73
   Susan 111
   William 51
Hawthon, Thomas 12
Hawthorn, Peter 12
Hay, Isaac 106
   James 127
   Ruben 59
Haygood, Archd. 61
   Archibald 78
   J. 128
   Middle (?) 126
   Middleton 78
Hayley, Holiday 47
Hayman, Staunton 12
Haymon, Stephen 12
Haynes, Bythol 55
   Emulia 56
   Ezekiel 47
   Levin 47
   Nathan 46, 57
   William P. 67
   Wm. P. 53
Hays, Andrew 12
   Arthur 12
   Isaac 50
   Queny 59
   Quinny 49
   Qunny 63
   Samuel 50
Haywood, Archibald 58
Head, James 32
   Richard 32
Headen, Louisa 12
Headspeth, Charles 12
Heard, (?) 86, 89, 92
   Bernard 12
   Jackson 75
   Jesse 12
   John 12
   John (Sr.) 12
   Joseph 12
   Stephen 12
Hearn, Wm. 99
Hearndon, Charles 43
Heart, Samuel 12
Hearthorn, William 12
Hearton, Thomas 12
Heartshorn, Andrew 131
Heath, Benjamin 32
   Daniel 49, 113
   Elizabeth 32
   Henry 62, 68, 114
   John 32, 97
   William 32, 114
Heaton, Robt. 85
Hebert, (?) 93
Heeth, Daniel 57, 64
   Sarah 58
Reethe, Sarah 45
Helton, (?) 85
   Abraham 45

Helton (cont.)
   E. 128
   James 32, 127
   Joseph 12
   Richard 43, 55
   Washington 114
   William 32
Hemp, Jos. 90
Hemphill, (?) 86
   Andrew 32
   Robert 131
   William 12
   Wm. 86
Henderson, (?) 86
   Dolly A. 78
   Levi 78
   Nichols 114
   Zachariah 12
Hendley, John 12
Henington, Betsey 46
   Jonathan 32
Henry, Isaac 32
Henson, Caleb 32
Herendine, Charlotte 65
Hergrove, Howell 92
   Renfro 93
Hern, Joseph 51
   Stephen 51
   Wyatt 51
Herndon, Charlotte 43
   George 12, 32, 126
   George (Jr.) 32
   James 32
   John 134
   Joseph 12, 32, 57, 97,
      132, 134
   Lewis 32, 132
   Stephen 32
   Wiatt 55
   William 32
Herren, Alexander 12
Herrill, William 12
Herring, James 86
   William 12
Herrington, Charles 131
   James 114
   John 60
Herrins, (?) 87
Hewett, William 12
Hewil, William 12
Hewitt, William 12
Hewlin, Joseph 76
Hewsom, Nancy 63
Hickinbottom, Burrows 12
   Joseph 12
Hicklen, Francis 70
Hicklin, Nancy R. 117
   R. N. 43
   Rubin 51
   William P. 78
Hickman, James 32
   Joseph 12, 100
   Theophilus 12
   William 12
   Wm. 86
Hickmon, Theo 97
Hicks, Adeline 124
   Henry 65, 76, 114
   James 12
   John 12
   Martha 124
   Nathaniel 12
   Nathaniel (Jr.) 12
   Samuel 12
   William 43, 114
Hidleberg, John 32
Higdon, (?) (Cpt.) 104
   Burel 104

Higdon (cont.)
   Charles 12, 86, 104
Higgs, Abraham 100, 132
   Elisha 32
   John 100
Highland, Nicholas 86
Highnote, Phillip 99
Hightower, Charnal 12
   Ephriam 76
   F. C. 64
   G. D. 43
   Joshua 114
   Lutetia 116
   Rolly 59
   Warren 113
Hill, (?) 81, 88, 90
   Daniel 32
   Edward 12
   Enoch 47, 101
   George 12
   James 12, 97, 113
   James J. 53
   Jno. 81
   John 12
   Joshua 12
   Moses 12
   Theophilas 63
   Theophilus 43, 54, 69
   Thos. 86, 88
   William 12, 69, 114
   Wm. 84, 94
   Zelphia 110
Hillar, (?) 85
Hillard, (?) 80
   Abigail 12
   James 12
   Majer 86
Hillary, Christopher 12
Hilliard, (?) (Maj.) 12,
   32
   Major 12, 32
   Martin 49
   Nancy 49
Hilson, John 32
Hilton, Abraham 32
   James 46
   Richard 46, 113
   Washington 73
Hilyer, James 12
Hines, Amarintha L. 118
   C. T. 73
   Churchwell 12
   Churchwell T. 63
   James 12, 84
   Richard 46
   Robert 12
Hinsley, Thomas 12
Hinson, John 32
   William 12, 62, 67
Hinton, Caleb 132
   Job 12
Hitchcock, Lucy Ann 112
   Mary 108
   Sarah 78
   Shadrach 114
   Turner P. 61
   Turner R. 114
   Turner R. (?) 61
Hitt, John 32
   William 32
Hobbs, Drury 32
   Jonathan 12
Hobs, Sarah 32
Hobson, Briggs 12
   Edward 12
   Griggs 12
Hocklin, R. N. 57
Hodge, Henry 52

Hodge (cont.)
  John 47
  Mary 67
  Mathew 32
  Robert 12
Hodges, Abel 55, 62
  Augustus G. W. 77, 114
  Barbara 122
  Benjamin 32
  Charles 32
  Charlotte 77
  Edward 32
  Elbert 43, 59
  Elizabeth 111
  Foreman 32, 52
  George C. 47
  Henry 43, 58, 62, 66,
    78, 114
  Henry C. 115
  James 32
  John 32, 50, 54, 66,
    78, 113
  John R. 71
  Jordan 59
  Julia 115
  Lemuel 50
  Martha 111
  Reddin 64
  Redding 12, 54, 70,
    114
  Reding 72
  Robert 32
  Samuel 32
  Sarah 43, 56
  Seth 53, 66, 101
  W. T. 62
  Wiley T. 43, 54
  William 46, 67, 114
  Wm. 66
Hoff, Samuel 12
Hogan, Edmond 32
  Griffin 32
  Griffin (Lt.) 138
  James (Cpt.) 102
  John (Jr.) 32
  R. John 32
Hoges, Lemuel 12
Hogg, Jacob 86
  James 12, 98
  James (Sr.) 12
  William 12
Hogin, John 97
Hoil, Edward 11
Holder, James 74
  James A. 76
  Nancy 115
  Sarah A. 117
Holderness, James 86
  Jas. 95
Holdness, James 12
Holeman, David 32
Holifield, W. L. 67
Hollaman, David 12
Holland, (?) 86
  Demsey 12
  Henry 98
  John 98
  Margaret 32, 55
  Sewel 132
Hollen, James 32
  Suel 32
Hollenger, Titus 12
Hollenworth, Stephen 86
Holley, Henry 32, 53
  Isaac 32
  John 43
  Thomas 32, 86
  Williaam 106

Holley (cont.)
  William 32
  William (Jr.) 32
Holliday, Ayers 12
Holliman, David 12
  Mark 13
  Richard 13
  Thomas 46
Hollin, William 32
Hollinger, William 13
Hollingsworth, Stephen
  13
Holliway, David 32
Holloman, Samuel 12
Hollomon, Mark 97
Hollon, Suel 99
Holloway, Barnes 13
Holly, Henry 47
  Jacob 13
  Jonathan 13, 86
  Nathaniel 13
  Thomas 13, 136
Holmes, John 61
  John J. 58
  Mary 79
  Nathaniel 46
  Robert 13
Holms, John 13
  Lewis 48
Holt, Ann 111
  Arrington 51
  Catherine 111
  Ellis 58
  Esau 127
  John 43, 127
  Kitchen 113
  Lewis A. 64
  Lewis H. 71
  Mary 65, 115
  Rachel 123, 127
  Susannah 43, 58
  Tapley 32
  Thaddeus 32
  Thomas 13, 32, 48, 106
  Willis 65
Holton, Elizabeth 58
  Francis 13
  Henry 72
  John 114
  Lavina 123
  Mary 60
  S. A. 128
  Salathel 32
  Salathiel 78
  Samuel 13, 86
  Sarah A. 112
  Selathul (?) 61
  Steph. 43
  Stephen 51, 125
  Thial 54, 125
  William 45, 57, 72
Holy, (?) 93
Homes, David 32
  G. Nathan 32
  J. William 32
  James 32
Hood, Allan 32
  Benjamin 13
  Edward 32
  J. 128
  James 113
  Jefferson 126
  Joseph 79
  Larkin 43, 67, 78
  Leutresia 110
  Lion 101
  Lucy 50, 51
  Nancy 120

Hod (cont.)
  Nathaniel 13, 86
  Reason 126
  Sean 54
  Seen (?) 50
  Sherod 78
  Sherrod 58, 61
  Simon 79
  Stephen 134
  Thomas J. 114
  Wiley 32, 43
  William 48, 54, 61,
    79, 114
  William (Jr.) 32
  William (Sr.) 32
  Willy 13
Hoodson, Abraham 50
Hook, James S. 67, 115
Hooker, (?) (Cpt.) 132
  Nathan (Cpt.) 99
  Stephen 136
  Stephen (Lt.) 97
Hooks, (?) 86
  Curtis 79, 115
  Hilery 79
  Hillary 58, 61
  Hopewell 63, 73, 113
  Sally 45
  Sarah 55, 63, 74
  Thomas 13, 32
  William 13, 32, 86,
    136
Hooper, (?) 93
  Absalom 13, 86
  Robert 13
Hopkins, Clara B. 74
  Jesse 45
  Lambert 13
  William 13
Hopson, (?) 95
  Amanda 73
  Briggs 13, 32, 86
  Edmond 32
  Edmond (Cpt.) 101
  Edward 131, 134
  Edward (Sr.) 32
  Hardy 32
  Nathaniel W. 114
  William 13, 32, 47, 53
  Wm. (Lt.) 101
Horn, (?) 52, 84
  Elizabeth 32, 72
  Hab. 89
  Jacob 13
  Joab 86
  John 32, 49
  Judy 46
  Richard 133
  Sherod H. 51
Hornby, Philip 13
Horne, John 13
  Phoebe 123
Horsley, Tarleton 13
Horten, Laban 78
Horton, (?) 86
  Daniel 13, 43, 52, 113
  Elizabeth 78
  F. K. 53
  Fred K. 43
  Frederick 50
  Frederick G. 56
  George W. 53
  Harrel 71
  Harrell 64
  Harrold 114
  Howel 57
  Howell 43, 52
  Hubbard 74

Horton (cont.)
Irena 121
James 62
Jesse 58
Josiah 114
Ketral 50
Labon 62
Laborn 56
Levi 32, 50, 133
M. 129
Martha 122
Nancy 117
Priscilla 108
S. 129
Sallie 113
Thomas 86
Wiley B. 58
William 50, 65
Hoskins, Miriam 13
Hotton, E. 43
Richard 127
Virgil 126
Houghs, Samuel 13
Houghton, James 13
Joshua 13
Thomas 13
William 13
House, Joseph 13, 86
Laurence 13
Housley, Weldon 13
Houston, (?) 89
James 13
William 13
Houstoun, Henry 13
John 13
Howard, (?) 80, 87, 95
Angeline 123
Ann 32
Benjamin 13, 32
C. 128
Charles 13, 48
David L. 125
Elizabeth 58, 66, 73
Franklin 67
George F. 66, 105
Harman 101
Harmon 48
Henry 48
Isaac 32
J. J. 73
James 13, 32, 45, 125,
    127, 133, 134
James (Lt.) 102
James (Sr.) 46
James M. 55
James W. 61
John 32, 114, 133
John R. 13, 59
Joshua 13, 48, 133
Lemuel 32, 46
M. E. 128
Martha 111, 125
Mary 62
Missouri 125
Morgan 127
N. 128
Nancy 13, 59
Nauflight 47
Naughflight 13
Penelope 60
Polly 54
Rhesa 13
S. A. 128
Sally 61
Samuel 13, 32, 46,
    114, 125, 127, 134
Sarah Orr (Mrs.) 120
Seaborn 73

Howard (cont.)
Sidney 117
Solomon 32, 45, 58,
    106
Solomon (Jr.) 47
Thomas 13
Thos. 92
W. 128
William H. 73, 125
Winefred H. 108
Howars, Solomon 136
Howel, (?) 87
Gabriel 100
Howell, Ashley A. 73
David 13
Elizabeth 32
Gabriel 133
Jehu 32
John 32, 133, 134
Joseph 13, 86
Nathaniel 13
Raford 114
Hoye, William 99
Hubert, Mathew 13, 86
Huckaby, Isam 13
Huckagy, (?) 96
Huckeby, John 86
Hudson, Benjamin 46, 71
Evan 47
George H. 78
Henry 43
Henry T. 127
Isaac 13
James 13
Nathaniel 13
Robert 13
Sarah 68
William 13
Wm. 86
Huff, Sam 83
Samuel 86
Huggins, Daniel 48
Hughes, Hardy 127
James 13
Nicholas 13
Hughs, James 13, 86
Nicholas 13
Hull, Daniel 65, 75
William 13, 65, 75
Humphrey, James 79
Humphries, Matchell B.
    113
Hunsham, Thomas (?) 48
Hunt, (?) 83
Ann 110
Daniel 13
Fitz 94
Fitz. 95
FitzMaurice 13
Fitzm. 95
James R. 67, 114
John 13, 54, 77
Mary A. 121
Thomas 32, 48
William 13, 55, 75
Wm. 65, 97
Hunte, John 13
Hunter, Dalziel 13
Miles 13
William 132
Huntington, H. N. 67
Hunts, (?) 83
FitzMaurice 13
Hurd, William 13
Hurst, Hardy 45
Henry 48, 50
Henry W. 114
Humphrey 52

Hurst (cont.)
James 45
Sarah 73
Huse, Hardy 126
Husky, Clayton 101
Hust, Barbara 61, 78
Easter 120
Gracy Ann 122
Henry 53, 61
Martha 120
William 64, 77
Hutcheson, Joseph 99
Hutchings, Thomas L. 78
Hutchins, James 13
Wiley 73
Zachariah 33
Hutchinson, (?) 84
James 13, 76, 83, 86
Joshua 76
Mary 121
William 52
Hutchison, Nathaniel 52
Richard 52
Hutson, (?) 89
Benjamin 33
Samuel 33
Sarah 66
Zadok 33
Hylliard, (?) (Maj.) 49
Major 49
Hynes, Churchwell 55
G. W. 55
IRwin, Jared 135
IVey, John 64
Ightner, Michael 33
Ikener, Michael 13, 52
Sampson 43
Ikner, Michael 57, 98
Phillip 59
Solomon 54
Ilands, Isiah 98
James 98
Ingram, Benjamin 115
Benjamin T. 72
Charles 33
Gilford 60
Richard 13
Thomas 72
Inman, Daniel 75
Jeremiah 115
Joshua 13
Shadrack 13
Irby, Edw. 86
Edward 13, 104
Hezekiah 115
Irvin, Alexander 13
Hugh 13
Lawson I. 13
William 13
Irwin, (?) 84, 85, 88,
    89, 92
(?) (Cpt.) 131
A. C. 132
Alex'r. 81
Alex. 33
Alexander 13, 43, 50,
    54, 64, 86, 131,
    135, 137
Charles A. F. 115
David 131
Hugh 13
Hugh (Cpt.) 99
Jared 13, 33, 51, 86,
    135
Jared (Col.) 102, 103,
    138
John 52, 135
John (Jr.) 33

Irwin (cont.)
John L. 13, 51
Margaret 108
Margaret M. 72
Nancy 33, 43, 117
Rebecca M. 112
Samson John (Sr.) 33
Thomas A. 53
W. 96
William 13, 33, 49,
131, 135, 137
William (Cpt.) 102
William A. 71, 115
Wm. 86
Islands, Absalom 13
Isiah 97
James 97
John 13
Iszele, Jesse 97
Ivey, James 64
John 64
Ivins, Ezekiel 46
Ivy, Edy 127
James 56
John 115
Joseph 72
Owin 56
S. 127
Jack, Samuel 13
Jackson, (?) 81, 82, 83,
85, 86, 87, 88, 89,
90, 92, 138
A. 92
Abraham 13
Absalom 13, 86
Absolm 87
Allen 13, 65, 76
Alsey 52
Andrew W. 116
Benjamin (Jr.) 33
Benjamin (Sr.) 33
Charles 13, 33, 49, 87
David 13, 87, 136
Edward 49
Erwim 75
Frederick 115
H. 128
Irwin 115
Isaac 13, 98, 99
Isham 133
Isiah 76
Jack 97
Jacob 33
James 13, 76, 104,
115, 138
James Henry 116
Jeremiah 33, 98
Job 13
John 13, 97, 127
Joseph 13, 87
Josiah 75
Julius 33
Kinchin 48
L. B. A. 54
Levi 33
Lewis 63, 75, 115
M. 128
Martha A. 110
Mary 79, 111
Nancy 119
Noel 75, 116
Paten 68
Peter 13
R. 80
Randal 13
Reuben 13
Robert 13, 97, 130,
131

Jackson (cont.)
Robt. 81, 85, 87, 88
Rosannah 59
Stephen 98, 99, 133
Steven 97
Thomas 14, 33, 98
Tobe 99
Walter 14, 85, 87
Warren 14, 49, 58, 65,
127
William 14, 57, 70,
97, 98, 115
William (Lt.) 102
Wm. 64
Jacob, (?) 88
Jacobs, Shadrack 48
James, John 33
Jamison, (?) 85
Wm. 87
Jarrell, James 98
Jarrott, Robert 14
Jarvis, Patrick 14
Jenkins, Ann E. 119
Arthur 14
Benjamin 14
Daniel 14
David 77
Drewry 57
Drury 14, 51, 63
E. 129
Elizabeth 124
Evan 49, 64
Evans 14
Evins 53
Francis 14, 87
Hezekiah 14, 48, 55,
63, 77
James L. 67
John 33, 76, 115, 116
L. 129
Lewis 14, 43, 48, 58,
106
Martin 76, 116
Moses 48
Owen 49
Richard 14
Robert 14
S. D. 43, 53
Thomas N. 53
Uriah 14, 48, 53, 63
Zachariah 87
Jennings, Sarah 14
Jernigan, Augustus 116
J. R. 63
Jeptha 115
Jeptha K. 71
L. A. 53, 66
Lewis A. 14
Jerrett, Robert 14
Jewell, Thomas 33
Jiles, Alexander 51
Jacob 51
Thomas 14
William 51
Jiner, John 99
Nathaniel 100
Jinkins, Allen 33
Wiley 33
Wm. 99
Jnoes, (?) 89
Jodun, Jane 52
John, Thomas (Cpt.) 97
Zephaniah 14
Johns, Arabella 118
James 101
Mary E. 61
Johnson, Abby 33
Alexander 136

Johnson (cont.)
Aron 101
B. 87
Benj. 87
Benjamin 14, 33, 77,
131
Chany 64
Charles 97
Chimia 59
Clary 33
Daniel 14, 45, 69
Danl. 87
David 14, 33, 87
E. 129
Elijah 14, 49, 57, 64,
77
Elizabeth A. 108
Ellis 60, 73
Emily 123
Equiny 14
Frances 118
Freeman 127
Freeman W. 67
Hansell 77
Hartwell 43
Henry 33, 54, 65, 126
Isaac 33, 43, 53, 115
Isard 76
Israel 49, 57, 64
James 14, 64, 76, 83,
87, 115
James (Jr.) 14, 87
James (Sr.) 14
James J. 115
Jane 70
Jared 14, 49, 125
Jas. 94
Jason 43, 59
Jesse 50
John 14, 49, 53, 73,
76, 87
John A. 115
Joseph 62, 78
Martha 68
Martin 132
Mary 123
Nancy 59, 116
Queny 59
Quincey 49
Rebecca 63
Sampson 33
Sarah 14
Sarah S. 118
Simon 33
Stephen 14
Thomas 46
Thomas (Cpt.) 97
Whitmill 33
William 14, 50, 78,
97, 135, 137
William (Lt.) 102
William C. 116
Willis 45, 49, 57, 64
Wilson 14, 33
Wm. 54, 62, 87
Wm. C. 55, 60
Johnston, (?) 84, 138
Abel 130
Benj. 99
Benjamin (Lt.) 103
Caleb 14
Charles 134
David 86
Jesse 14
John 14
Malcolm 14
Martin 90
Samuel 14

Johnston (cont.)
Simon 133
Thomas 14
William 14, 136
William (Lt.) 103
Wm. 99
Joice, Edward 33
William 45
Joiles, William 14
Joiner, Abraham 43, 47,
48, 106
Benjamin 14
Carolina 116
Cherry Ann 123
Edmund 14, 48
Elias 14, 76, 115, 116
Elisha 48
Ezekiel 56
Hardy 48
Hewett 115
Hull A. 70
Jabes 72
Jabez 50
James 68
Jared 115
Jesse 116
John 63
M. 77
Malachi 63, 115
Malichi 48, 59
Mary 55
Moses 66, 67, 115
Rachel 109
Sarah 76
William 67, 115, 133
Joines, Edmond 33, 57
Edmund W. 66
Ezekiel 33
Jabaze 54
James 43, 56, 63
Jared 43
Joel 33
John 33
Joseph 33
William 43, 56, 101
Wm. 66
Joins, Edmond 87
Edmund 47
Edward W. 43
Ezekiel 101
Jone, Henry 84
Jones, (?) 80, 81, 87,
88, 96
Abel 73, 116, 125
Allen 73, 116
Amos 33
Bassel 57
Benjamin 14, 33, 48,
54
Celia 63
Charles 14
David 14
Doctor F. 78
Elias 14
Elijah 50
Elizabeth 33, 123, 124
F. (Dr.) 78
Francis 14
Frederick 14
H. P. 14
Henry 47, 57, 61, 73,
98
Howel 53
Howell 62, 74
Isaac 64, 66, 75, 105,
115
Isaiah 48
Isiah 125

Jones (cont.)
James 14, 33, 43, 54,
66, 99, 135
James (Jr.) 33, 99
Jesse 14, 87
Jobey 66
Joel 33
John 14, 33, 50, 63,
72, 73, 87, 99, 116,
135, 136
Jonathan 14, 33, 100
Joshua (Jr.) 33
Joshua (Sr.) 33
Josiah 50, 73, 116
Leonard (Jr.) 33
Leonard (Sr.) 33
Martha 113, 126
Mary 113
Nancy 126
Nathan 14
Needham 115
Philip 14
Phillip 87
Redding 74
Robert 14
S. A. H. 66, 79
Samuel 101
Seaborn 14, 70, 115
Seaborn A. H. 115
Seaborn J. 115
Seaborn N. 115
Sherrod 70
Silas 115, 116
Thomas 14, 94
Wilas 67
Wiley 33
William 14, 33, 47,
59, 60, 73, 115
William B. H. 72
William J. 77
Jonson, Eliza 126
Elizabeth 125
Freeman 125
Isaac 125
Mary 125, 126
Jordan, Alesberry 79
Ann B. 122
Archibald 68, 115
Asa 14, 43, 46, 57
Baxter 99, 115
Benj. 60
Benjamin 14, 46, 56,
115
Benjamin S. 116
Britton 14
Burrel 47
Catherine 122
Cornelius 14, 58, 60,
73, 115
Dempsey 14
E. D. 61, 70
Elisha 60
Elisha W. 77, 115
Elizabeth W. 112
Elsbury F. 115
Emily 123
Henry 48
Jacob 45, 55, 115
James 55, 101, 115,
116
John 47, 56, 62, 63,
75, 106, 115, 116
L. H. 68
Laurence 116
Lewis 14
M. 128
Margaret 57
Mary 60, 72, 79

Jordan (cont.)
Mary Ann 109
Middleton 69, 115, 127
Nancy 123
Nancy A. F. 112
Richard 99
Rolin 46
Stephen 115
Thomas 14, 45, 58, 115
Thomas (Jr.) 60
Thomas (Sr.) 60
Thomas J. 68
W. (Mrs.) 56
William 14, 45, 47, 56
William F. 115
Wm. 62
Wm. D. 54
Zina 108
Jordon, Richard 135
W. 43
Winnafred 43
Josey, Henry 115
Henry A. 74
John 69
John W. 70, 116
Mary 74
R. L. 70
Robert J. 116
Samuel 74, 115
Jourdan, Asa 33
Baxter 33
Burwell 33
James 79
Levi 33
Lucius 72
Thomas 33, 73
Jourden, Catherine 73
William D. 79
Joy, Turner 33
Jukins, Dempsey 14
Justice, Dempsey 14
Isaac 14
Karr, Ezekiel 14
Kay, (?) 94, 95
Keath, Samuel (Jr.) 14
Keaton, Benjamin 33, 43
Cader 33
Charles 33
Jesse 33, 43
John 14
Keen, Coleman 71
William 55, 71
Willis 116
Wm. 64
Keener, Mariah 116
Kellam, Seth 33
Keller, Lewis 116
Kelley, David 97
Edward 33, 98
George 33
Jacob (Lt.) 103
Jesse 97
John 97
John (Lt.) 103
Lloyd (Cpt.) 103
Thomas 97, 98
William 33, 97
Kellums, Russel 47
Kelly, (?) 81, 84, 85,
90, 92, 93, 94, 96
(?) (Cpt.) 132
Abner M. 73
E. W. 66
Edward 14
George 45
Jacob 14, 83, 135
James 14, 62
James B. 14, 68

Kelly (cont.)
  Jesse 99
  John 14, 53, 66, 87,
    98, 116
  Lidia 55
  Lloyd 87
  Loyd 83
  Lydia 61
  Martha 119
  Michael 33
  Morgan 127
  Rebecca 77
  Thomas 14
  William 14
  Wm. 87
Kemp, (?) 92
  (?) (Cpt.) 103
  Benjamin 33, 100, 134
  Elitha 49
  Harris Floyd 90
  James 14
  Joseph 100
  Lucy 33
  Mary 50
  Morgan 126
  Reuben 43
  Reubin 33
  Stephen 100
  Thomas 14, 33
  William 14, 33, 100
  William (Cpt.) 102
  William (Jr.) 33
  Wm. 87
Kendal, David 14
  Jeremiah 14
  William 14
Kendall, (?) 95
  David 87
  Jeremiah 87
  Susannah 33
  Wm. 88
Kendrick, (?) (Cpt.) 132
  Ann D. 117
  Benjamin 33
  Benjamin (Lt.) 103
  Burrel (Cpt.) 133
  Burrell 14
  Caroline 117
  Eliza E. 117
  Harvey 101
  Hezekiah 14
  James 14, 48, 55, 63
  James (Jr.) 14
  Jones 33
  Martha 33
  Martin 33
  Tabithy 33
  William 33
Kenedy, James 70
  Sarah 71
Keniday, John 14
Kenman, Austin 43
  Kendrick 64
Kenneda, David 64
  Thos. 64
Kenneday, S. 43
Kennedy, Alexander 116
  Andrew 14, 136
  Archibald 116
  David 50
  James 50
  Jane 52
  John 14, 33
  Joshua 14
  Leroy 116
  Rebecca 122
  Samuel 14, 50
  Samuel W. 116

Kennedy (cont.)
  Sarah 33
  Thomas J. 116
  William 33
Kenner, Jordan 116
Kennida, David 56
  Elizabeth 56
  Samuel 53
Kent, John 33
  Levi 33
Kerr, Henry 14
Kersey, Jane 124
Ketcher, Benjamin 131
Ketrale, Noah 64
Ketrell, Noah 53
Kettle, Mary 14, 88
Key, Henry 47, 55
  James 46
  Jane 71
  Sion 116
  Warren 64
Keyton, Repsey 76
Kibriel, Elizabeth R.
    109
Kicklighter, Fred 116
Kilb, George 15
  Sarah 50
Kilgore, John 14
  R. 80
  Ralph 14
  William 14
Killebrew, Hezekiah 116
  John C. 116
Killeyworth, Franklin W.
    73
Killingsworth, F. W. 120
  Freeman 70
  Jane 64, 71
  John 33
  M. C. 116
  Mathew C. 71
  Randal 55
  Randall 43
  Wm. 51, 55
Kilpatrick, (?) 14
  Austin 43
  David 56
  James 97
Kimbro, John 33
Kimbrough, (?) 88
  Allen 14
  John 15
  William 15
Kimmea, William 15
Kimmey, William 134
Kimmon, Kendrick 15
Kimmy, John 49
  William 33
Kindman, Mary 118
Kindred, Kinman 116
Kindrick, (?) 87, 96
  Barrie 88
  James 87
  Jonas 88
  Nathaniel 15
King, Ann 51
  Anna 33
  B. 128
  Benajah 126
  Blanay H. 126
  Calvin 65
  Caroline 115, 121
  Charles 15, 56, 61, 77
  Charles C. 53
  Chloe 33
  Clarisa 68
  Clarissa 66
  David 33

King (cont.)
  Elisha 50, 56, 64
  Ephraim 33
  H. 128
  Henry 61, 79, 127
  James 33, 127
  Joel 43
  John 15, 33, 43, 48,
    50, 75
  John (Jr.) 56
  John (Sr.) 59
  John C. 54
  Joshua 33
  Josiah 65
  Josiah F. 116
  Josiah T. 15, 75
  M. 128
  Mary 55, 65, 122
  Matilda 113
  N. 128
  Nancy 109, 127
  Parks 15
  Thomas 52, 57, 126
  Thomas H. 59
  William 75, 116, 126
  William R. 43
  William T. 116
Kingary, Abraham 116
Kingman, Fanny 123
Kinman, Alston 116
  Kindrick 71
  Levi M. 71
  William 33
Kinney, John 33, 99, 132
Kirk, Jno. 86
  John 15, 88
  Thomas 49
Kirkham, Joseph 15
Kirkland, John 15
Kitchen, (?) 88, 90
  Benj. 88
  Benjamin 15
  Boze B. 116
  Laurence 33
Kitchens, (?) 88
  Benj. 88
  Benjamin 132, 134
  Bethany 111
  Sarah 51
Kitrell, Noah 116
Kitril, Noah 71
Kitrill, John 67
Kittrell, Noah 70
Kitts, John 15
Kneeland, Mary A. E. 111
Knight, Abel 116
  Allen H. 69
  Charles 45
  Eli 65
  Elijah 15
  Elijah L. 75
  J. B. 65
  Jess B. 15
  Jesse B. 43, 76
  Lewis 43, 60, 68
  Martha C. 116
  Robert 47
  Russell 125
  Silvanus 33, 60
  Sylvanus 45
  Temperance 108
  Treacy 116
Kolb, George 33
Koonce, George 15, 33
Lackey, (?) 15
Lafearse, Isaac 131
Lafever, John 15
Lamar, (?) 82, 87, 88,

Lamar (cont.)
  95
  John 15
  Luke 15
  Samuel 15
  Thomas 15
  William 15
Lamb, Abraham 15
  Jesse 15, 88
  Quincy 74
  Quinny 117
  Thomas 15
Lambert, Alfred 116
Lamborn, Noel 49
Lamkins, Parting 134
  Samuel 15
Lancaster, (?) 83, 90
  James A. 116
  Wm. 88
Land, Henry 15
  John 15
Landcaster, James A. 43
Landers, Abraham 15
  Jacob 15
Landon, Milla M. 121
Landrum, William 15
Lane, Bryant 54
Lang, Henry C. 117
  John 15
Langarn, Richard 101
Langdon, Samuel 131
Langford, Elizabeth 121
  James 15, 77, 98
  James L. 117
Langham, Richard 54
Langhurn, Richard 51
Langmade, E. S. 67
  Edward 117
  Eliza E. 68
  John S. (?) 117
Langston, Benjamin 15,
  34, 135
  David 50
  Dorcas 45
  James 34
  Samuel 15
Lanier, Sarah 47
Lankford, Josiah 15
  Moses 15
Lard, Lodowick 34
  Sarah 34
Larimore, John 15
Larkin, Samuel 133
Lasler, Hardy 55
Lasseter, (?) 88
  Hansil 15
Lassiter, Brinkley 34
Laten, Hillary 76
Lathrope, Eliza 47
Laton, Hillary 63
  Hillery 117
  James 63, 116, 117
  John 43, 54
  Leonard 77
  Phoebe 117
Laughen, Noel 15
Laurance, John 63
Laurence, Devereaux 34
  Henry 34
  John 34, 43, 47, 106
  Susan 47
Law, Samuel 116, 117
  Samuel M. 67
Lawhon, John 15, 53
  Nathaniel 15
  Noel 15
Lawhorn, Bryant 61
  Nathaniel 34

Lawhorn (cont.)
  Noel 34
Lawrence, Homer 68
  Homer M. 77
  John 15, 56, 84
  Martha A. M. 110
  Newton 117
  Sherrod 117
  Sherwood 15
Lawson, (?) 81, 84, 86
  Andrew 15
  Charles 34
  Elexander E. 77
  Hugh 34, 135
  Hughrea 67
  Jno. 88
  John 15, 34
  John (Jr.) 34
  R. 96
  Reubin 34, 134
  Roger 34, 62
  Roger (Jr.) 15
  Sarah 34
  Thomas 15
  Thompson 52
Layton, James 77
  John 47
  Zilpha 15
Lazeron, Edward 74
  Morris 67
Leapham, Aaron 15, 88
  Frederick 15
  Moses 15
Leaptrot, A. 57
  Avy Mirany 108
  Bolin 62
  Bolin P. 78
  Milbra 62, 78
  Rolin 56
Leath, James 34
  Peter 34
Ledbetter, Ephraim 34
  Fred'k. 15
  Isaac 15, 88, 100
  James 97
  John 15
  Samuel 34
Lee, Bud 15, 48
  Cato 15
  Elias 15, 47, 54
  George 98
  Ira 49
  Iry 34
  John 106
  Joshua 15
  M. 77
  Milley 59
  Milly 43
  Ransom 98
  Richard 134
  Sampson 48, 106
  Sampson (Sr.) 15
  Temple 98
  William (Jr.) 43
Leeper, John 49
Leggett, Abner 15
  Jaramiah 97
  John 15
Leghorn, William 131
Lenair, Isaac 15
Leneves, Samuel 34
Lenier, James 55
  Lewis 58
Lennill, (?) 94
Lennon, Gabriel 133
Lenton, Thomas 134
Leonard, John 15, 34
Lesley, Joseph 15

Lester, Thomas 15
Lethgo, Robert 15
Lethgore, Andrew 15
Lett, Reuben 15
Leverett, Daniel M. 117
  Henry 15
  J. P. 78
  Joel P. 62
  John 15
Leveritt, Daniel M. 78
  George W. 78
Levily, Jesse 132
Levin, Richard 88
Levingston, John 34
Lewas, Daniel 98
Lewcos, Moses 98
Lewis, (?) 15, 87, 96
  Aaron 75
  Asa 51
  Daniel 34
  Edward G. 77
  Emeline 124
  George 34
  Ira 51
  Ire 101
  J. E. 79
  James 65
  James E. 117
  Joel 133
  John 34
  Rebecca 74
  Redding R. 43, 58
  Samuel 51
  Thomas 15
  W. B. 60
  William 15
  William B. 79
  William H. 72
Licett, David 34
Lides, (?) 94
Lightfoot, John 15, 88
  Martha 43, 56, 66
  Philip 43
  Richard 45, 68
  Robert 43, 56
  Temperance 121
  William D. 43
Liles, John 99
  Sherwood 34
Lilly, (?) 99
Linch, John 100
Lindey, William 117
Lindsay, David 48
  Dennis 15
  John 15
Lindsey, Celia 112
  Henry 34
  John 34, 76
  Mariah B. 112
Lineacum, Hezek. 97
Lingo, (?) 86
  Arrenia 114
  Elijah 15
  John 34, 98
  Martha 114
  Moses 15, 34, 45, 88
  Patrick 15
  Peter 43, 60, 117
  Pinkston 52
Lingould, William A. 77
Linn, Charles 15
  John 15
Linnum, Juda 113
Linsey, Dennis 15
  John 43, 84, 88
  Nelson 63, 68
Linton, John 15, 34
Linzey, Anna 113

163

Marshall (cont.)
Levi 16
M. 82
Mathew 16
Moses 16
Solomon 16, 89
William 34
Martain, John 104
Reubin 104
Marten, John 96
Martin, Augustus 67
Bird 43, 54
Charles 34, 50
David 34
Dolly 113
Edy (Widow) 107
Elizabeth 60, 71, 115, 124
Ezra 74
Francis 50
George 43
Green 56, 71
Henry 16, 43, 117
James 16, 34, 35, 54, 56, 64, 70, 99, 117
John 16, 35, 43, 53, 57, 59, 65, 70, 72, 101, 125, 135, 136, 137
John (Jr.) 16, 35
John O. 66
Joseph 16, 70
Julius 35, 101
Lemuel 43, 64, 70
Levi 16, 35, 50, 99
Mary 113
Miley 123
Nancy 65, 70
Noah 50, 101
Oliver 138
Osborn O. 70
Pressilla 64
Pricilla 71
Richard 16, 35, 49, 57
Simon 70
Thomas 35, 50, 99
William 16, 35, 54, 71, 89
Zachariah 35
Mashburn, Daniel 48
Mason, (?) 95
Eliza A. 111
George 16, 49, 59, 64
Henry 75
James 35
Jno. 93
Thomas 16, 89
Turner 35
Massey, (?) 83
Abel 51, 58, 64, 71
Abraham 46, 58
Banakias (?) 50
Bennett 53, 64
Budd 70
Corde 117
Cordy 56
Elizabeth 55, 66, 70
Elizabeth A. 112
George W. 67
Isabella Jane 116
J. B. 66
James J. 71, 118
John 69
John B. 53, 67
K. W. 63
Kinchell W. 117
Kinchen W. 77
Mary 108, 116

Massey (cont.)
Mary F. 116
Sampson 43
Sarah 110
Massy, Artamass 109
Mathew, James 16
Mathews, Ann Mariah 124
Daniel 35
Frances 70
Isaac 35
Isham 35
Jacob 35
John 35, 57, 58, 59, 117
Reuben A. 68
Reubin 35
Stephen 16
Temperance 35
William 16
Mathis, Amandy 108
Isaac 66
John 43, 46, 47, 52, 58, 106
John (Sr.) 35
Lewis 46
Littleton 55, 63, 67
Logan 66
Lorinzo 66
Lovey 64
Mary S. 108
P. (Mrs.) 56
Sally 45
Sealy 114
Tempe 45
Thomas 97
Tilly 121
Trecy 124
William 35
Matlock, (?) 90
Day 90
Matthew, Rebecca 76
Matthews, John 16
Lodowick 57
Mesheck 16
Moses 16
Reuben A. 117
Thomas 16
William 16
Mattocks, Leonard 135
Lewis 35
Spencer 134
Maxfield, Feliz 48
Maxwell, Felix 56, 65, 74
Josiah 16
Margaret 119
Mary 119
Polly 119
Robert 16, 77
May, Appy 119
Dread 35
Drury 71
Edmond 35, 58
Edmund 16, 46, 60, 73
Edmund (Jr.) 43
Francis 35
George 54
Hardy 35
James 16
Jas. 86
Jethro 46, 55, 60
John 16, 47, 96, 98, 133
John E. 61
Jonas 89
Joseph H. 117
Luamber J. 74
Lumber (?) J. 118

May (cont.)
Martha 73
Martha Ann 109
Mary 108
Moses (Lt.) 103
Nancy 120
Reuben 117
Sarah 115
Tempe 46, 118
Temperance 114
William 16, 35, 72, 73, 135
William (Jr.) 60
William (Sr.) 60
Wm. (Jr.) 43
Wm. (Sr.) 43
Mayo, Benj. 61
Benjamin 57, 117
Dempsey W. 118
Elizabeth 123
Howel 68
Howell 62
James J. 117
Jane 116
Mark 16, 89
Mary 115
Nancy 121
Nancy A. 124
Reuben 61, 67
Temperance (Widow) 107
William 47, 54, 61, 117
William W. 69, 118
Mays, Etheldred 16
Jemima 43
William 101
Maze, John E. 16
McAfee, Arthur 43, 56, 64, 72
E. 129
Eason 71
James 57, 65, 71
James (Jr.) 65
Jesse 64, 71
John 65
Jordan 72, 118
Lydia 121
Mary 71
McAllister, Sarah A. C. 110
McAlvay, George R. 117
McAnless, William 48
McAvin, Matilda 72
McBeth, James 53, 117
McBride, Elizabeth 79
Thomas J. 117
William G. 70, 118
McCain, Catherine 120
McCall, Thos. 89, 94
McCallister, Nancy 113
McCandless, Patience 123
McCandliss, Asam (?) 126
Esair 126
Ezre 126
Godfrey 126
P. 129
McCanless, Wm 43
McCarcal, James 16
McCarley, Samuel 34
McCartie, John 16
McCaughy, John 16
McCavy, (?) (Cpt.) 99
McCeymore, Emily 89
McClayne, Allen 133
McClenden, Joel 98
McClendon, (?) 87, 90, 95
Isaac 16

McClendon (cont.)
Jacob 16
Job 99
Joel 16, 89
John 16
Lewis 16, 34, 89
Mason 34
Willis 34
Wilson 16, 34, 99
McCliven, W. P. 76
McClung, Wm. M. 97
McCoan, Andrew 16
McColester, Richard 66
McCollins, Nancy 120
McCondachies, John 16
McConley, Andrew 68
McConnel, Clark 118
Clark O. 67
McCorcle, (?) 89
James 89
McCord, David 16, 34
McCorkdale, Daniel 57
McCorkle, James 16
McCormac, (?) 84
McCormack, (?) 89
Benjamin 16
James 16, 99
McCormic, (?) 82
McCormich, James 16
John 16
Thomas 16
McCorquedale, Daniel 49
Malcolm 49
McCory, Andrew P. 78
McCoy, Daniel 53
N. A. 128
Nancy 57
Robert 56, 61
William 43, 62, 117
McCrary, Jonathan 16
McCreary, Isaac 34
McCullars, Bryant 89
McCullen, Bryant 16
McCuller, Sarah J. 121
McCullers, Bryant 16
Charles 16
David 16
Drury 16
Elizabeth 114
Elizabeth A. 121
Mary 16
Susan J. 68
Thomas 34
McCulloch, Patrick 16
Samuel 16
McDade, Charles 34, 101
James 34
William 34
McDaniel, Anna 61
C. 128
Daniel 47
Edward 53
Ennis 47
J. 128
John 34
M. 128
Mary 16, 52, 128
Susannah 46
Thomas 45, 46
Zaddock 101
McDanil, Charles 73
McDearman, Mary 108
McDonald, Charles 16
Hugh 34
Lovett 43
Mathews 34
Thomas 16, 136
McDougal, Alexander 45

McDougal (cont.)
Andrew 34
Robert 34
McDougald, Dugald 43
McDougall, Alexander 16
Daniel 45
McDouglad, Daniel 16
McDowel, (?) 93
(?) (Cpt.) 97
McDowell, (?) (Cpt.) 97,
130, 131
Daniel (Cpt.) 134
John 34
Thomas 16, 34, 46
Thomas (Cpt.) 102
Thos. 89
William 16
McDuffee, Christia 58
McDuffie, John 51
Malcolm 16, 49
Mary 61
McEwen, William P. 118
McFarlan, (?) 94
McFarland, James 16
John (Jr.) 16
McFarlin, (?) 97
John 131
McGab--, Daniel 51
McGaha, Andrew 101
McGarr, Owen 16
McGary, Robert 17
McGearman, Sarah 118
McGee, (?) 90
Lewis 17
Shadrack 17, 89
William 136
McGeehe, (?) 90
McGeehee, Thomas 17
McGehee, (?) 81, 94
Nathan 117
Samuel 17
Thomas 17
William 17
McGill, John 17
McGilton, James 17
McGinty, Jos. 98
McGomary, John 98
McGonders, (?) 82
McGowan, David 17
Jinsy 118
Robert 17
McGowen, Nancy 74
McGregor, Alexander 17
McGruder, Ninian 17
Zadok 17
McGwain, Patrick 17
McIntosh, John 17
Lachlin 17
McIntyre, Thomas 64, 118
McKaskill, Peter 17
McKee, John 34
McKensey, (?) (Cpt.) 98
McKenzie, Aaron 98
John (Cpt.) 98
Randal 98
Randall 134
Wm. 98
McKey, Mike 34
William 34
McKigney, George 34
McKinley, Joseph 52
McKinney, Henry 17
Tabitha 34
William 17
McKinvale, James 34
McKinzee, Aaron 34
Rachel 34
McKinzey, Randolph 98

McKinzey (cont.)
William 98
McKissick, Mack 34
McLane, (?) 89
Daniel 17, 89
McLaughlin, Sally 69
McLean, John 17
Laughlin 46
McLendon, Burrell 117
Mark 132
Mason 48
Thomas 132, 133
McLeod, Angus 17, 49
Daniel 47
Neal 17
Niel 49
McMath--, (?) 17
McMath, Philip 34
McMellon, Malcom 54
McMillan, A. 45
Mathers 17
McMillen, Adolphus 118
Angus 34
Archibald 34
McMillion, Matthew 89
McMillon, (?) 80, 90
Malcolm 69
Matthew 90
McMullen, James 130
Mary 117
McMum, John 17
McMurphy, Daniel 17
McMurray, John 34
William 17, 34
McMurry, Augustus 68
Kirkland 95
William 17, 89, 136
McNabb, Rebot 17
McNair, JohnA. 118
McNatt, Benjamin 34
McNeel, Turguil 34
McNeely, Daniel 17
Mary 17
McNeil, Archibald 17
Archiblad 46
Daniel 17
Daniel (Sr.) 17
James 17
Jesse 17
Michael 17
McNiel, David 17
Mary 46
Niel 34
McNully, Hugh 17
McQuathy, Thomas 17
McQueen, John 49
McRae, Charity 57
John 43
McRea, Elizabeth 115
McSwain, Patrick 17
McSwane, Catherine 61
McVay, David 47
John 47
Walter 117
Wiley C. 118
McVey, David 34, 53, 117
Martha 119
Wiley 71
Winney 120
Yancy 117
McWhirter, Moses 34
McWilliams, Gracy 34
John 17
Thomas 17, 49
Thomas N. 118
Meak, Washington 118
Meakes, Benjamin 58
Meanly, John 17

Moore (cont.)
Lemuel W. H. 78, 118
Levi 35
Luke 35
Mathas 62
Mathew 45, 54, 68
Nancy 125
Richard 17, 90
Richd. 83
Sarah 75, 117
Shadrach 48
Shadrack 35, 43
Shadrick 55, 65
Thomas 17, 90
William 17
Winnaford 58
Winnifred 65
Moorman, Charles 17, 136
More, Underhill H. 43
Morehead, Kite 135
Moreman, Charles 35
Lucia Ann 116
Morgain, Garlant 99
Morgan, (?) 76, 96
James 17, 97
James (Lt.) 103
Jery 98
Jesse 17
Jesse F. 118
John 17
John M. 17
Philip 17
Robert 17
Stephen 17
William 18, 98
Wm. 90
Morganson, Asa 18
Morgin, Assa 97
Morrel, Fanny 66
Morrell, Enoch 61
Enoch C. S. 117
Mary 121
Morris, Benj. 43
Calvin 69
H. 127
Israel 35
Jacob 47, 59
John 18, 69, 118
Nimrod 35
William 18, 35, 76,
118
Wm. 63
Morrison, Alexander 125
Angus 35, 72
Angus A. 118
Catherine 125
John 51
John (Sr.) 57
Joseph 125
Margaret 60, 74
Martha 125
Morssie, Cashford 100
Morton, James 99
John 35
Moseley, Benjamain 18
Littleberry 18
Robert 18
Thomas 18
Thomas (Jr.) 18
Moses, John 35
Joshua 35
Robert 35
Samuel 35
Mosley, William 18
Moss, Howell 35
Leonard 18
Motley, Benjamin 48
Robert 35, 52, 99

Motley (cont.)
Wilson 35
Mott, Hiram 58, 72
Joseph 18, 55, 117
Lovelace 35
Nathan 35, 46, 59, 106
William 18, 97
Motte, Jos. 97
Joseph 18
Nathan 18, 97
William 18
Zepaniah 18
Motts, Wm. 90
Mounger, Sampson 90
Moy, Duran 55, 66
Duren G. 76
Geo. 63
George 55, 64
Isaac 62, 117
John 55
John E. 69
Thomas 55
Thomas E. 63
Moye, Benajah A. 43
Caroline 115
Cherry A. E. 120
Devran 47
George 48, 51
George W. 118
Isaac 71
John E. 76
John R. 118
Martha 119
Mary A. 120
Matida 123
Sarah 118
Thomas E. 71
Mullins, Clement 18
Mullowney, Laughlin 35
Mumford, Jeffry 35
John 35
Joseph 35
Thomas 35
Munford, Robert 35
Mungin, John 76
Munk, Mial 98
Murchant, Isaac 90
Murchants, John 90
Murkerson, John 35
Murkeson, George M. 117
Murkinson, Franklin 126
M. 128
Wm. M. 57
Murkison, Green 43
John 50
Murph, (?) 83
Murphey, Daniel 98
Elizabeth 114
Rebecca 115
Smithey 114
Murphry, Edward 18
Morris 18
Murphy, (?) 94
Bartholomew 90
C. 136
Chisnel (Lt.) 99
Cornelius 35
Cullen 62, 74
Daniel 35
Drury 35
Edward 18
Henry 118
James 35
Miles 135
Samuel 58, 74
William 35, 43, 45, 54
William B. 18
Wm. 62

Murray, John 49
Muse, Eli 62
Musslewhite, G. B. 43
William 49
Myers, Brittania 111
Martha 112
Mary 65
Thomas 47
W. A. 76
William 76, 118
Myors, Thomas 56
Myres, Delany 68
Nail, Elisha 18, 90, 95
Reubin 94
Nails, E. 87
Nall, Martin 18, 90
Nals, Elis 88
Napier, Polly 35
Rene 18
Thomas 18
Nash, Clement 18
Naylor, George 18
Neal, David 18
Tho. (Cpt.) 97
Thomas 18, 90
Thomas (Cpt.) 97
Thomas (Jr.) 18
Nealon, John 18
Neel, Antony 100
Elias 18
John 35
Reubin 134
Thomas 35
William 18
Neeland, Elizabeth 73
James 35, 133
John (Sr.) 35
O. David 35
Polly 46
Neeley, Julia 18
Richard 18
Thomas 18, 35
Neely, Elizabeth 108
John 90
Julia 64, 72
Thomas 51, 58
Thomas (Sr.) 49
Neil, Thomas 18
Neile, George 18
Neiley, John 18
Neland, William 18
Nellson, Ambrose 35
Nelms, John (Jr.) 132
John (Sr.) 132
Nelson, William 18, 90,
134
New, Daniel 57, 65
Ezra 65, 74, 118
John 75, 118
Liddy Ann 114
Mary 116
Rachel 75
Stephen F. 18, 118
Newberry, William 18
Newcom, Ellafair 61
Newdigate, John 18
Newman, Barsheba 74
Eliorll 58
Elwell 61, 79
Francis 35
James 51
John 18
Mark 67, 118
Walter 45
William 99
Newnham, John 18
News, John 18
Newsom, Agnes 35

Page (cont.)
Allen A. 119
Britain 75
Britton 58, 65
Elizabeth 114
J. H. 65
James 48, 98
James J. 71
John 18, 43, 55, 64,
  65, 75, 77
John D. 18, 119
John M. E. 119
John M. R. 69
John W. 76
Joseph H. 55, 68, 79
Julia A. 121
Mary 55
Mary (Widow) 107
Mary E. 119
Nancy 75, 121
Nathan 50
Sarah 114
Solomon 36, 54, 65,
  119
Solomon (Jr.) 44, 55
Solomon (Sr.) 47, 48
Thomas 36
Wilson 36
Pain, Isham 36
John 36
Joseph 36
Samuel 18
Paine, James 54
Painter, Joseph 18
Pair, Zachariah 131
Pall, James 100
Palls, James 18
Palmer, Isabella 65
John 18, 36
Jonathan 18
Samuel B. 75
Solomon 18
Panill, Joseph 18
Paradis, Mary 65
William 55
Paradise, James 119
John D. 75
Mary 68, 76, 118
Parash, Hezekiah 98
Parham, Hadden 36
Haden 45
James 36
Paris, James 36
Parish, Charles 50
James 18, 52
James G. 78
Josiah 98
William 18
Parker, Aaron 18, 90
Abel 100
Benjamin 98
Cader 36
Daniel 18, 91
Eliza W. 122
Elizabeth 60, 73
Emily 122
Francis 18
Hardy 44, 53
Henry 51, 101
Isac 45
Jacob 97
James 47
Jeremiah 64, 76
John 18, 64
Jonathan 36, 56, 64,
  77
Joseph 36, 45, 134
Joshua 58

Parker (cont.)
Keder 47
Lewis 62, 78
Mary 36, 110, 119
Mason S. 44
Sarah E. 120
William 18, 91
Wm. 36
Parkerson, Jacob 18
Parks, John 18
Parmenter, John 98
Parmer, Isabella 59, 70
Samuel 36
Samuel M. 70
Parneel, James 133
Parrish, Benjamin 36
James 57, 62
William 57, 62
Parrot, (?) (Cpt.) 132
Parrott, (?) 81
B. (Cpt.) 134
Benj. (Cpt.) 100
Benjamin (Sr.) 132
Parrymore, James 49
Sarah 49
Partain, Robert 18
Partridge, Payton 44,
  119
William 45
Parum, Peter 18
Pasmore, Housman 45
John 36
Pate, Ann 114
Elizabeth 64
Ellen 118
John 48
John W. 55, 65
Patrick J. 76
Patrick Y. 119
Redding 54, 119
Redding H. 72
Thomas 98
William 98
Patrick, Henry 18
Patridge, Henry 36, 53
Paten 68
Peyton 66
Patten, James 36, 99,
  132
Patterson, Alicia 109
Drewry 133
Drury 36
Gideon 18, 89
Gidion 36
John 18
Robert 18
William 18
Paul, (?) 80, 94
Brice 36
James 36
John 36
Pauls, (?) 86
Pavys, Dial 18
Paxton, William 18
Payne, James 44
Samuel 18, 19
Zachariah 19
Peabody, John 56
Peace, John 119
William 119
Peacock, A. 53
Archibald 19, 49, 63,
  106
Asa 53, 68
Asa P. 19, 63
George B. 68
Green B. 119
Greene B. 65

Peacock (cont.)
John 19, 36, 49, 53
John (Jr.) 63
Jonathan 36, 49
Levi 36
Lewis 68, 119
Mary 119, 125
Mary E. 119
Michael 36
Moalton 19
Molton 49, 63
Moulton 68
Pamealann 121
Pierson 36
Pilson 49
Right 49
Samuel 36
Samuel (Sr.) 36
Tinker John 49
Uriah 53, 63, 66, 67,
  105, 106, 119, 125
Urian 19
Washington 49
Willia 57
William 47, 53, 76
Wm. 63
Zachariah 76, 119
Peak, (?) 82
John 19
Peal, John 19
Pearc, John 98
Pearce, Abram 71
Martha 70
Wiley Cox 70
Pearrie, Nathaniel 19
Peddy, Betsy 47
Beverly 36
Bradford 36
Jeremiah 19, 36
Julius 101
Julius C. 47
Juslous (?) 55
Nehemiah 19, 36
Rachel 36
Peeler, Frederick 19
Pendleton, (?) 81
Solomon 19
Pennington, Henry 36
Thomas 19
Penson, Enoch 131
Isaac 19
Perce, Abner 97
Peres, John 131
Peret, Robert 19
Perison, John 19
Perkins, Abraham 19
Adam 19
Bedy 78
Benjamin 36
Jackson 62, 119, 127
John 19, 69, 132
Joseph 36, 45
Peter 19
Phillip 127
Robert 127
Shelton 79
Susan C. 112
Virgil H. 74
Virgil T. 74
William 19, 46, 134
Pernell, Scarbro 47
Perrett, John 19
William 19
Perrey, James 36
Joseph 36
Perrit, James 36
Perritt, William 133
Perry, (?) 91

Price (cont.)
65, 119
M. 128
Marady 98
Mary 75, 115
Mary E. 123
Matilda 109
Moor 65
Moore 19, 74, 119
Morning 75
Nancy 61, 121
Nathan 65, 75, 119
Pledge 44, 72
Rice 19, 48, 57, 65, 119
Richard 36, 46
Sarah A. 120
Warren 75, 119
William 19
Zachariah 36
Prichard, Thomas 119
Prichet, Thomas 36
Pridgen, Ann 111
Edward 74
Edwin 54, 62
Priget, James H. 69
Prince, George 37, 56
Hamelton 37
Hamilton 50
Martha G. 124
Mary A. M. 119
Rebecca 61, 114
Silvenes 99
Sylvanus W. 79, 119
Procter, Mary 120
Proctor, Joshua 37
William 37
Prosser, Elly 52
Jesse 101
Oty 57, 106
Samuel C. 19
Pruett, (?) 87
Pugh, D. Guilford 37
Elijah 19
Francis 19, 137
James 19
James (Jr.) 19
Jane (Mrs.) 137
Jesse 19
John 19
Mary 37
Philophilus 19
Theophilus 92
William 137
Pullen, Henry 37
Thomas 19
Thos. 92
William 37
Pullin, Thomas 37
Purce, Philip B. 119
Purkins, Adam 91
Elisha 98
John 99
Joseph 56
Stephen 53
William 53
Purnell, William F. 19
Purser, Alfred 126
John 126
William 126
Pusser, James 44
Quails, John 130
Quarles, Roger 19
Queens, John 19
Quick, William 49
Zachariah 43, 49
R?ellin, Charles B. 69
Raburn, John 97

Rabutton, Almira 124
Rachaels, Burwell 72
William 46
Zadoc 72
Rachel, James 92
Miles 19, 92
William 58
Zadok 19
Zedoc 58
Rachels, James 37
John 19
Joseph 120
Miles 37, 86
Myles 55
Valentine 97
Zacock 60
Rackels, Burrel 97
Radcliff, Polly 49
Rafforty, Michael 19
Raford, H. W. 68
Ragan, John 19
Nathaniel 19
Ragland, (?) 94
Evan 19
William 19
Raiford, Morris 19, 136
Raines, Dartha (?) 118
Datha 118
Elizabeth 109
John 19
Richard 120
Winny 49
Rains, Allan 51
Allen 57
Alphair 112
Amaline 121
Griffin 120
John 49, 57, 77
Nancy 115
Richard 70
Washington 51, 56, 120
William 120
Winnifred 59
Raley, Charles 37
Ramsay, William 73
Ramsey, (?) 92
Isaac 19
John 19
Randol (Jr.) 19
Randolph 19
Samuel 19
Thomas 19
William 19, 46
Randolph, (?) 92
Isaac 19, 92
Ranes, Jane 117
John 64
Needham 64
W. W. (?) 64
Raney, Benj. 92
Benjamin 37
James 132
John 19, 37, 92, 134
Joseph 99
Smith 92
Thomas 20
William 99
Raskee, James 99
Ratcliff, (?) 86
Benjamin 20
Joseph 20
Rausaw, William 20
Rauzey, William 56
Rawlings, Frederick 120
Mary 67
Sarah 122
William 45, 53
Wm. 66

Rawls, Dempsey 52
John 20
Mary 119
Ray, (?) 84
Ambris 98
Ambros 58
Ambrose 20, 37, 61
Ambrose (Sr.) 51, 101
Charles 20, 37, 137
Francis 37
Gabriel 37, 51
Hardy 51
James 20, 61, 79, 92, 120
John 37, 120
Mary 110
William 20, 37, 133
William (Jr.) 37
Zachariah 20, 92
Rayfield, Spencer 20
Rayford, Mauris 92
Rayley, Sarah 20
Rayne, Joseph 20
Raynolds, James 78
Razar, Isaac 20
Read, (?) 85
John 20
Thomas 20
Reason, Margaret M. 110
Reatherford, Robt. 99
Reaves, Joseph 20, 92, 120
William 97
Recton, Joseph 97
Red, James 20
Samuel 20
Reddick, (?) 82
William 20
Reddin, Anderson 98
Thos. 63
Redding, Anderson 37
Arthur 37
Charles 37
George 20
William 37
Reddix, Abraham 20
Redfeard, Branson 74
Redfern, Branson 60
Rees, Joel 20, 81
Reeves, Greene 37
John 20
John L. 20
Simon 37
Spencer 20
Thomas 20
Regan, Frederick 134
Regester, Benj. 62
Nole 61
Register, Abel 56
Ann E. 124
Benjamin 44
Jesse 47, 120
John 47, 56, 62, 120
John N. 120
Mary 116
Noel 120
Rebecca 121
William 47
William K. 120
Reiley, Delia G. 71
Joseph 20
Renals, Washington 68
Rener, Michael I. 62
Philiip I. 62
Renfore, James 58
Renfree, Margaret 114
Renfro, (?) 85
D. 128

Scott (cont.)
Harriett 117
Hiram 44, 56, 64
James 48, 65, 76
Joseph 21
Margaret 116
Mary 63, 113
Peter 21
Thomas 122
William 21
William T. 126
Winfield 71, 121
Scrogging, Josiah 37
Scroggins, Eliza 113
Scurlock, Presley 98, 99
Scurry, Nicholas 21
Seal, Matilda 120
Seale, Wm. 94
Seals, William 21
See, Jesse 37
Sehlvy, Moses 51
Self, William 21
Sellers, Anna 61, 76
Cassa 112
Catherine 121
Daniel 121
Debby 117
Margaret A. 120
Martha Ann 116
William J. 76
William James 121
Sess, (?) (Col.) 94
Sessions, (?) 81, 85
Benj. 54, 64
Benjamin 51, 72
Daniel 38
Delilah 38
Elizabeth 109
Frederick 38
George 50
Jos. (Jr.) 53
Joseph 21, 38, 44, 45,
51, 53, 94
Levi 54
Lewis 48
M. L. W. 63
Martha W. 115
Mary 112
Sherrod 53, 129
Sexton, Hugh 98
William 38
Shackleford, John 21
Shaddock, Thomas 21
Shadrack, (?) 91
Shaffer, David 21
Shafford, John 137
Sharks, Josiah 94
Sharp, John 21
John (Sr.) 21
Joshua 21
Michael 21
Wiley 21
Sharpe, Malton 50
Shaw, David 21
Thomas 21
William 21
Wm. 94
Shealds, Thomas 131
Shearling, James 62
Sheffell, Mark 21
Sheffield, John 21
John C. 49
Robert 21
William 21
Sheffle, William 21
Sheftall, Mordecai 21
Shehe, Allafair 47
John 47

Shehe (cont.)
Thomas 47
Shehee, Alafair 113
Ellafaw 60
Sheke, Daniel 38
Shelby, John 21, 38
Sheler, Ellafair (?) 55
Shellman, John 135
Shelman, (?) 89
I. 21
Jno. 94
John 21, 94
Michael 21, 94, 95
Shelsee, A. B. 45
Shelton, Henry 21
Shelvey, (?) 94
John 94, 99
Shelvy, John 101
Shep, John 56
Shepard, Green L. 21
Sheperd, Sarah A. S. 109
Shepherd, Andrew 38
Charles 38
Charles H. 73
Chas. 96
David 44, 138
Eaton 75
Francis 127
James 38
John 38
John (Jr.) 38
John (Lt.) 102
John (Sr.) 38
Lewis 44
Mary 38
Rebecca 74
Thomas 21, 38
William 38
Sheppard, (?) (Cpt.)
131, 132
Andrew 21
Benj. 60
Charles 47, 56
Charles H. 121
Chas. 61
Daniel 121
David 21, 48, 57, 63,
66, 69, 121
Elefair 124
Elena 123
Frances 57
Francis 21, 63
Green L. 121
Henry 49
James 21, 48, 134
Jno. 88
John 21, 48, 54, 61,
66, 68, 69, 70, 121,
135, 136
John (Cpt.) 134
John (Jr.) 61
Lewis 56, 63, 73, 75
Malinda 119
Martha 122
Mary 119
Mary Ann E. 122
Robert J. 121
Rutha 118
Sarah 122
Thomas 21, 48, 58
William 21, 122
Zachariah 121
Sheppeard, David 76
Elizabeth 76
Zachariah 79
Shepperd, David 44, 76
Francis 76
James 21

Shepperd (cont.)
John 21
John W. 79
Lewis 44
Nancy Ann 109
Rebecca 114
Shepward, (?) 83
Sherlin, E. 128
James 49, 77, 126
James H. 77
John E. 126
Sherling, Elizabeth 117
James 121
James (Sr.) 121
James H. 121
Susan C. 112
Sherman, Robert 55
Sherod, Joel 21
Sherrer, James B. 70
Sherry, Isaiah 38
Sherwood, Benjamin 38
Shery, Jno. M. 56
Shick, Frederick 21
Shield, Robert 21
Shields, Andrew 21
Margaret 21
Mary 116
William 21, 137
Shilton, Henry 21
Shiney, Benjamin 44
Shinnon, Kendrick 44
Shipley, Robert 21
Shira, John M. 64
Margarette 64
Samuel 64
Shire, Eliza 110
Shirey, B-- 121
Silas 44
Shirling, James 56
Richard 121
William F. 122
Shirly, James 49
Shiry, Benjamin 54
Isian B. 71
Jno. M. 56
Margaret 71
Samuel 56, 71
Shivers, C. T. 73
Jacob 75
Shoals, Dennis 88
Show, Adam 21
Shuffle, William 21
Shurlock, Samuel 136
Sikes, Daniel 21
Daniel (Lt.) 138
Elizabeth 138
William 21
Willoughby 38
Simkins, Charles 21
Simmerson, Elizabeth 112
Simmons, Charles 21
Debro 73
James 21
John 21, 131
Joseph T. 44
Steve 21
William 53
Simms, James 38
Simonson, Isaac 21
Simpkins, Charles 21
Simpson, Ezekiel 51, 58
James 21
Samuel 21
Thomas 98
Sims, James 21, 54, 130
M. John 38
Mann 21
Singleton, Hansel 49

Singleton (cont.)
James 46
Sinquefield, Aaron 21, 135, 137
Asa 101
Emeline 116
Moses 38, 47, 56
Samuel 21, 38, 99, 135, 137
Wm. 47, 56
Sitten, John 21
Sizemore, William 21
Skener, Michael 21
Skinner, Isaac 21
Skrine, Benj. (?) 66
Benjamin 38
Benjamin 121
Q. 66
Quintilian 21
Sarah 45
Virginia 72
William A. 55
Slade, Elefair 68
Jethro 38
William 44, 53, 66
Slappey, Henry 21
Slappy, Henry 38, 136
Sled, Joshua 21
Slocom, John 97
Slocomb, John A. 98
Smallden, Peter 62
Smalley, Michael 21
Smart, Robert 21
Smiley, A. 128
Elizabeth 38
William 38
Smith, (?) 83, 93, 96, 125
(?) (Cpt.) 131
Abraham 21
Alan 48
Alexander 38, 71
Allen 54, 56, 64, 65, 71
Allen B. 79
Arena (Mrs.) 120
B. R. 70
Benajah 21
Benjamin 99
Benjamin G. 75
Bennett 21
Britton 38
Caleb 38
Catherine 120
Cato H. 121
Caty 46
Celia 114, 115
Charles 21, 38, 134
Colbey 21
Colesby 49
Colsbey 44
Colsby 106
Cooper John 49
Cornelius 21
David 21
Dempsey 38
E. B. 55
Eli 21
Elijah 22
Elijah M. 121
Elizabeth 64, 114
Elsey 75
English 50, 58, 62, 77
Etheldred 76
Francis 38
Frank 67
George 22, 49, 59, 64, 75, 94, 125

Smith (cont.)
Gideon 44, 55, 64, 68
Hamilton 64
Harbert 38
Hardaman 69
Hardeman 127
Hardy 38, 50, 51
Henry 38
Isaac 22, 38, 49, 57, 63, 69, 125, 127
Isaac L. 77
Israel 131
J. F. 76, 121
J. R. 63, 66
Jacob 22, 133
James 38, 51, 75, 121, 125, 127, 133, 137
James F. 22
James R. 67, 121
James S. 121
Jane 133
Jeremiah 38
Jesse 38, 52, 99, 101
Job 49, 106
John 22, 38, 49, 53, 65, 75, 94, 131, 132, 133, 135, 136
John (Jr.) 38, 63, 71, 101
John (Sr.) 101
John B. 74
John C. 22, 63
John M. 121
John Y. 75
Jonathan 75, 121
Jordan 38, 48, 55
Jordan R. 44, 69
Jordon 22
Joseph 22, 63, 87
Joseph D. 76
Joshua 38
Ladden 51
Lavenia 110
Lew 85
Lewis 22, 38, 44, 49, 58, 65, 75
Liby 71
Lydia 38
Martha 112, 115, 117, 121
Martha A. 109
Martha Ann 116
Mary 38, 48, 65, 111, 112, 115, 126
Mary Ann 121
Mary E. 124
Mary N. 121
Matilda 54, 64, 71
Micajah 49, 53, 63
Miles 38
Milly 38
Milton C. 68
Mourning 123
Nace 98
Nancy 126
Nancy A. 119
Nathaniel 22
Needham 38, 51
Nehemiah 22
Nicholas 22, 98
P. P. 56, 65
Patience 118
Patrick 55, 120
Peter 22
Peter P. 79, 121
Phillip 38
Phineas 120
Powel 38

Smith (cont.)
Rachel 117
Rebecca 38
Reddick 38
Richard 38, 51, 56, 64
Richard (Sr.) 38
Robert 101
Robt. 94
Samuel 22, 38, 44, 53, 64, 66, 75, 79, 132
Samuel G. 55
Samuel R. 49
Samuel T. 49
Sarah 38, 56, 61, 71, 120
Sarah A. 114
Sarah Ann 109, 114
Sarah G. 116
Simon 22
Syntha 114
Tabitha 111
Thomas 22, 47, 49, 56, 63, 99, 101, 132
Thomas (Sr.) 38
Thomas B. 76, 121
Thomas R. 121
Thomas S. 71, 121
Thos. 81, 91, 94
William 22, 38, 51, 52, 55, 68, 102, 121, 125, 131, 135
William (Jr.) 38
William A. 70, 121
William F. 121
William K. 121
William L. 69, 72, 121
Wm. 65, 94
Wm. (Cpt.) 98
Wm. F. 44, 46
Smithson, Floristino 22
Snead, William 68
Sneder, Jacob 51
Sneed, (?) 88
Anderson 38
Ansel 45, 101
Ansil 38
Charles 22
Chs. 94
Dudley 22
Sarah 45, 56
William 55, 120
Wm. 64
Snell, (?) 81
Christopher 22, 81, 94
Martha A. C. 122
Snelson, Thomas 22
Snider, Jacob 59, 62, 78
Thomas B. 121
Solbury, (?) (Widow) 84
Solomon, David 22, 53, 66
Soulard, E. A. 66
Soulder, Scantling A. 138
Soullard, Edward 53
Spaight, Jonathan 57
Spaldin, (?) 83
Spann, (?) 94
(?) (Cpt.) 131
Francis 22
Geo. 80, 94
Geo. (Cpt.) 134
George 38, 136
George (Cpt.) 99
John 58, 120
Sparks, John 22, 38, 46
Josiah 22, 137
Margaret 113

Taber, John 131
Tabutton, Joseph 122
Taff, George 39, 133
  James 39
Taft, George 132
Tait, Sally 46
Talbert, Edmond 39
Talbot, Brabazin (?) 73
  Brabazor (?) 122
  Thomas 22
Tallonton, Thomas 101
Talor, Hodg 22
Taner, Mitchell 69
Tankersley, John 22
Tanner, Ardenna 108
  Becky 47
  David 79, 122
  E. 128
  Franklin 22, 79, 122
  Isaac 65, 76, 122
  Joel 22
  Joseph 47, 54, 66
  Mathew 122
  Miles 122
  Mitchell 122, 127
  Morgan 126
  Noah 95
  Rebecca 55, 61
  Richard 61
  Solomon 69, 122
  Thomas 22, 39, 57, 74,
    122
  Thomas J. 61
  Thos. 62
  Thos. J. 44
  Vincent 54, 61, 126
  William 56, 74, 101
  William (Sr.) 74
  William H. 69, 122
  Wm. 61, 63
Tannet, William 130
Tannyhill, John 22
Tant, William 98
Tanton, Henry 39, 46, 59
  Nathan 39
  Newsom 46, 56, 101
  William 46, 55
Tapley, Jno. 95
  John 22
Tarbutton, Benj. 53, 66
  Benjamin 22, 68
  Elizabeth 121
  Joseph 22, 54, 64, 67
  Susan 120
  Winnefred H. 112
  Wm. 63
  Wm. (Sr.) 53
Tarver, Ben 53
  Benjamin 44
  Bryan 53
  Elijah 22
  Fred. 50
  Frederick 39
  Jacob 39
  James 47
  Martha A. 110
  Nancy 109
  Penny 59
  Robert 50, 53
  Robt. 64
  Starling 44
  Stephen 44, 54
  Sterling 48
Tate, Robert 22
  Robert (Cpt.) 102
Tatom, John 39
Taunton, Asa 72
  Eli 122

Taunton (cont.)
  Elizabeth 74
  Henry 106
  Hilsey 74
  Newsom 74, 122
  Sarah 114
  William 44
  Wm. 60
Taver, Charlotte M. 121
  Delania 115
Taylor, D. 128
  Drewry 22, 59
  Drury 46, 62, 79
  Elbert D. 68
  Elizabeth 108
  Faith Ann 111
  George 39
  H. S. 56
  Henry 22, 39, 98
  Henry S. 45, 62, 68
  Hodge 39
  Isaac 39, 51
  Isaiah 44
  James 22, 39, 132
  James (Jr.) 39
  James R. 22, 76, 122
  Jared 44
  John 22, 39, 44, 61,
    79, 122
  Joshua 22, 39, 84, 95
  Josiah 22, 39
  Kinchen 50, 64
  Kinchin 39, 54
  M. 128
  M. James 39
  Martha 110
  Martha L. 114
  Mary 119
  Nancy 123
  P. T. 64
  Right 100
  Shachack 132
  Sofiah 59
  Thomas 22, 39, 50
  William 22, 52, 70,
    79, 122
  William P. 74
  William R. 122
  Wm. 95
  Wright 22
Tedder, Zachariah 54
Tendol, Jacob 54
Tennell, W. A. 44
Tennelle, A. S. 66
  Alex. St.C. 44
  Francis T. 63
  Robert 63
Tennill, Benjamin 23, 39
  Francis 23, 39
Tennille, (?) 80, 82,
    85, 86, 88, 92, 94,
    95, 96
  Benj. 95
  Benjamin 135, 137
  F. 94, 95
  F. G. 53
  Frances 95
  Francis 122
  Francis D. 68, 122
  Fras. 84, 91
  G. 80
  John P. 47
  Mary 45
  Robert 55, 67
  Sarah W. 124
  Wm. A. 45, 54
Terlington, Thomas 54
Terrell, Benjamin 23

Terrell (cont.)
  Joel 23
  Margaret 117
Terrett, Robert 23
Tervin, George 23
Tetterton, John 39
Tharp, Charnick 39
  John 23, 59, 64, 75,
    122
  Wiley 95
Thigpen, Catherine 74
  Dennis 74, 79
  Elizabeth 109, 114,
    116
  Green 122
  Green B. 76
  Ivey 60, 79
  James 48, 53, 60, 74
  James R. 74, 122
  Jesse 79, 122
  John 65, 70, 122
  Jonathan 39
  M. A. 128
  Mary 121
  N. 128
  Parmelia 108
  Randal 23, 59
  Randall 60
  Randol 69
  Sarah 114
  William 56
Thiner, Michael (?) 95
Thom, William 23
Thomas, Benjamin 106
  Darius 39, 50
  Etheldred 23
  Euphama 55
  Euphema (?) 66
  Euphemy 68
  G. 92
  Gideon 23, 95
  James 23, 78, 95, 135,
    136, 137
  John H. 44
  Maning 76
  Mary (Widow) 107
  Peney 112
  Robert F. 55
  Sarah 69
  Simon 75
  Troy 78
  William 39, 77, 100,
    122
Thomason, William 57, 78
Thompkins, Benj. 95
  Burwell 54
  Eliz. 95
  Elizabeth 23
  John 95
  Partin 39
  Samuel 39
Thompson, (?) 84
  Alexander 23
  B. 80
  Benjamin 23
  Charles 39
  Edmund 127
  Elijah 98
  Gideon 130
  Hardy B. 68
  Isham 39
  James 39
  Jeremiah 39
  Jesse 23, 39
  John E. 69
  John H. 59
  John P. 60, 122
  Joshua 23

Thompson (cont.)
  Laban 23
  Lustatia 66, 105
  Penelope (Widow) 107
  Robert 23, 48, 101
  Samuel 23
  Sarah 56, 61
  William 23, 39, 133
  Wm. 87
Thomson, Jesse 98
  Swan 97
Thorn, David 23
Thornton, Azariah B. 122
  Elam 23, 95
  John 23
  Samuel 23
  Solomon 23
  William 23
Thorp, Jane 124
Thrasher, George 23
Thrift, Robert 39, 45
Thurman, Absolom 23
Tibbett, William 47
Tillet, Geo. 39
Tillman, Malaki 44
Tillmon, Littleberry 23
  Stephen 23
  Stephenson 23
Tilman, Littleberry 95
Tindal, Joshua 23, 106
Tindall, Jacob 47
  Joshua 47
  William 23
Tine, Henry 23
Tiner, Lewis 39
Tinny, Isaac 50
Tinsley, John 50
Tison, B. 129
  Daniel 127
  E. 129
  Fred. 53
  Frederick 23, 59
  Fredrick 63
  Gideon 64, 126
  Jacob 127
  John 55, 126
  M. 128, 129
  Mary 125
  N. 129
  Nancy 113
  Noah 23, 53, 127
  Rachael B. 116
  Stephen 45, 53
Titman, Alfred 44
Todd, Hardy 51
  M. 128
  Susan 56
Tolar, Lewis 99
Tolbert, Patrick 60
Toler, Joel 23, 39
Tomalson, Wm. 44
Tomerson, Wm. 62
Tomkins, Burrel 50
  Rubin 50
  Samuel 50, 99
Tomlin, Thomas 39
Tomlinson, Aaron 95, 106
  Benjamin 39
  David 23
  Harris 44, 57
  John 39, 134
  William 106
Tomme, Joseph 23
Tompkins, Burrell 122
  Burwell 39, 66, 69
  C. C. 66
  Charles 69
  Cullen C. 69

Tompkins (cont.)
  Dolly Emeline 121
  Eliz. 95
  Elizabeth 70, 122
  Elkin 44
  F. Y. 69
  Francis 122
  James 44, 69
  James M. 66, 122
  John 131
  John Y. 53, 62
  Mousora 117
  Robert 69, 122
  Rukin 54, 66, 69
  Rukin (?) 44
  Samuel 57, 62, 122
  Sarah E. 110
  William 69
  William P. 122
Tomplins, Chas. 95
Tompson, John P. 73
Tomson, John 100
Tomston, William 61
Tood, Jourdan 72
Took, Ann S. 115
  David 122
  John A. 44
  Mary 68
  Thomas 67
Tooke, Allen 39, 63
  Arthur 39
  Jesse B. 53
  John 23
Toolle, Enoch 64
Tooten, Sarah 52
Tootle, Alley 120
  Fereby 49
  Rebecca 77, 122
  Sarah 123
  Shadrack 122
Townsed, Eli (Lt.) 97
Townsend, Henry 23
  Thomas 23
Townshind, Henry 49
Townsley, Ann C. 113
  Job 45, 97
  Lott 56
  V. S. 53
  Victor Sikes 45
Towsand, Aaron 122
Towson, Henry 57
Trammell, Jared 39
Trapnell, Archibald 100
Trapp, John 23
  Joseph 23
Travis, Gidion 23
Trawick, Anson 125
  Elizabeth 51
  Francis 23
  James 67
  John 79
  Mary 125
  Moses 51
  Moses W. 79
Tray, John 23
  Mary 23
Traywick, Lunsford 59
  Moses 39, 57
  William 58
Tribble, Morris 63
Trice, James 23
Tripp, Henry 23
  John H. 73
Trotman, Blount 50, 54
  Thomas 57
  Winnefred 39
Trowick, Jesse 97
Troy, Mary 95

Truelock, Sutton 39
Trussel, Josepus 68
Trussell, James N. 71
Trussill, Frances A. 118
Tucker, (?) 96
  Ann 50
  Anna 44
  Annabella 113
  Benjamin 39
  Daniel R. 58
  Elijah 122
  Eliza R. 115
  Harper 54
  Henry C. 44, 56
  John R. 44, 55, 62,
    69, 78, 122
  Nancy 77
  Reubin 39, 133
  Robert 23
  T. H. 64
  Thomas (Jr.) 23
  Thomas (Sr.) 23
  William 49, 56
  Wm. 64
Tufts, Francis 39
Tuke, Robert 77
Tull, Isaac 57, 62
  Nancy A. E. 77
  Pennina 118
Tully, William 23
Tunis, Nehemiah 23
Tunnell, Francis 23
Turknett, Henry 23
Turlington, Henry 76
  T. 44
  Thomas 48, 75
  Thos. 65
Turner, Alfred 23, 75
  George J. 65
  I. D. 52
  John B. 73
  Jonathan 39
  Miles 73
  Samuel 39
  William 23, 39, 48
  Zadock 122
Tuter, Shadrack 44
Tuttle, Pherraby 59
Twilly, William 56
Tyler, Elisha 47
Tyson, Elizabeth 125
  Frederick 50, 76
  Frederick (Sr.) 50
  Isaac 23
  John 23, 50
  Moses 39
  Noah 50
  Sarah 112
  Stephen 44
Ubanks, Daniel 46
  Mary 48
Umphreys, Mitchell B.
  122
Umphy, Jaames 122
Underwood, Benj. 95
  Benjamin 23, 39
  Daniel 39
  Elizabeth 64
  George 39
  Isham 39
  Isum 23
  James 65, 71
  John 39
  Josiah 23, 39, 132
  Mary 108
  Reuben 56, 64
  Reubin 39
  Ruben 49

Ward (cont.)
Jesse 40
John 24, 40, 136
John (Jr.) 24, 40
John (Lt.) 98, 102
Joshua 24
Moses 24, 40, 96, 97
Ware, A. G. 66
Arthur G. 123
Nicholas 24
Warlick, Robert Hudspeth
138
Warmack, Margaet 75
Sarah 75
Warren, Margaret A. 119
Wars, Samuel 132
Warthen, Catalina 122
F. J. 66
Graves 96
Green H. 60
Hannah A. 118
I. M. 60
Lovard 124
Minerva H. 111
Reb. (Widow) 107
Richard 60, 96, 133
Sarah Ann 111
William 135
Warthern, Victoria 116
Warthin, Green H. 105
Wm. B. 66
Warthon, Richard 24
Wm. 44
Wash, William 24
Waters, Charles 24
Margaret A. 115
Martha 50
Richard 48, 64, 71
Simon 44
Watkins, Alaphen 117
Ann 115
Ansel L. 45
Arthur 70
Bryant 73, 123
Daniel 53
E. 116
Isaac H. 60
Jonas 55
Lydia F. 79
Malinda 116
Mary P. 108
Mildred (Mrs.) 67
Mitchel 72
Mitchell 44, 45, 55,
61, 62, 123
Mitchell (Sr.) 107
Redden 77
Reddin 63
Redding 55
Richard 57
William 78, 107, 123,
124
Watley, Daniel (Lt.) 102
Watson, Averat 24
Benj. 96
Benjamin 24
David 24, 40, 96, 99
David (Jr.) 40
Elijah 24, 40, 44, 57,
64
Elisha 99, 133
Everett 40
Ezekiel 40, 49, 107
Fereby 49
Green 75
Isaac 133
Isaiah 40
J. W. 71

Watson (cont.)
Laban 40, 77
Labon 24, 64
Levi 24
Peter 24
Phillip 40
Reddick 40
Redick 24
Silas 40, 133
Thomas 24
William 40
William J. 124
Watters, Lodowick 49
Watts, Jacob 24, 40, 96
James 40
Jesse 96
John 24, 96, 133
John (Col.) 102
Josiah 24
Tabitha 40
Thomas 24
Waudin, John 24
Waugh, W. H. 66
Wauls, William 130
Weakly, Lewis 24
Weathers, Edward 24
Weaver, James 61
John 24, 40
Othinal 40
Othneil 136
Webb, Benjamin 124
Crawford 64, 123
Elizabeth 119
G. G. 76
Giles 44
Gilles 49
Hollan 59
Holland 123
James 54
Jesse 40
John 40, 49, 54, 56,
64, 70, 101
John C. 124
Josiah 40, 99
Kinchin 40
Mary 114
Saml. 40
Samuel 49
Sarah 121
Susannah 40
William 56
William A. 70, 124
Webster, Abner 24
Jane 110
Lewis 54, 66, 71, 123
Nancy 113
Richard 56, 66, 70
Samuel 24
Thomas 24
William 66, 70
Weeks, (?) 82
Henry 73
Kaleb 69
Wiley 79
Welborn, Curtis 24
David 98
Welborne, Courtice 24
Welch, (?) 86, 116
Allen H. 123
Asa 46, 58, 63, 73,
123
Benjamin 24
Elizabeth 73
Emanuel 60, 73
Jacob P. 68
Joshua 24
Nicholas 130
Warren 124

Welch (cont.)
Washington 60, 74, 123
William 50, 124
Welcher, Jeremiah 24
Nathaniel 40
William 24
Weldon, John 24
Welker, Dorsett 57
Wells, (?) 84
Benjamin 24
Benjamin (Sr.) 24
E. H. 59
Eligah 97
Elijah 40
Francis 52
James West 24
John 24
John R. 123
Joseph 24
Sion 24
Tavener 24
Taverner 40
William 24
Welsh, Benj. 96
Welton, James 132
Wesley, Lemmons 130
Leumons 96
Wesson, Sarah 44
West, Charles 40, 47
Elbert W. 75
Hamlin 40
Isham 40
Jacob 61
John 51
Matthew K. 75
Wester, Elias 133
Lucinda 118
William 24
Westers, Elias 24
Westley, Lemon 24
Westly, Lemans 40
Whatley, (?) (Cpt.) 130
(?) (Lt.) 103
Alan 98
Allen (Lt.) 103
Dan'l. (Lt.) 97
David (Cpt.) 103
Elisha 98
Jesse 24, 98
John 24
Michael 24
Richard 24
Samuel 24
Walton 24
Wharton 24
Whatly, (?) 86
Wheddon, Demp. 44
Wheeler, Amos 24, 40,
134, 137
Reuben 40
Zachariah 24
Wheelis, Isham 24
Wheelon, Amos 132
Where, William 24
Whiddon, Dempsey 123,
127
Dempsy C. 68
Eli 127
Eli B. 67, 124
Green 24, 44, 68
Greene 62
Hampton 123
Jared 127
M. 128
Mary A. 117
R. A. 128
Rhoda 62
S. 128

Williams (cont.)
66, 105, 107, 125
Wilson 40
Winford 116
Winnifred 40
Wm. K. 44
Williamson, (?) (Cpt.)
133
Anderson 101
Benjamin 51, 55
Charles 25, 45
D. 120
Daniel 65
E. C. 67
Francis (Jr.) 40
Francis (Sr.) 40
Harriett 120
Littleton 25
M. C. 70
Malachi 47
Malichi 59
Malinda I. 121
Mary Ann 122
Mathew C. 123, 124
Micajah 25
P. G. 53
Rebeca 70
Richmond N. 124
Robert 25
Sarah 62, 121
Wiley 40
William 25
Wm. 50, 54
Willie, Britton 25
George 25
Isaiah 25
Wm. 25
Williford, (?) 95
Nathan 25, 96
Nathan (Lt.) 97
Willingham, Memory P.
124
Nancy 71
Willis, J. B. 74
James 40
Jeremiah 124
Mary 40
Willson, Barbar 50
Daniel 40, 49
Wilson, Alexdr. 40
Archibald 25, 64, 75
Augustine 53
Augustus 44
Barbary 56, 63
Daniel 57
Eliza 115
Elizabeth 119
Frances 115
James 75, 97, 98, 99
John 25, 44, 58, 65,
75, 123
John (Jr.) 64
Mary 122
Moley 76
Nancy 119
Robert 40, 98, 99
Robert L. 123
Samuel 25, 98
Samuel (Lt.) 102
William 127
Wimberly, D. Fredericks
40
David 25, 47, 53
David (Lt.) 101
Ezekiel (Sr.) 40
John 40
Mary 40
Noah 40

Wimberly (cont.)
Thomas 40
William 40
Windham, Benjamin 46
Winfrey, (?) 91
Jesse 25
Wingate, Martin 40
Winn, Peter 99, 131
Robert 40
Thomas 40
William 40
Winne, John 25
Winsket, Samuel 25
Winters, John 133
Wise, Elizabeth 117
John 44, 50, 58, 61,
70, 124, 127
John J. 76
Mary 123
Nancy 56, 61
Sheridy 25
Wit, Michael L. 67
Witherspoon, David 133
Wm's., (?) 85
Wm., (?) 88, 96
Wodall, David 97
Wodsworth, John 57
Wolder, Joseph 97
Womack, Jesse 25
Joseph 25
Sarah 59
William 25, 53
Womble, Egbert 48, 125
Elisha 45, 74
Elizabeth 57
Frances 122
James 70
Jeremiah 125
Jordan 127
Lucretia 108
Martha 60, 79
Phoebe 122
T. 128
Thomas 57
William F. 79
Wood, (?) 81, 96
Abraham 25, 40, 96
Abrahm 96
Anderson 78
Aron 98
Balenger 25
Balinger 65
Benjamin 98, 124, 131
Black 84
D. 135
David 25, 96
Dempsey 25, 95
Druscilla B. 122
Edward 25
Elizabeth 111
Etheldred 98
George 51
George R. 25, 55, 64
Green 78
Greene 62
Harriett C. 124
Harrod 56
Henry 25, 44, 56, 64,
71, 78, 123
Henry H. 65, 71, 123
James 25, 40, 63, 69,
96, 98, 137
James (Cpt.) 138
James H. 123
James N. 69, 124
Jared 44, 51, 64, 123
John 25
Jonathan 25

Wood (cont.)
Levina 113
Mary 44, 62
Miesels (?) 57
Misel 40
Misuel 48
Penelope 113
Peter 40, 51
Polly 57
R. T. 65
Rebecca 113, 114
Rich. 97
Robert 40
Solm. 86
Solomon 25, 89, 96,
136
Temperance 119
Thomas 25, 40, 44, 63,
75, 123
William 25, 71, 124,
135
Willis 40
Woodard, Warwick 25, 96
Work 97
Woodburn, John A. 71,
124
Woodham, Edward 47
Woodruff, Joseph 25
Woods, Benjamin 71
Nathaniel 25
Tabitha W. 118
Woodward, James 98
Wooford, Benjamin L. 72
Woten, Henry 99
James 25
John 134
Nathan 25
Thomas 25
Woton, Hardy 98
Works, James 40, 99
Worsham, William (Lt.)
102
Worthan, Elijah 97
William 97
Worthen, (?) 90
Elijah 40
Elijah (Jr.) 46
Elijah (Sr.) 46
Green H. 56
James M. 72
Rebecca 58
Richard 25, 40, 58, 67
Thomas 25
Thomas J. 55, 69
W. J. 72
William 25, 40, 46,
72, 107
William B. 68
Wm. B. 55
Worthy, Elison 45
John 101
Peggy 46
Robert 56
Wright, Abednego 25
Benjamin 25, 40
Elijah 40
Elizabeth 40
Geo. 62
Habucker 25
Isaiah 25
John 25
John B. 64, 71, 123
John M. 49, 54
M. John 40
Thomas 25, 49, 64, 70,
123
William 25, 40
Winfield 41

Wright (cont.)
  Wingfield 25, 123
Wyat, Wiley 75
Wyatt, Peyton 25
Wyche, Baille 25
  George 25
Yankerfield, John 25
Yarborough, Benj. 51
  James 25
  Littleton 25
  Thomas 25
  Wm. 98
Yarbrough, Ambrose 41
  Joseph 41
  Wm. 97
Yates, Harriett 115
  James 45
  James E. 74
  John 55
  Mary 60, 79
  Peter 79
  William F. 79
Yearly, Henry 25
Yeates, James 44
  Mary 44
Yolden, Matthew 132
Yorke, James 25
Yost, Wiley W. 73
Young, (?) 96
  A. J. 127
  Alfred 125, 127
  Andrew J. 124
  Daniel 25
  David 44, 124
  Edward 25, 131
  Elizabeth 41, 49, 57
  G. W. 67
  George 127
  Green 44, 70, 125, 127
  Jacob 41
  James 57, 127
  Jesse 49, 59, 64, 77
  M. 128
  Mahala 109
  Malachi 125
  Martha 65, 111
  Mary 119, 125, 126
  Mills 41
  Nancy 109
  Pierson 49
  R. John 41
  Rebecca 110
  William 25, 49, 53,
    75, 76
  William (Jr.) 76
  William G. 76
  William Green 124
  Wm. 63
Youngblood, Arther 97
  Henry 41
  I. R. 57
  Isaac 52
  Isaac R. 62
  Jacob 41
  James 25, 41
  John 25, 41
  John L. 70
  Jonathan 25, 41
  Nathan 97
Younge, John 25
Younger, William 25
Zinn, Jacob 25